WAIT

THE USEFUL ART
OF
PROCRASTINATION

FRANK PARTNOY

P

PROFILE BOOKS

This paperback edition published in 2013

First published in Great Britain in 2012 by
PROFILE BOOKS LTD
3A Exmouth House
Pine Street
London EC1R 0JH
www.profilebooks.com

First published in the United States of America by
Public Affairs, a member of the Perseus Books Group

Copyright © Frank Partnoy, 2012, 2013

10 9 8 7 6 5 4 3 2 1

Printed and bound in Great Britain by
CPI Group (UK) Ltd., Croydon CR0 4YY

The moral right of the author has been asserted.

A CIP catalogue record for this book is available from the British Library

ISBN 978 1 84668 595 8
eISBN 978 1 84765 818 0

MIX
Paper from
responsible sources
FSC® C020471

For Fletch, again

CONTENTS

INTRODUCTION

The dog on the cover of this book—let's call her Maggie—is a role model for those of us who want to make better decisions. Maggie could have devoured the biscuit resting on her snout in the blink of an eye. Instead, she is holding back, showing us she can keep her instincts and emotions in check, delaying the pleasure of the snack she can smell all too well. Although this book is mostly about human beings, not animals, its central point is that we can learn a lot from Maggie.

Maggie is, in a limited way, thinking about the future. She is acting a lot like my own dog, Fletch, a fourteen-year-old yellow Labrador retriever I trained as a puppy not to immediately go for a treat. Fletch probably can't think about the future for more than a few minutes, but his limited ability to anticipate consequences and delay gratification has served him well. If anyone in my family leaves food on the table after dinner, Fletch won't leap for it right away, when we probably would catch him. Instead, he'll quietly follow us into the living room and lie down at my feet. We won't realize he has moved until we hear the crash of dishes from the kitchen.

Recent experiments confirm that Fletch and Maggie are not exceptional. In 2012 researchers from Scotland and France published a study demonstrating what many pet owners know: dogs of various breeds are able to make future-oriented decisions about food.[1] Most dogs can learn to suppress their snap reactions for at least ten to twenty seconds if doing so gives them a chance at a better or bigger treat. Many have much longer tolerance. One working sheepdog held a small chicken chew treat in her mouth for more than ten minutes while waiting for a chance to trade it for a piece eight times bigger.[2]

—

In recent years, scientists have made great progress in comprehending how we make decisions. Psychologists have suggested we have two systems of thinking, one intuitive and one analytical, both of which can lead us to make serious cognitive mistakes. Behavioral economists have said our responses to incentives are often irrational and skewed, sometimes predictably so. Neuroscientists have taken pictures of our brains to show which parts react to different stimuli.[3]

Yet we still don't understand the role time and delay play in our decisions and why we continue to make all kinds of timing errors, reacting too fast or too slow. Delay alone can turn a good decision into a bad one, or vice versa. Much recent research about decisions helps us understand what we should do or how we should do it, but it says little about *when*. Sometimes we should trust our gut and respond instantly. But other times we should postpone our actions and decisions. Sometimes we should rely on our quick intuition. But other times we should plan and analyze.

Although time and delay have not occupied a prominent spot in decision-making research, these concepts lurk behind the scenes, especially in discussions about human nature. Many scientists say the key skill that distinguishes human beings from animals is our superior ability to think about the future.[4] However, thinking about the future is different from predicting it.

As a professor, I have studied law and finance for more than fifteen years. In 2008, when the financial crisis hit, I wanted to get to the heart of why our leading bankers, regulators, and others were so shortsighted and wreaked such havoc on our economy: why were their decisions so wrong, their expectations of the future so catastrophically off the mark? I also wanted to figure out, for selfish reasons, whether my own tendency to procrastinate (the only light fixture in my bedroom closet has been broken for five years) was really such a bad thing.

I interviewed more than one hundred experts in different fields and worked through several hundred recent studies and experiments, many as yet unpublished, in divergent areas of research. I noticed that decision researchers with different types of expertise do not cross paths very often.[5] Frequently, they haven't heard of each other. Decision research has become so sprawling that experts in one sub-area often don't know experts in another, even if they are tackling the same questions.

I decided, after a couple of years of thinking about decision-making and time, that in order to understand these concepts we should not look only to psychology or behavioral economics or neuroscience or law or finance or history—we should explore them all, simultaneously. I tried to assemble the mass of evidence from these disciplines as any good lawyer would, to illuminate and clarify arguments we might not see if we look from only one perspective.

The essence of my case is this: given the fast pace of modern life, most of us tend to react too quickly. We don't, or can't, take enough time to think about the increasingly complex timing challenges we face. Technology surrounds us, speeding us up. We feel its crush every day, both at work and at home. Yet the best time managers are comfortable pausing for as long as necessary before they act, even in the face of the most pressing decisions. Some seem to slow down time. For good decision-makers, time is more flexible than a metronome or atomic clock.

During superfast reactions, the best-performing experts instinctively know when to pause, if only for a split-second. The same is true over longer periods: some of us are better at understanding when to take a few extra seconds to deliver the punch line of a joke, or when we should wait a full hour before making a judgment about another person. Part of this skill is gut instinct, and part of it is analytical. We get some of it from trial and error or by watching experts, but we also can learn from observing toddlers and even animals. As we will see, there is both an art and a science to managing delay.

Throughout this book we will return to two questions that are central to decisions in our personal and professional lives. First, how long should we take to react or decide in a particular situation? Then, once we have a sense of the correct time period, how should we spend our time leading up to the moment of decision? We will begin by exploring these questions at superfast speeds, when reactions take just a split second. Then, as the chapters move along, we will telescope out to longer-term decisions.

As we will see over and over, in most situations we should take more time than we do. The longer we can wait, the better. And once we have a sense of how long a decision should take, we generally should delay the moment of decision until the last possible instant. If we have an hour, we should wait fifty-nine minutes before responding. If we have a year, we should wait 364 days. Even if we have just half a second, we should wait as long as we possibly can. Even milliseconds matter.

0 **FIRST**

So, what do you think of this book so far?

1 HEARTS AND MINDS

tephen Porges, a psychiatry professor and neuro-scientist at the University of Illinois at Chicago,[1] believes the key to our psychological development as human beings lies not solely in our brains but below them, along the nerve that serves as the two-lane racetrack for the signals that zip back and forth between our brains and the rest of our bodies. He focuses on the tenth cranial nerve, known as the vagal nerve, a strip of fibers that originates in the medulla oblongata, a part of the brain stem, and winds around the most important parts of our bodies, from the head and throat to the lungs, heart, and digestive system.[2] It's like a miniature speedway running around our most vital organs. Not very many people understand the crucial role it plays in our decisions.

Porges began his doctoral research on this neural racetrack during the late 1960s, just as the discipline of psychology was splintering: some researchers were advocating psychotropic drugs, while others were preoccupied with death. Porges joined the Society for Psychophysiological Research, a relatively obscure cluster of practical-minded academics who wanted to combine psychology and physiology. The dream of this group's members, including Porges, was to improve our understanding of human behavior by monitoring people's bodies in real time. They were frustrated by the increasing reliance on subjective questioning and self-reporting, and they had limited interest in having patients lie on sofas and talk about their childhood three times a week.

Instead of trusting the words that came out of patients' mouths, these researchers wanted to test the changes in patients' bodies. As Porges explained it to me, "The goal was to understand patients' psychological states without having to talk to them."

Porges decided to study the heart. He thought the high-speed nerve connections between our brains and hearts were central to understanding human emotion. He wanted to prove he could assess our psychological health simply by measuring the changes in our heart rates to the nearest millisecond. He envisioned that future psychologists might diagnose, and even predict, mental disorders simply by timing the hearts of their patients.

Like many genius insights, Porges's ideas seem downright crazy at first. Why would tiny changes in our heart rates matter to our mental health? Yes, our hearts beat faster when we are agitated and slower when we are calm, but we barely perceive any of that; the variance is a fraction of a second. And although it's interesting to know that our heart rates go up when we inhale and down when we exhale, it doesn't affect our sanity or emotional health. Our heart rates vary, but the changes don't suddenly make us go crazy. Try it: Breathe in and out. In, out. In, out. You can't feel that your heart is speeding up when you breathe in and slowing down when you breathe out, but it is. Nor will you feel more or less manic or depressed, because you aren't. So what was Porges thinking?

Before Porges wrote his dissertation on heart rate variability and reaction time, research on the topic hadn't progressed much since Charles Darwin, over a hundred years ago, speculated, based on the earlier writings of French physiologist Claude Bernard, that human emotional states might be driven by a rapid-fire brain-heart feedback loop. Just as Darwin anticipated so many later discoveries in other areas, he suggested in one passage that the vagal nerve, then called the pneuma-gastric nerve, was a road carrying signals from the brain to the heart and back. As Darwin wrote in 1872:

> When the mind is strongly excited, we might expect that it would instantly affect in a direct manner the heart; and this is universally acknowledged . . . when the heart is affected it reacts on the brain; and the state of the brain again reacts through the pneuma-gastric nerve on the heart; so that under any excitement there will be much mutual action and reaction between these, the two most important organs of the body.[3]

During the following century, scientists didn't know enough to confirm or deny Darwin's theory. In 1969, when Porges attended his first meeting of the Society for Psychophysiological Research, the precise workings of the brain-heart feedback loop were still speculative. The field needed less theory and more practice.

Porges designed new heart rhythm tests.[4] He recorded how his subjects' heart rates changed when they focused on a task. He recruited students, hooked them up to Beckman cardio tachometers, and figured out a reliable way to measure heart rate variability, which he tested against a range of psychological factors, particularly in infants. He studied heart rate patterns of various living creatures, from rats to babies. More than one hundred laboratories around the world adopted his method of quantifying variations in heart rates.

In one study, Porges and his colleagues tested a group of kids, first as infants (at nine months) and then as toddlers (at three years).[5] At the initial stage of the experiment, the infants sat quietly in their mothers' laps for three minutes. Then they were presented with toys, blocks, and shapes as part of the standard Bayley Scales of Infant Development evaluation. Meanwhile, Porges measured their hearts' responsiveness by timing their heartbeats to the nearest millisecond. Finally, the mothers completed several standard questionnaires about how their children behaved. More than two years later, Porges retested the children as toddlers. Once again, his team gathered data about the kids' behavior. Then they compared the two sets of results.

They found that the infants' behavior indicated in the answers on the questionnaire at age nine months was unrelated to their later behavior. You couldn't tell whether a toddler would be depressed or aggressive or destructive at age three by asking his parents whether he had behavioral problems at age nine months. Babies who refused to play turned out just fine, whereas once-beatific nine-month-olds became three-year-old monsters.

But the infants' heart rate patterns told a more compelling story. According to the study, "the best predictor of behavior problems at 3 years of age was the infant's ability to decrease cardiac vagal tone during the Bayley test."[6] In other words, the infants who had the most flexible heart rates—who could quickly accelerate and brake their snap reactions while they confronted new toys, blocks, and shapes—had fewer behavioral problems later. The infants who instantly regulated their heart rates had fewer difficulties later with social withdrawal, depression, and aggression. The ability to manage their heart rates over a few hundred milliseconds at nine months helped these kids operate more smoothly at three years.

This study embodied Porges's goal of understanding patients' psychological states without relying on their opinions. Of course, nine-month-old babies don't say much, so listening to them is not fruitful. But Porges found that listening to their mothers isn't helpful either. Nor is observing the babies' behavior for several seconds or minutes. Instead, what matters is what is happening inside their bodies, where their little hearts are shifting gears millisecond by millisecond.[7]

Over more than two decades, to the surprise of many psychologists, Porges repeatedly showed that heart rate *variability*—having a wide range of heart rate acceleration and deceleration—is a measure of good mental health in the same way blood pressure or cholesterol generally are measures of good physical health.[8] It is especially true of babies and children. As infants, we watch new visual stimuli longer and are less easily distracted when our heart rates are more variable.[9]

Young children with a resting heart rate of 100 are less likely to suffer emotional distress later in life if their heart rate varies in a wide band from 90 to 110 when they are surprised or scared than if it varies more narrowly from 95 to 105. It isn't the resting rate that matters, but how much the rate varies in response to stimulus. Children who have a wider range of instant heart response have a more efficient feedback system, and this increased efficiency helps them regulate their emotional state: their hearts speed up more when they are excited, and slow down more when they are calm.

Think of the heart as being like the engine and brakes of a car. If you are driving down a winding two-lane road in a car that doesn't reliably accelerate or slow down, your travels are going to be unpleasant and stressful. If it gets dark or the weather turns bad, you might panic and overreact.

But if you are confident that you can easily speed up to pass or slow down at a dangerous curve, you will be more secure about your maneuvers. You won't necessarily gun the accelerator all the time or slam on the brakes. But sometimes you will need a wide range of variation, maybe a burst of speed followed by several minutes at a calm and steady pace. A car's superior performance will give you a lot of comfort during the drive.

————

When I first read that milliseconds-long reactions in our hearts affect longer-term responses in our brains, which is tantamount to saying how we react and make decisions, I was skeptical. Porges's experiments weren't cited in the leading books on decision-making. The top decision-making researchers I interviewed hadn't even heard of him. Yet numerous studies, by him and others, confirm the benefits of high heart rate variability, particularly for children. And low heart rate variability is bad—it is associated with higher levels of anger, hostility, stress, and anxiety.[10] It is a counterintuitive result, but having a heart that can respond rapidly helps us delay gratification and remain calm, even in the face of great temptation or fear. Being fast in our heart helps our brain go slow later.

John Gottman, the scientist made famous in Malcolm Gladwell's book *Blink* for his ability to assess marriages by watching couples for just a few minutes, learned about Porges's theory and wanted to see how kids' hearts responded to disapproval from their parents. Sure enough, he and his colleague Lynn Katz found that four- and five-year-olds who are better at quickly, and unconsciously, adjusting their heart rates in response to stressful interactions with their parents are better able to regulate their emotions later at age eight. Gottman and Katz didn't observe the kids' conscious reactions or behavior at all. Instead, they looked at what was going on inside the kids' bodies and found that children are emotionally better off if they can tweak their heart rates in response to criticism from Mom and Dad.[11]

Another group of researchers asked sixty-eight cohabiting heterosexual couples to sit on a sofa and talk about their relationships, sort of like the couples from the film *When Harry Met Sally,* except that their bodies were wired with electrodes connected to a four-channel bio-amplifier that continuously measured their heart rate responses.[12] As they talked about their partner's character and behavior and what it was like to be away from him or her, computers recorded millisecond-by-millisecond changes in their heart rates. Then, over the next three weeks, the couples kept detailed records of their interactions and how they felt about each other.

Although the results were complicated and differed by gender, the overall pattern was that both women and men reacted more favorably and recorded more positive interactions when their *partner's* heart was more responsive. Somehow, people sensed what was happening inside their partner's body. These results suggest that heart rate variability matters not only to our own emotional reactions but also to our partners' reactions to us. Our hearts really do skip a beat when we're in love.

—

Stephen Porges's experiments inspired a generation of new research that connected heart rate variability to emotional good health. But in September 1992—just after Porges had published an article showing that healthy full-term newborns have more variable heart rates and premature babies less variable ones—he received a letter from a neonatologist that forced him to rethink everything he had discovered. The letter said Porges's article was interesting and helpful. But the neonatologist also noted that the results seemed to contradict something he had learned in his practice: quick reactions from the central nervous system's fast track could be extremely dangerous. A highly responsive heart rate could be bad for newborns. So bad that it killed them.

The neonatologist was referring to bradycardia, a sudden and massive slowing of the heart rate that deprived an infant's brain of oxygen. He said the vagal nerve caused this decline. In other words, the same neural speedway Porges was studying seemed to carry two very different kinds of signals to the infant heart, with opposite effects. Sometimes the signals were healthy for a baby because they caused its heart to be speedier and more resilient, but sometimes the signals slowed down a baby's heart so much that they put it at risk of sudden death.

Porges says, "I had gone through an intellectually expansive period, with many discoveries, and I thought I had it. I had solved a big problem. My data showed that heart rate variability was always helpful. But this letter was a confrontation. I was totally challenged, and was forced to rethink everything."

Porges put the letter in his briefcase, where it stayed for two years.

In 1994 Porges was invited to give the presidential address at the Society for Psychophysiological Research. It was a kind of intellectual homecoming, a great honor from a group that had grown just as much as he had during the previous twenty-five years. By October 8 of that year, he had figured out how to respond to the neonatologist's challenge and was finally ready to propose a new big-picture theory that covered both the positives and negatives of highly responsive heart rates.

In his speech, Porges said the vagal nerve that runs from our brain stem throughout our bodies is really two tracks of fibers wound together: one crude strand we inherited from our common ancestry with reptiles, and one sophisticated strand we developed more recently as mammals.[13] Both operate at high speed, within milliseconds, but they do very different things. The crude reptilian part controls our digestive and reproductive systems, while the more modern mammalian part controls the muscles of our head and face, along with our cardiovascular system. Basically, the old stuff controls our gut, and the new stuff controls everything above it.[14] But, Porges carefully noted, both systems are connected to the heart.

The reptile part of the nerve has an early evolutionary history; imagine tiny tortoiselike signals traveling up and down that strand. The mammal part of the nerve evolved later; imagine tiny harelike signals traveling up and down that strand. Both signals race back and forth along these two interwoven tracks. Both are superfast. The strange part about the race between them is who wins when, and why.

According to Porges, when we confront a stimulating event—something scary or exciting—both strands of the nerve affect the heart, but in opposite ways. The tortoise part instantly sends signals to withdraw and shut down, like the emergency brake of a car. Porges cites iguanas, whose heart rate plummets when they confront fear, and hog-nosed snakes, whose heart rate drops so precipitously when stimulated that they appear to be dead. Although reptiles are among the slowest animals in the world, their nervous reactions of withdrawal are really fast. Many scientists refer to a fight-or-flight response, but Porges thinks of it as "fight, flight, or freeze."

In contrast, the mammal part of the vagal nerve reacts to stimulation more flexibly, revving up and slowing down the body, as appropriate. It also can let up on the reptilian brake, which otherwise might shut everything down. So while the old reptile part of the nerve immobilizes, the newer mammal part of the nerve mobilizes. One nervous response is like a panic freeze; the other is to heighten our awareness so we're at our most alert and ready to face whatever the newly challenging situation is. We inherited both reactions, so our vagal nerve responds in two wholly different ways. According to Porges, the reptile part acting alone would either slow our heart rate so much that we would faint or perhaps stimulate our gut so much that we would defecate—rarely ideal responses, in childhood or adulthood.

With this new theory, Porges could answer the challenge posed in the neonatologist's letter. Infants generally are healthier when their hearts are more variable—when the mammalian signals are more active. But if the reptilian signals predominate, the infant is in trouble. Reptilian signals aren't slow and steady—they are superfast protective reflexes that shut the heart down when they sense danger. That is why infants in fetal distress have virtually no observable variation in heart rate. The old part of their nervous system, sensing peril, flips off the switch.[15]

These vagal responses, although just milliseconds long, might explain all kinds of physical disorders and emotional problems, particularly those related to stress. Asthma, for example. A reptile, with its primitive brain stem, needs to radically conserve oxygen when it is under attack. But that same shutdown could be lethal for an oxygen-hungry mammal. An asthma attack might be a defensive move by the reptile side of the nervous system, when it senses that the cardiovascular system has been working too hard in response to a dangerous situation.[16]

Or autism. Although the idea is controversial, some studies suggest that autistic children have less responsive heart rates and are more vulnerable to the reptilian shutdown response. Apparently, when the reptilian part of the vagal nerve dominates, it doesn't necessarily shut down the heart entirely, but it can shut down the mammalian response. According to Porges, stimulating the newer mammalian part of the nervous system— making the heart more responsive—can reduce autistic-like behaviors in some patients.[17] Autism might be an example of the tortoise winning the battle, shutting down the emotional and social responses that otherwise would be available to a child.[18]

Or borderline personality disorder. Researchers have found a correlation between heart rate responsiveness and BPD. In one experiment, when a control group viewed some highly emotional film clips, their heart rate variability increased. But when subjects with BPD viewed the same film clips, their heart rates became less responsive than they were before. Why? Again, the reptilian part of the vagal nerve seemed to be the culprit: it appeared to be blocking the mammalian part of the vagal nerve, which otherwise would have instantly caused the heart to beat faster during a scary scene and slower during a calm one.[19] According to Porges, in each of these instances, there was a deficit in how the mammalian strand of the vagal nerve regulated the heart.

Measuring heart rate variability is now a straightforward process: it takes just a few minutes, and the equipment is virtually foolproof. If heart rate variability proves to be as important as studies suggest, we might add it to newborn tests such as the APGAR (Appearance, Pulse, Grimace, Activity, Respiration) assessment. We also might test the heart responsiveness of young children to understand which ones are at greatest risk of mental disorders. For adults, we might add a measure of heart rate variability to our standard battery of periodic medical tests, such as blood pressure or cholesterol, to see how much our hearts speed up and slow down when we are stimulated. Psychologists and doctors could consider heart rate variability as a factor in their diagnoses, just as we all might develop some intuition about when our own heart rate becomes more or less variable, or when its fluctuations influence others, particularly our loved ones.

Since the research is new, we shouldn't draw too many absolute conclusions. Nor should we panic if our children have relatively stable heart rates. There is no need to rush out to test the heart rate responsiveness of a potential spouse. Not yet, anyway.

One of the most important applications of this new research is the treatment of trauma victims. People who have reported being abused as children have less variable heart rates later in life, the idea being that a traumatic event not only shut them down then, but also persists in their memory, continuing to mute their heart's responsiveness.[20] The cliché about the broken heart might, it seems, have a large measure of anatomical truth to it.

Some of the most successful trauma treatments today are designed to teach victims techniques to control their heart rate, from yoga programs that help traumatized women manage their breathing patterns to inner-city theater programs that help traumatized teenagers learn rhythmical movements and sounds. Although slow breathing, meditation, and exercise all help increase heart rate variability, the extent to which these therapies can repair the damage done by a traumatic event remains unclear. If nothing else, the new research on hearts and mental health gives us yet another reason to engage in activities we should be doing anyway for our physical health—in case you need another reason to jog or do yoga.

I asked Porges what his research says about raising children. Unsurprisingly for a researcher who prefers to observe physical responses rather than listen to verbal cues, he focused on the physical. He spoke of the environment that surrounds children, especially very young ones, who are least able to consciously understand their circumstances and rationalize their experiences: "Avoid loud sounds and traumatic situations. Pay attention to physical details. Think about how your actions might cause them to shut down. Be as aware as you can of their bodily states, as well as your own and those of friends and family. Pay attention to children's physical reactions."

We like to think we know what safety means. But what an adult considers a threat might be different from what a child's body actually experiences as one. Just the perception of danger to a child is enough—it doesn't have to be real.[21] We already know that many psychological disorders are related to traumatic early life experiences, such as sexual abuse and family dysfunction. But children also withdraw because of less blatant, even unintentional behavior; an angry reprimand or a scary Halloween costume could be enough to trigger this reaction. We might think it's a good idea to shout "*No!*" when we see a small child reach toward a hot stove or a sharp knife. Or we might not think about shouting at all. But our reactions can hurt our children's longer-term emotional well-being.[22] The lesson, according to Porges, is that we should provide babies and children with a safe environment where they can develop their central nervous system's ability to respond quickly without shutting down.

—

Porges's discoveries arrived just as the interest in children's decision-making and self-control was catching fire. Much of that interest was stoked by a widely publicized series of experiments at Stanford University's Bing Nursery School, where researchers presented four-year-old children with one marshmallow and gave them a choice: eat the marshmallow right away or wait fifteen minutes and get two marshmallows instead. They tested these children later in life and found that those who were able to delay gratification performed better on standardized tests in high school, were less prone to impulsive behavior, and were more likely to become emotionally well-adjusted adults.[23]

Since those tests, researchers have found, again and again, that children who can delay their reactions end up happier and more successful than their snap-reacting playmates: they are superior at building social skills, feeling empathy, and resolving conflicts, and they have higher cognitive ability.[24] Kids with good preschool-age delay skills have higher self-esteem later in life, cope better with stress, are less likely to use cocaine and crack, and aren't as fat.[25] Children who can decide to wait do better.

Educators and parents are well aware of these results—often too well aware. Many schools emphasize self-control as part of their curriculum. The KIPP (Knowledge Is Power Program) Academy in Philadelphia gives its students shirts emblazoned with the slogan DON'T EAT THE MARSHMAL-LOW.[26] Obsessive mothers and fathers fret about whether they have a (doomed) One-Marshmallow Child or a (triumphant) Two-Marshmallow Child. Blogs such as Raising CEO Kids and Growing Rich Kids advise how to teach children about the pecuniary blessings of delayed gratification. Some parents have taken to rewarding good behavior not with immediate praise or presents but with tickets that are redeemable only at a later date.

Yet concluding that children are better off delaying gratification doesn't tell us why waiting is so much easier for some than others. The marshmallow tests might be widely known, but their results are not well understood. Although we have some understanding of the brain regions that are triggered by these kinds of tests, we don't really know whether some four-year-olds are naturally able to wait fifteen minutes to get a second marshmallow and therefore do better in life, or whether we can save impatient children by training them to delay gratification for a few extra minutes. This is a new version of the old debate about nature versus nurture.

Nor do we understand precisely how long children should be able to wait. We think a four-year-old who is only capable of waiting a second or two before scarfing down a marshmallow might be in trouble because children without impulse control are more likely to encounter emotional problems. It makes sense that a kid who can wait several minutes for a second marshmallow would end up better off, because that amount of delay reflects a useful degree of willpower and self-control. However, these experiments don't tell us how short is too short, how long is too long, or which factors affect the ideal amount of delay. Arguably, we should worry less about the impatient child who grabs the marshmallow right away than the one who is still staring it down hours later, obstinately refusing to give in. We might conclude that such an obdurate child is more likely headed for prison than Princeton.

Experts assume the time periods that matter most to a child's mental health are at least a few seconds long. Assessments of pervasive developmental disorder and attention deficit disorders—including autism, Asperger's syndrome, and attention deficit hyperactivity disorder—examine children's reactions over that sort of period. Psychologists who diagnose these disorders watch children as they play, talk, fidget, squirm, and become bored, all of which take at least several seconds, often longer.[27]

Brain research concentrates on a similar time frame. Scientists use functional magnetic resonance imaging to map our brains' reactions, showing that different regions "light up" as our responses change.[28] But the changes in blood and oxygen flow that fMRI machines capture do not occur until several seconds after our neurons fire. Although many techniques allow scientists to track brain changes faster, until recently even the fastest fMRI machines could not take pictures more often than once per second.[29]

All of this means that when we think about delay and child development, we tend to focus on time periods that last at least a few seconds. We overlook Porges's time frame—of the milliseconds-long responses carried by the vagal nerve. But what if a child's ability to manage superfast delays of just a fraction of a second is the key to his or her emotional development and psychological health?

Neither kids nor their parents and teachers are even aware of this kind of unconscious time management. No one wears shirts that say DON'T REACT IN MILLISECONDS. Ultrarapid reactions seem more like animal responses than human emotions. We can't even begin to reason during half a second, any more than my dog Fletch, though moderately well trained, can think through what to do when I toss a hunk of steak in his direction. At such fast speeds, any response seems automatic and unconscious, what the philosopher William James labeled "passive-involuntary."

However, children react faster than "marshmallow time" in ways that are crucial to the ultimate decision to eat or not to eat a marshmallow right away. Our understanding of how we make decisions is incomplete if we overlook the essential physical contribution that our bodies make during the milliseconds of preconscious time when a threat or a temptation is first put in front of us. In decision-making, our hearts can be at least as important to our ability to wait as our minds.

———

Time is a slippery concept, and we are often wrong about it. If we focus on how our brains react over the course of seconds and minutes, we will not see quicker reactions. This is a general problem we have with thinking about decision-making, for both children and adults. All too often, we find ourselves looking in the right places at the wrong time.

Research on the vagal nerve has revealed a high-speed world inside our bodies, one so fast that we cannot consciously access it. Yet when we are asked to make a decision, such as whether to eat a marshmallow right away, it is these rapid-fire responses that help determine what kind of a decision we will make. A speedy response in our hearts can help us delay a speedy response in our brains and bodies. It is a strange idea, but being fast at first really can help us go slow later on.

Heart rate variability is a tool that helps us manage delay at very high speeds. It is an unconscious skill that we can use, as children and adults, when we need to be patient. Medical science has not shown us exactly how to optimize the split-second changes in our heart rates—not yet. We cannot give four-year-old children a pill or procedure to enhance their heart rate variability and help them wait fifteen minutes for a second marshmallow. We don't have the tools to manage the timing of our superfast reactions. All of this helplessness can be unsettling.

And yet some human beings are nevertheless able to manage their ability to delay their quick reactions beautifully, even at preconscious speeds. Their bodies instinctively react at precisely the right time, even when they have only a split-second. That skill makes them some of the most admired and widely watched people in the world.

2 SUPERFAST SPORTS

I n 1974 *Jimmy Connors won* the Wimbledon men's singles title, and Chris Evert won the women's title. He was twenty-one; she was nineteen. Each of them had grown up in a tennis family and studied with professional coaches. They met, played mixed doubles, started a romance, and got engaged. He ultimately won 148 titles; she won 157. Both were ranked first in the world for more than five years. But what they shared most, even after the wedding was called off, was an incredible ability to return serves.

A tennis court, baseline to baseline, is seventy-eight feet long. First serves are launched, by men and women alike, at over one hundred miles per hour. A player returning serve has just four to five hundred milliseconds from when the ball leaves the server's racquet until it hits his or her own. Just half a second.

David Foster Wallace, the novelist, essayist, and regionally ranked junior tennis player, was an expert on service returns. He recognized that of all the shots played in tennis, apart from quick volleys, the return of serve is unique because the decision about how and where to return the ball must be made in a time period so short that it precludes deliberation: "Temporally, we're more in the operative range of reflexes, purely physical reactions that bypass conscious thought. And yet an effective return of serve depends on a large set of decisions and physical adjustments that are a whole lot more involved and intentional than blinking, jumping when startled, etc."[1]

Wallace was pointing out that returning serve is a paradoxical act. On one hand, it is a largely unconscious physical reaction. It has to be, given the speed of the ball. There is not enough time to consider spin or angle. Conscious contemplation takes at least half a second, so anyone who even tries to think about how to return a serve will end up helplessly watching the ball fly by.

On the other hand, returning serve involves a range of sophisticated and creative responses. Ideally, a player should react to both the placement and trajectory of the ball. The position and movement of the server are crucial. Great tennis returners respond to the information cascade of a serve as if they had taken time to process it consciously, even though we know that is not possible.

Connors and Evert knew precisely where the ball would hit the ground and how it would spin. They processed huge amounts of data and then often hit a perfect return. If you hired a dozen physicists and coaches to analyze recordings of Connors and Evert in slow motion, you could not plot better reactions. (Computer sports game programmers understand this, which is why they increasingly rely on video of top players instead of mathematical algorithms.)

How did Connors and Evert do it? One way to understand their success is to divide the time available to return a serve into two parts. The first part is the time it takes the brain to react to seeing the ball after it is served—the purely visual reaction time. We can measure visual reaction time by having a tennis player simply press a button when he or she first sees the ball leave the racquet.

Visual reaction time is about the same for all of us. Most people can react to a visual stimulus in about two hundred milliseconds, but no faster, and the range of reaction times is surprisingly consistent across people and activities.[2] A teenage driver sees a red brake light. A middle-aged stock trader sees a low price. A professional athlete sees a ball coming. All of them, and all of us, can react at top speed in about two-tenths of a second, roughly half the time it takes an eye to blink. That means virtually anyone who can see a distance of seventy-eight feet can react to the visual stimulus of a ball being served in plenty of time to meet the incoming serve, even if it is zooming in from Andy Roddick or Venus Williams.

The remaining period of, say, three hundred milliseconds is the time we have to react *physically*—to adjust ourselves to what we know about the ball's flight and then try to hit it how and where we'd like. The split between the time available for visual reaction (we'll call that "see") versus physical reaction (we'll call that "hit") looks something like this:

See (200 ms)	Hit (300 ms)

As even the slowest video gamer can attest, if all you had to do was "see" and then press a button to swing—if you didn't even have to get off the sofa—anyone could return a professional-speed serve. The difficulty in real tennis arises in the second stage of the service return.

The "hit" part is a serious problem for most of us. The physical reaction time available to hit a professional serve is barely long enough for us to adjust our racquet by a few inches. Amateurs cannot move to the correct spot and produce a swing with accuracy or power in three hundred milliseconds. Many solid professionals cannot do it either. Andy Roddick, who held the record for the fastest serve ever recorded in professional tennis, 155 miles per hour, until March 2011 (when Ivo Karlović hit one 156 miles per hour), says that even if a court surface is slow, "if you hit it 140, hit your spot, it's going to be an ace."[3]

Connors and Evert did not successfully return every serve. But for most of their returns, they had plenty of time. They were so skilled and practiced that they could produce near-instantaneous muscle contractions to move their bodies and execute a swing in perhaps one hundred milliseconds. For them, the physical part of returning a serve was almost as easy as pressing a button.

———

To understand why some tennis professionals are so good at returning serve, I made an appointment to see Angel Lopez, one of the most sought-after tennis coaches in the world and a return-of-serve guru. Lopez has coached numerous professionals and is a contemporary of Jimmy Connors; they trained with the same instructor and coached World Team tennis against each other.

Lopez explained how Connors revolutionized the return with his speed and focus: "Connors put pressure on the server. He trained to be really quick, and violent. He practiced repeatedly at high speed. It's all training, to get a feel for where the ball is going. That's why they say you only get better at returning serve by returning serve. He focused his vision on the precise point where the ball leaves the strings. He didn't worry about what the server's body was doing. His eyes were fixed at the point of impact. And his eyes were huge, like Charles Manson's. Connors looked like a mass murderer when he returned serves."

Lopez's mantra is "ball identification"—the preparation phase that precedes the decision about exactly how to hit the ball back. He told me to watch his eyes as they darted around and then froze. "Most players train their hands and feet. But you need three things to be fast: hands, feet, and eyes. Fast means fast eyes too. That doesn't just mean picking the ball up—this isn't a video game. It means focusing on the ball, and then translating that focus into an attack."

According to Lopez, ball identification is becoming even more important with advances in technology and serving skill. "At the highest levels, you can't get any information from what the server does before the ball hits the racquet. Nothing. I've analyzed Pete Sampras in detail with other coaches, in super-slow motion. You can't see anything. He's like a great baseball pitcher disguising his release. Everything looks exactly the same, regardless of where the ball is going. So you have to focus on impact. The theory of returns used to be that you should hit the ball as early as possible. But as players got faster and equipment improved, they learned to hang back and hit harder returns. They spend more time on ball identification, getting a chance to read the ball, and then really punish it."

Connors and Evert didn't have substantially faster visual reaction times; no one does. But they were much faster at reacting physically. Their physical speed freed up time for them to prepare during the phase Lopez calls "ball identification." This was when they absorbed the crush of data generated after the ball left the server's racquet. They split up the time available during a service return; because they were so fast, they had extra time to gather and process information. Finally, at the last possible instant, they committed to their choice of return and swung. They sandwiched a lot of preparing between seeing and hitting.

See (200 ms)	Prepare (200 ms)	Hit (100 ms)

Because Connors and Evert needed less time to hit a return, they had more time to gather and process information. They saw, they prepared, and finally, only after they had processed as much information as possible, they hit. Their preconscious time management—what their brains did during the "prepare" period—was crucial to their success. Their talent enabled them to stretch out a split-second and pack in a sequence of interpretation and action that would take most of us much longer.

Robert Levine, a psychologist who has written widely about how people perceive time, compares the athlete's experience during this preparation phase to the Zen task of becoming "liberated from time." According to Levine, Jimmy Connors exemplified this Zen-like quality. Talking about Connors, Levine describes "transcendent occasions when his game rose to a level where he felt he'd entered a 'zone.' At these moments, he recalls, the ball would appear huge as it came over the net and seem suspended in slow motion. In truth, of course, Connors's seeming eternity lasted only a fraction of a second."[4] Yet he felt that he had all the time in the world to decide how, when, and where to hit the ball.

Connors and Evert were able to stretch time and gain an advantage from their ability to delay. They practiced to become as fast returning serves as they possibly could. Sometimes they used that speed to pick off a serve right away, on a short hop, returning it quickly to surprise an opponent. But more typically their speed enabled them to return serves as slowly as they possibly could. They got fast first in order to go slow later.

———

Tennis is not unique. In other sports that require a superfast hit, such as baseball and cricket (or fencing, car racing, or table tennis), the best athletes are no faster than we are at "seeing." What distinguishes top baseball and cricket batsmen—such as Ted Williams (career batting average of .344) and Sir Donald Bradman (career average in international Test matches of 99.94)—is their ability to gather and process information before they hit. Top batsmen excel not because their visual reaction times are fast, but because their fast physical reaction times enable them to go slow.

Laboratory studies of baseball and cricket confirm that the best professionals are better, not because of what they do during the "see" phase, but because of what they do during the "prepare" phase. When professors from Kyoto University put professional baseball players in a dimly lit room and measured how quickly they responded to images on a computer screen, they confirmed that professionals were no faster at visual reaction than amateurs or even non-athletes: everyone was in the range of two hundred or so milliseconds. The authors concluded that "simple reaction time is not a particularly accurate predictor of experience, performance, or success in sports."[5] Instead, it was what batters did after their visual reaction that distinguished professionals from amateurs.

The leading experiments comparing the ball identification and reaction skills of amateurs and professionals were performed on cricket batsmen of widely varying abilities by Peter McLeod of Oxford University. I visited

25

McLeod in one of the common rooms at the Queen's College, where he is a fellow. At first glance, McLeod might seem like an antiquarian—an Oxford don talking about a centuries-old sport at a college founded in 1341. But McLeod is a distinguished neuroscientist and experimental psychologist who works at the leading edge of both fields.

"The best cricket players seem to have a lot of time," he told me, "whereas the less good ones always seem hurried. Everyone sees this, but we wanted to test whether these observations are true in fact, so we precisely measured how long different players took to swing and when they began their swings. We looked at three different levels of players, ranging from true amateurs to top professionals. Interestingly, all of them employed essentially the same strategies. The professionals were quicker, but not by much—just in the range of tens of milliseconds quicker. When we watch them play, the gap in skill appears to be enormous, but in truth it is a very small time difference. What matters crucially is just a tiny time window of about fifty milliseconds in all. That makes all the difference."

According to McLeod, a cricket batsman who is just fifty milliseconds slower than an average professional—in other words, someone who is slower by just a fraction of the time it takes an eye to blink—simply has no chance of competing with the pros. This slight time disadvantage is overwhelming because cricket professionals are so adept at using that extra time for ball identification, the same processing and preparation that Angel Lopez says is so important to returning serves. From studying high-speed film of cricket batsmen, McLeod has concluded that "their skill, it seems, lies in how they use visual information to control motor actions once they have picked it up, not in the more elementary process of picking it up."[6]

There is something uniquely animal-like about the rapid-fire ball identification required in superfast sports. These sports are all forms of one-on-one duels: tennis server versus returner, cricket batsman versus bowler, baseball pitcher versus hitter. Superfast sports tap into the most primal, survivalist parts of our nervous systems. They mimic a fight to the death, a civilized version of a pistol duel, or of two wolves lunging at each other's throats. One opponent watches the other move and then instantly reacts.

Fencing is perhaps the fastest sport of all. The speed of a fencing bout is mind-boggling: to score a hit in épée, for example, you must hit your opponent forty milliseconds before he or she hits you.[7] A fencer's actions depend on preconscious anticipation, like returning a serve or hitting a baseball. Fencing might be a gentlemanly sport, but it tests largely primeval instincts.

———

We tend to lump together all sports that appear fast. Yet few sports require reactions as quick as those needed to hit a major league fastball or defend against a fencing parry. National Football League quarterbacks are often called the ultimate athletic quick-decision-makers. In the first chapter of *How We Decide,* Jonah Lehrer marvels at the ability of Tom Brady, the quarterback for the New England Patriots, to slow down time.[8] Professional quarterbacks often talk, as Jimmy Connors did, about being in a Zen-like zone where they see linebackers moving in slow motion and are liberated from time.

Yet a quarterback's decisions are leisurely compared to hitting a professional tennis serve or a cricket fastbowler's opening ball.[9] Quarterbacks typically have a few seconds, a relative eternity, to decide where to throw. Football does not seem slow—especially compared to cricket matches, which can last for several days, with breaks for lunch and tea—but the "prepare" phase for the key decisions in football is relatively long.

The point here is not that quarterbacking is easy and slow; it isn't easy or slow. The point is that superfast sports (tennis, baseball, cricket, fencing) are categorically different from merely fast ones (football, soccer, basketball). This is a distinction with a difference. At superfast speeds, we have to rely exclusively on our hardwiring to react quickly.[10] Superfast athletes aren't making the kinds of slower, more conscious decisions we will explore later in this book. (Some football-related decisions by coaches are coming up in Chapter 5). Football, soccer, and basketball are played in seconds; tennis, baseball, and cricket are played in milliseconds.

Superfast sports are a kind of showcase for us to watch how quickly human beings can respond under rapid-fire attack. Incredibly, the best athletes are able to observe their opponents, process information about their opponents' actions, and then react, all in a few hundred milliseconds.

How do these insights about tennis serves and baseball pitches matter to those of us who cannot compete with professionals at superfast sports? As we will see in later chapters, the decision-making framework that professional athletes use is precisely the same framework we should use for all kinds of non-sport decisions at slower speeds. The superfast athlete's approach of first observing, second processing, and third acting—at the last possible moment—also works well for our personal and business decisions. What is different, and most remarkable, about superfast athletes is that they follow this decision-making framework, and teach us this valuable lesson about delay, without thinking.

Benjamin Libet, a physiology professor at the University of California at San Francisco for nearly fifty years, thought about superfast reactions more than just about anyone. His pathbreaking experiments uncovered a strange phenomenon: a consistent half-second delay between a person's unconscious reaction to a stimulus and his or her conscious awareness of the stimulus. Libet found that we don't become aware of a reaction—even our own reactions—for half a second. This half-second consciousness-time barrier is a bizarre, almost magical, finding. It also is what makes superfast sports special.[11]

It is no surprise that the scientist who discovered the five-hundred-millisecond consciousness barrier in the brain also would gravitate to sports that pose five-hundred-millisecond challenges. Nor is it a coincidence that the two sports Libet used as examples in his writings about preconscious reactions were tennis and baseball.[12] (As a typical American, he didn't think about including cricket; I didn't either, until I found Peter McLeod.) Libet was fascinated by how professional athletes use preconscious delay, so these two superfast-reaction sports naturally were of special interest to him.[13]

Libet explained that the professional tennis serve is a special test at the boundary of preconscious human skill. It is designed for periods longer than the fastest visual reaction time but shorter than the minimum conscious reaction time. The serve forces the returner to act within a set period, before the ball goes by, but it favors those who can wait the longest during this period. And it does all of this so fast that conscious thought is impossible. These features are what make service returns so interesting to watch.

Libet had similar views about baseball. What he found most remarkable about professional baseball batters was not merely their speed, but what their speed enabled them to do:

A baseball batter faces a pitched ball at 90 mph. He must decide whether to hit that ball and to swing the bat in a path that can meet the ball.

Because the pitcher is 60 feet from the batter, the ball reaches the batter in a total of 450 milliseconds. The batter has only the last 200 or so milliseconds of the ball's approach to recognize the speed and trajectory of the ball and to make the decision to swing. Both that recognition and decision are presumably initially unconscious. Great baseball hitters are probably those who can successfully delay these processes as much as is physiologically possible.[14]

It is a marvelous evolutionary story that some sports arrived at this superfast-but-not-too-fast timing. Tennis and baseball could have been structured to demand faster reactions, which would have tested pure reflexes. Or they could have allowed for slower reactions, which would have tested conscious responses. But if the service line or pitching mound had been just thirty feet away—or two hundred feet away—the games would have been less compelling. At closer distances, the players would have had just enough time to react and hit, but not enough time to show off their preconscious preparatory skills. And at longer distances, players could have planned too much; incoming serves and pitches would have been lobs. Our fascination with the professional tennis serve and the major league fastball comes not at a response time of two hundred milliseconds or at one full second, but somewhere in between. Four to five hundred milliseconds is a kind of sporting sweet spot.

Libet found that in this time zone what distinguishes top tennis returners and baseball batters is not their ability to react quickly to visual stimulus, but rather their ability to create extra time, and then get the most out of it, before they have to react. They expand the available time period, slow it down, gather more information, and then end up in the right place to hit the ball with the optimal speed and angle. They are delay artists. They can react quickly, but only do so when it is truly necessary. As Libet concluded, "The great home run hitters . . . can swing the bat with extraordinary speed. That enables them to delay their decision to swing until the minimum required time to hit the ball."[15]

Libet's conclusions apply to all kinds of decisions. Professional tennis and baseball players follow the same two-step approach to good decision-making that we should follow in our longer-term personal and business decisions. First, they figure out roughly how much time they will have available to respond. Second, they delay their response as long as they possibly can within that time period. If you watch Albert Pujols hit a baseball in *really* slow motion, he looks just like Warren Buffett buying a stock: study the pitcher, watch the ball carefully, and don't respond to any opportunity until you have taken time to decide if it is a good one. Wait as long as you can so you'll have a better chance of swinging only at fat pitches.

Much of the battle between superfast athletes is too fast to see. It requires careful research using high-speed cameras. As with heart rate variability, much of what matters to our reactions and decisions over the course of milliseconds is so quick that it is largely hidden from view.

The superfast tools we have developed to replicate human behavior are likewise hidden from view. Computers and software algorithms that are modeled on our own decision-making circuitry are hard to tell apart from us at high speeds. That isn't surprising and has been a central part of discussions about artificial intelligence for decades.[16] However, what perhaps is surprising in the high-speed world of computing is that delay may prove beneficial and speed is not everything.

3 HIGH-FREQUENCY TRADING, FAST AND SLOW

I n the middle of 2006, the stock trading firm UNX, Inc.,
found itself in trouble. The company was seven years
old, nearly a lifetime in the dog-year world of high-
frequency securities trading. Its technology was dated. Its computer plat-
forms were falling behind, and its clients, including sophisticated hedge
funds and Wall Street banks, were shifting to competitors. To survive,
UNX needed to build a more efficient trading platform that could compete with other superfast trading firms.

André Perold, then the chair of UNX's board and the head of Harvard
Business School's Finance Department, understood the problem, and he
knew just who to call. The core of UNX's business was trading securities

on behalf of sophisticated clients who wanted to buy and sell cheaply, quickly, and anonymously. At one level, Perold understood that UNX needed a "quant," someone who grasps mathematical algorithms. But he also knew there is an art to split-second securities trading. Scott Harrison, the man Perold called, told me about Perold's pitch: "He said we were going to save UNX. We'd raise money from some Wall Street banks and build a brand-new platform with the best trading technology. It was going to be a serious challenge, but also an exciting opportunity. Our goal was to become faster and cheaper than anyone."

Harrison was one of a handful of people in the world who had the two skill sets the UNX job required. He had managed algorithmic trading operations, including complicated computer programs with names like Triton and QuantEX. But Harrison also was a visionary and a builder. Most managers of high-frequency firms spend their careers trading stocks and crunching numbers. Before Harrison began working in finance, he was an architect at Skidmore, Owings & Merrill.

When I first spoke to Harrison, on a fall weekday in 2010, he wasn't trading. He was cooking, taking a break from a home renovation project. Harrison was what some technology CEOs call "in between brilliant ideas." (He later joined Liquidnet, a large global trading network, as global head of product.) He was eager to tell me what had happened at UNX after he joined: "I'm not sure anyone really understands what happened. I think about it all the time, but I still don't get it. There's no word for it. It was just weird."

Harrison joined UNX in July 2006, and after a three-month transition he took over as the firm's chief executive. When André Perold made the public announcement, he praised Harrison and proclaimed, "We are confident UNX has a bright future under his management." Harrison and UNX quickly raised money and built a cutting-edge computer trading system. Both the hardware and software were designed to be faster and therefore more efficient. Harrison set up the new machines in a second-floor office in Burbank, California, two blocks east of Interstate 5, three thousand miles from Wall Street. Then he flipped the switch.

—

"High-frequency trading" might sound complicated, but it's just superfast stock trading by computers. It's different from "day trading"—the rapid buying and selling of stocks by humans, not machines, during the day. The computers involved in high-frequency trading buy and sell faster and more frequently than any person possibly could.

The industry dates back to the late 1990s, when regulators first authorized electronic stock exchanges. Before then, the bulk of trading in stocks listed on the New York Stock Exchange was done through specialists— human beings who walked around a vast trading floor covered with cigar ash and paper trade records. I still remember joining the bedlam of the NYSE floor one day in the 1990s when a law school friend arranged a tour. It was frantic, with men shouting, lights blinking, and phones ringing.[1] At the time, a trade was fast if it took less than a few seconds.

Today, high-frequency trading accounts for 70 percent of U.S. stock trades. The Securities and Exchange Commission calls high-frequency trading "one of the most significant market structure developments in recent years."[2] Computers dominate the modern market, and they aren't patient enough to wait for a specialist to shout or a phone to ring. Even the blinking lights are barely fast enough as trading signals approach the light-speed barrier. Electronic trading networks are booming, while the NYSE's famous floor and the people who work there are becoming irrelevant. Now a trade is fast if it takes less than a few milliseconds.

Scott Harrison believed a faster trading system would be more profitable. He thought UNX's speedy new computer platform would enable it to compete with larger, better-funded firms. He was right: Harrison and UNX won the arms race of high-frequency trading, at least for a while. But it wasn't for the reasons they anticipated.

When UNX switched on its new computers, its trading costs immediately plummeted. The new platform supercharged UNX's business. Suddenly the firm could buy and sell shares at a lower cost than just about anyone else. Clients rushed to do business with them.

As word spread, other Wall Street brokers struggled to figure out how UNX had become so good so quickly. As Harrison put it, "We were fighting against people who were really fast—Lehman, UBS, Jones Trading—and now we were winning. One day we were nobodies, and then overnight we were the best. They used to call all the time and ask, 'Who are you guys, and why the hell are you at the top of the list?'" Harrison was thrilled, and he was a hero.

By the end of 2007, UNX was in fact at the top of the list. The Plexus Group rankings of the leading trading firms hadn't even mentioned UNX a year earlier. Now UNX was at the top, in nearly every relevant category.

Harrison is the sort of leader who is always asking how things can be improved even when they are going very well. Although UNX's new trading platform was a huge success, he thought they could do even better by moving their computers three thousand miles from Burbank to New York, closer to the trading facilities of the New York Stock Exchange and NASDAQ, where most trades were completed. At the time, few people had focused on the travel time of trades. But Harrison understood that geography was causing delay: even at the speed of light, it was taking UNX's orders a relatively long time to move across the country.

He studied UNX's transaction speeds and noticed that it took about sixty-five milliseconds from when trades entered UNX's computers until they were completed in New York. About half of that time was coast-to-coast travel. Closer meant faster. And faster meant better. So Harrison packed up UNX's computers, shipped them to New York, and then turned them back on.

This is where the story gets, as Harrison put it, weird. He explains: "When we got everything set up in New York, the trades were faster, just as we expected. We saved thirty-five milliseconds by moving everything east. All of that went exactly as we planned."

"But all of a sudden, our trading costs were higher. We were paying more to buy shares, and we were receiving less when we sold. The trading speeds were faster, but the execution was inferior. It was one of the strangest things I'd ever seen. We spent a huge amount of time confirming the results, testing and testing, but they held across the board. No matter what we tried, faster was worse."

"Finally, we gave up and decided to slow down our computers a little bit, just to see what would happen. We delayed their operation. And when we went back up to sixty-five milliseconds of trade time, we went back to the top of the charts. It was really bizarre. I mean, there we were in the most efficient market in the world, with trillions of dollars changing hands every second, and we'd clearly gotten faster moving to New York. And yet we'd also gotten worse. And then we improved by slowing down. It was the oddest thing. In a world that values speed so much, you could be slower, yet still be better."

What happened to UNX seems strange, almost mystical. Yet UNX's experience is common in modern communication technology. For some tasks, the best approach is to send data as quickly as possible. But for others, the earliest signal is too early. How fast you should be depends on what you are doing. Sometimes it is better to be later.

Indeed, managing "latency," the amount of delay in a system, has become a multibillion-dollar business, and not just in stock trading. When you have a problem with a cable or Internet connection, a technician will *ping* a destination to measure the round-trip latency, the time it takes a packet of data to leave your cable box or computer, arrive at a destination, and then return. We often want that ping to return as quickly as possible. It is irritating to talk to someone via satellite and have to wait more than a half-second to hear each response.

When latency is too high, the back-and-forth of data signals is too slow. A conversation doesn't work. Live video games are worse: even at the speed of light, a long satellite delay ruins interactive play. Likewise, a surgeon performing a procedure remotely needs immediate feedback, so a satellite feed can be too risky. For phone calls, live video games, and remote surgery, speed is often crucial, and slower means worse.

But other times we don't need a faster signal. Unlike satellite delays, latency for a domestic phone call is almost always less than 150 milliseconds, faster than the human reaction to sound, so we rarely notice the delay. Telephone companies could invest in systems that reduce latency below 150 milliseconds, but they don't. A faster communication wouldn't improve our experience. Indeed, when computers are programmed to receive data packets within a particular amount of time, sending information too early can create inefficiencies or high-tech traffic jams. This is why computer programmers frequently write pauses into their code, to be sure destination computers will be ready for incoming data. In all of these areas, speed is marginal and slower can mean better.

Technology consultants recommend that companies assess the trade-off between time and cost and make latency budgets, partly to ensure that data arrive in time, but also to avoid paying to speed up a signal too much.[3] There is an optimal amount of delay. Not everyone needs to be faster.

Latency in the telecommunications industry might seem esoteric, but managing latency is similar to managing people. A company that asks its sales force to arrive at meetings an hour early has to cover the cost when they stop for lattes; a company that asks everyone to arrive a full day early has to cover hotel and meals. If clients don't care when salespeople arrive, as long as they are on time for meetings, why send them early? Not every company wants to pay extra for its salespeople to arrive first.

The bottom line is that how much latency we want depends on what we are doing. Do we care more about time or cost? If time is the key, we want to move as quickly as we can. We want to *minimize* latency. But if cost is more important, we can move a bit later, when the time is best. We want to *optimize* latency. Minimizing delay and optimizing delay are two very different things.

Optimizing delay is what a professional athlete does when faced with a speeding ball. It is what an emotionally well-adjusted child does when faced with a tempting treat. Instead of reacting instantly, they benefit from using an extra split-second to identify a ball or vary their heart rate. Computers that optimize delay don't always respond instantly at high speeds either, any more than superfast athletes and children do. Their goal is not necessarily to be first, but to be just right.

What about minimizing delay? Consider this extreme example: one of the most popular fiber-optic cable routes for carrying securities trades runs between Chicago, where most options and futures are traded, to New York, where most stocks are traded. Many firms are perfectly content to send their Chicago–New York trades along the cables that zig and zag along old railroad tracks running through Indiana, Ohio, and Pennsylvania. They don't care much if their trades arrive a few milliseconds faster, any more than we would care if a package sent by overnight mail arrived at 8:59 AM instead of 9:00 AM.

But other firms demand a faster route, and this demand led a company, Spread Networks, to spend two years and several hundred million dollars digging a new straight-shot trench from Chicago to New York. It costs a fortune to send trades through the cables along this more direct new route, like a superfast version of Federal Express, but many firms are willing to pay to minimize latency. After all, they save *three whole milliseconds.*[4]

Why are three milliseconds so important? For some traders, having an electronic buy or sell order arrive first can be the difference between making money and losing money. If only one share is available at a low price, the first buy order to arrive will secure that price. Any later orders might pay more. High-speed trading can be a kind of temporal arms race, like a superfast version of holiday shopping. If you aren't among the first customers in line on Black Friday for the post-Thanksgiving sale, by the time you get in the door the best bargains will be gone.

High-frequency traders say this kind of superfast computerized trading is good for all investors because we can buy or sell whenever we want at the lowest possible cost. Others argue that the increasing speed of trading is not only socially wasteful but dangerous. Critics believe we have been fortunate to avoid a market crash caused by high-frequency trading and that someday we will not be so lucky. One fundamental concern is that although stock prices quickly reflect new information, short-term price swings are too volatile and do not reflect a company's long-term value; at some point, if automated trading programs push stock prices too far in one direction, they will abruptly reverse. At its core, the debate is about computer versus human decision-making. Is it better to let computers trade on their own at preconscious speeds, or do we need conscious human intervention?

———

At 2:32 PM on May 6, 2010, an employee of Waddell & Reed, a mutual fund company headquartered about a mile from my childhood home in Overland Park, Kansas, clicked Start on a computerized trading software program.[5] The firm's goal was to reduce its exposure to $4.1 billion of stocks it owned by selling something called "E-Mini" futures contracts. The E-Mini is based on the Standard & Poor's 500 Index of top stocks, except that it is traded in small amounts (hence "Mini"), and it goes through an electronic trading platform instead of the frenzied "open outcry" method still used for other futures contracts (hence "E-"). To hedge $4.1 billion of stocks, Waddell & Reed would need to sell 75,000 E-Mini contracts.

Instead of having its own employees manually enter these orders or call a broker, Waddell & Reed used this automated computer program. Each minute the program calculated the number of E-Mini contracts traded in the market during the previous minute. It then automatically sold 9 percent of that number. The program was designed to take several hours, or perhaps even days, to sell 75,000 E-Mini contracts.

Instead, the program triggered the fastest roller-coaster ride in the history of financial markets. At first, when Waddell & Reed's computers started to sell, various high-frequency traders, with their own computer programs, stepped in to buy. The market was calm and balanced. For about nine minutes.

41

But then, at 2:41 PM, high-frequency traders began selling the contracts they had accumulated to zero out their positions. During the first minute, as they switched sides, trading volume increased and Waddell & Reed's automated program responded by selling a larger number of E-Mini contracts. During the second minute, more traders sold and so did the automated program. During the third and fourth minutes, everyone sold even more, in a kind of high-speed computerized trading death spiral.

By 2:45 PM, trading volume was exploding and the E-Mini futures contract was collapsing. Its price had fallen 5 percent in just thirteen minutes. The high-frequency computer programs were a big chunk of the market at this time. During one fourteen-second period, high-frequency traders accounted for 27,000 E-Mini contracts, about half of the total trading volume.

The decline in the value of the E-Mini contracts instantly spread to the rest of the market. Computer programs were triggered to sell, not just E-Mini contracts, but shares of companies represented by those contracts. As those shares declined, there was tremendous additional selling pressure, so much so that there were no remaining offers to buy shares of some companies. As a result, the brokers' legitimate orders to sell shares were matched with "stub orders" to buy shares at absurdly low prices. ("Stub orders" typically were placed to comply with legal rules that require some firms to keep open a certain number of offers, whether or not they are at realistic market prices.)

Some of the selling pressure came from computer algorithms that hadn't anticipated this kind of shock. Many high-frequency traders exited their positions entirely, running for the virtual hills. Stock indices other than the E-Mini also collapsed, as did the individual stocks represented by the E-Mini contracts. At 2:47 PM, shares of Accenture plc, the consulting firm, fell from nearly $40 to $30 and then suddenly—in just seven seconds—

plummeted to one cent. Although some shares were bought and sold at these absurdly low stub prices, trading instantly dried up. A few minutes later, shares of Procter & Gamble, the consumer products company, fell from more than $60 to $40. Shares of blue-chip companies such as IBM, Apple, 3M, and General Electric also declined abruptly.

But then, within a couple of minutes, the market snapped to life. Accenture traded near $40 again; Procter & Gamble was back above $60. The E-Mini contract and all of these stocks recovered.

By 3:08 PM, the market had settled and prices were about the same as they were before Waddell & Reed had started its trading program. When the firm's computers finished selling 75,000 E-Mini contracts, they ran out of instructions and shut down. The entire ride, the bust and the boom, had taken just thirty-six minutes. It became known as the "flash crash."[6]

Numerous studies show that under normal conditions high-frequency traders are a powerful positive force in the markets. They improve liquidity, making it easier and cheaper for us to buy and sell stocks. They reduce volatility, particularly in the short term, so that stock prices remain relatively stable.[7] However, other studies show that during periods of high uncertainty, such as May 6, 2010, high-frequency trading is associated with increased volatility and sudden, abrupt swings in the prices of stocks.[8] Overall, the evidence is mixed.

What, then, should we do about high-frequency trading? The first lesson for us as individual investors is simply to beware. Although high-frequency trading firms make billions of dollars in profits, most of us who actively trade stocks are like weekend warriors who try to compete with professional athletes: we definitely will lose, and we might get hurt. Most of us should just buy stocks and hold them, selling only when we absolutely must. However, it is hard for many people to follow this simple lesson. We trade more than we should for the same reasons we overeat, drink too much, and gamble. (More on all of these vices later.)

Although Charles Perrow, a Yale sociology professor, didn't write directly about high-frequency trading, his proposal to add "slack" to complex systems to bring them into sync and reduce risk applies to stock trading as well as it applied to the risks of nuclear power plants, air traffic, and dams. Perrow's pioneering book, *Normal Accidents,* was inspired by the nuclear accident at Three Mile Island.[9] Might stock trading be a similarly complex system, in which there inevitably will be a "normal accident" that will bring down the system? It isn't a pretty thought, and Perrow's proposals for complex systems are radical—either redesign the system to minimize risk or abandon the activity entirely. His broader point, fast-forwarded three decades, is that we can understand the dangerous tendencies of a complex system if we have more time and perspective.

Another lesson is that, although high-frequency trading seems to be driven by computers, there is a lot of human wisdom that goes into the programming and monitoring of those computers. Essentially, the most profitable high-frequency trading firms are managing time—they speed up when appropriate, but they also slow down.[10] Several leading high-frequency traders told me they encourage employees to take more time to reach decisions and they program their computer algorithms to anticipate how other traders will react, and then wait for those reactions. Sometimes these computer algorithms are set to minimize delay. But more often they are optimizing delay—buying and selling only a few shares during the first milliseconds, like the initial feint of a fencing duel, to test how other traders respond.

Today the top trading firms teach internal decision sciences classes in which they ensure their human traders understand why their computer algorithms react the way they do in different scenarios. They emphasize strategy more than quick math. For example, when interviewing prospective employees, one leading high-frequency trader likes to ask which fraction is larger, $\frac{8}{13}$ or $\frac{11}{18}$, not so he can see who gets the right answer first, but to get a window into how people think. He is less impressed by the math whiz who can quickly divide both fractions to the thousandths place and say $\frac{8}{13}$ is larger. He is more impressed by the contemplative type who can see-prepare-hit like a tennis professional by stepping back and quickly talking through the fact that the common denominator is 234 and then conclude that $\frac{8}{13}$ is $\frac{144}{234}$, while $\frac{11}{18}$ is $\frac{143}{234}$.

Increasingly, top firms are also teaching poker strategy to emphasize the importance of thinking through alternatives instead of just being fast. Poker requires not only the calculation of probabilities but also the anticipation of what opponents will do. It helps us develop the kind of strategic, future-oriented thinking that is crucial if we want to make good decisions about buying and selling stock. Susquehanna International Group, a leading firm, has run a ten-week training class, with one-quarter of the time devoted to extended analyses of poker betting. The director of recruiting at Susquehanna has hosted poker competitions at top schools and even has taught a class at the Massachusetts Institute of Technology based entirely on one poker hand.

Not very many individual investors can compete with these smart, well-trained traders. And not very many regulators can keep up with them either. Although some politicians have argued for regulators to police high-frequency trading, it is unlikely that regulators would have much of a chance against computer trading algorithms, any more than they would be able to beat a computer at chess or Jeopardy. By the time the federal government's report on the flash crash was published on September 30, 2010, market participants already had switched to new strategies. No one would use Waddell & Reed's trading program today.

Although regulators won't have much of a chance battling high-frequency traders directly, there is one policy they might implement to help protect against future flash crashes: instead of trying to keep up with the markets, regulators could help slow them down by introducing explicit pauses. Stock exchanges already use circuit breakers to force markets to shut down when they have declined by certain amounts.[11] So here is one concrete proposal to help traders slow down: force them to take a lunch break.

When I worked in Morgan Stanley's Tokyo office during the 1990s, I was struck by the positive impact of the required ninety-minute lunch break on the tempo of trading. Not that Morgan Stanley's traders were models of propriety during lunch: some of the most egregious trades described in my book *F.I.A.S.C.O.* were created in Tokyo and conceived during those breaks. Still, as a general matter, the pause in trading led to more rational thinking about the trading day and often helped cooler heads prevail. We read. We contemplated strategy. Sometimes we even ate lunch.

Historically, stock exchanges in Hong Kong, Shenzhen, and Singapore followed a similar approach, with ninety-minute midday breaks. In contrast, all of the world's other stock exchanges, including those in the United States, are open continuously, from morning bell to closing bell. Now the Asian markets are moving toward the Western model. In February 2011, the Tokyo Stock Exchange announced it would shorten its lunch break by thirty minutes.[12]

Unfortunately, there is no constituency to implement market pauses such as a required lunch break. Continuous trading is supported by the masses, including day traders, who consistently lose money. Wall Street banks oppose lengthy breaks, as do many regulators. The markets overall are moving to global around-the-clock trading. Interestingly, the leading proponents of taking breaks include some of the fastest, most sophisticated traders, who frequently use pauses in their own trading strategies. They understand that being fastest isn't always best.

———

There are trade-offs in managing trading delay, and the optimal amount of delay changes every day, perhaps every second of every day. For a relatively brief period in 2008, the optimal delay in the markets that UNX traded was around sixty-five milliseconds. The basic answer as to why UNX did better is that, at least then, the best strategy was to let other firms go first, and then follow up by entering the market later. UNX did that beautifully. Today that kind of delay would be unacceptable to many high-frequency trading firms. And yet for other firms, and other strategies, it might make sense to wait even longer.

Although many superfast trading algorithms make money by being the first to trade based on new information—using computer programs to estimate where stock prices are headed or to piggyback on orders submitted by others—increasingly, high-frequency traders prefer to test the trading waters first by placing a few small orders initially to see how others react. Depending on the supply and demand that instant, they might offer higher or lower prices a few milliseconds later. They might dive in or pull back. They live in a complex ecosystem where hundreds of computer algorithms react to each other's strategies. Like professional athletes playing superfast sports, they essentially play a kind of high-speed war game, doing whatever it takes to get a slight advantage. Sometimes the best strategy is to buy or sell just a little bit later than the other computers. Sometimes there is a first-mover disadvantage. Sometimes the second mouse gets the cheese.

The first milliseconds of stock trading are like the first round of an Easter egg hunt. Some children rush in to fill their baskets. Others wait behind. Which children are following the correct strategy? It depends. Rushing in might be the right thing to do if what you care about is maximizing the number of eggs you take, particularly if everyone else also is planning to rush in. But if not everyone is going to rush in, or if you think those who rush in will leave enough eggs behind, you might be better off waiting. This is particularly true if you want to avoid the cost of the rush (potentially injuries or traumatic memories) and just have a nice time while you pick up some remaining eggs. Then you'd be better off waiting for the ruckus to subside before doing a leisurely, less costly hunt during the second round. How long you should wait depends on what you care more about: time or cost.

Like professional athletes, Scott Harrison, André Perold, and UNX learned there is an art to delay, even for preconscious reactions that take only milliseconds and even if those reactions are implemented by a computer, not a human being. By delaying its trades slightly, UNX avoided the extra costs that arose from the rush of instantaneous trading. Our initial reaction might be to criticize UNX for being slow, for not getting there first. But that wasn't the company's game. It got better results by waiting a few dozen milliseconds—by procrastinating at the speed of light.

4 **FRONTAL NUDITY IN *FIGHT CLUB***

I*am going to violate* the first two rules of *Fight Club,* but only to pursue further insights into decision-making at preconscious speeds.*

Among *Fight Club*'s many fascinating, sometimes outrageously mind-blowing subplots and ideas is the notion that a movie projectionist would splice a single frame of male frontal nudity into a family film, just to see

---

* As Tyler Durden, played by Brad Pitt in the film, says: "Welcome to Fight Club. The first rule of Fight Club is: you do not talk about Fight Club. The second rule of Fight Club is: you *do not* talk about Fight Club!" IMDb, "Memorable Quotes for 'Fight Club,'" http://www.imdb.com/title/tt0137523/quotes.

how the image would affect the audience. *Fight Club* itself contains such an image spliced at the end (I rented the DVD and checked, just to be sure), as well as other frames scattered throughout with strange clues and messages. Although the movie premiered more than a decade ago, it retains a cult following, and there are extensive online discussions about the meaning of its various subliminal messages, which obsessive viewers have teased out by closely examining the film frame by frame.[1]

If you see the movie, you will not be consciously aware of these messages. Traditional video formats, including *Fight Club*'s, are "24p," meaning twenty-four frames per second. That works out to about forty-two milliseconds per frame.[2] We cannot react to visual stimulus in anything close to forty-two milliseconds. If we had to press a button during a movie when a single-frame image appeared at that speed, we would fail.

But might a movie's subliminal messages nevertheless affect us, even though we cannot consciously respond to their superfast appearance? More generally, might preconscious flashes of information from other sources—advertising, television, or even from the corners of our eyes— change our behavior in ways we do not understand? Do we indeed make different decisions after we see that spliced image from *Fight Club*?

—

Subliminal messaging has a volatile history. James Vicary, a controversial businessman and researcher, coined the term when he announced the results of a 1957 experiment he might or might not actually have conducted.[3] Vicary claimed that when he put a high-speed tachistoscope in the projection booth of a Fort Lee, New Jersey, movie theater and flashed frames of "Hungry? Eat Popcorn" and "Drink Coca-Cola," sales of popcorn and Coca-Cola rose 58 percent and 18 percent, respectively.

Vicary called a press conference to report that these results held throughout a six-week test period and to announce that he had just formed the Subliminal Projection Company. He wouldn't give out his data, or even tell anyone which movie theater he had used, but he said that he and his new company were available to help advertisers capitalize on his findings.

Vicary's move came at a time of intense controversy about the advertising industry. It was the era of Don Draper, the lead character in the television series *Mad Men,* when advertising was profitable and flashy, but also under attack. Consumers had begun to understand how advertisers were influencing their decisions, and they didn't like it. Paranoia about mind control was widespread. George Orwell's novel *1984* had just been made into a film. Vance Packard's exposé of the advertising industry, *The Hidden Persuaders,* was a best-seller.

Vicary's Fort Lee study outraged the public. The National Association of Broadcasters banned subliminal advertising, as did the governments of Britain and Australia. Lobbyists for media companies advocated to protect thirty-second advertising slots, fearing that competitors would reach the public more effectively in a flash of a second. But as scientists looked more closely at Vicary's results, they could not replicate them. After years of investigation, Vicary finally admitted to lying about the experiment. Later studies concluded that subliminal advertising was ineffective. It didn't lead consumers to buy more popcorn and Coca-Cola. It didn't seem to change behavior at all.

Still, people remained concerned about subliminal messages, and every few years there were bursts of outrage. One notable scandal was during the 1973 holiday season, when the Pressman Toy Corporation ran a television ad for the Norwegian children's game Hūsker Dū with a one-frame subliminal message: "Get It."[4] Again, consumers were furious. The Federal

Communications Commission held hearings and issued a new ban. So did other governments, including Canada, where the game was popular.

More recently, subliminal messaging has become a cat-and-mouse game among advertisers, consumers, and regulators, with activists scouring film and television for objectionable content.[5] In 1999 the Walt Disney Company recalled the home video version of its 1977 animated classic *The Rescuers* after a viewer found two frames that depicted, not just a couple of cute mice, but also a topless woman.[6] In 2000 the FCC accused George W. Bush's presidential campaign of including the word "RATS" in one frame of a television attack ad. In 2007 anti–fast food protesters uncovered a single-frame McDonald's logo that flashed during an episode of *Iron Chef,* a show on the Food Network. And so on.

Our opinions about subliminal messaging vary. On one hand, it seems threatening. If unconscious stimuli work, then "Big Brother" could change our behavior just by flashing the right image and we would never know it. If subliminal influences are that powerful, we should be aware of them and perhaps seek to avoid or prohibit them. At minimum, we should moderate our behavior when we know we have been exposed to such influences.

On the other hand, subliminal messaging can seem absurd. Could the topless woman in *The Rescuers* substantially influence a viewer's behavior? Many subliminal advertisements just seem like gimmicks.

Research on subliminal messaging has been nearly as volatile as our opinions. Until recently, there seemed to be scientific consensus that although subliminal stimuli might influence our behavior, the effect is rarely powerful or enduring. Studies found subliminal messages are most effective when they prime us to do something we already are inclined to do, or to think something we already are inclined to think. Many experts have said subliminal messaging doesn't change our behavior very much, if at all.

However, new evidence suggests that the impact of subliminal messages can be lasting and influential, especially if these messages tap into our life experience. Recent studies show that people can retain trace memories of subliminal images for hours, or even days.[7] When the subjects of one experiment experienced a subliminal flash of the Apple computer logo instead of the IBM computer logo, they were more creative at work that day[8] (sorry, IBM). People exposed to a photo of an exclusive restaurant displayed better manners at dinner that night[9] (though someone who had never been to an exclusive restaurant, like the high school kids in *The Wire,* presumably would not have been affected). When people see words generally associated with the elderly, such as "bingo," "gray," and "sentimental," even for just a few milliseconds, they walk more slowly, have worse memories, and espouse more conservative political views.[10] Maybe the topless woman in *The Rescuers* really did affect some teenage boys.

Today more experts believe subliminal messages can make us do things we otherwise would not have done, for better or worse. Their claims might seem as far-fetched as James Vicary saying he could make us crave popcorn and soda, but this time they are backed by facts and peer-reviewed academic research.

—

Sanford DeVoe is an assistant professor of organizational behavior and human resources management at the University of Toronto's Rotman School of Management. He is one of several young scientists who are reexamining how people think about incentives and time. As a PhD student at Stanford University in 2007, he published two important studies showing how hourly wages distort our behavior. Then he began thinking about fast food.

When most of us see a McDonald's restaurant, we don't consider the stimuli bombarding us. Many of us just want to order a Quarter Pounder and eat it. Even if we understand precisely what is in the food and how it will affect our diet, we aren't conscious of how the company's logo and colors change our non-food-related behavior. I never imagined that the stimuli at McDonald's would alter my decisions outside the restaurant, even though in a prior life I was a McDonald's junkie, worked at McDonald's during high school, and campaigned for the presidency of the University of Kansas student body wearing a McDonald's uniform and advocating, as my primary platform plank, that McDonald's be permitted to open a restaurant on campus. (I lost the election.)

DeVoe sees McDonald's stimuli through a more skeptical lens. He craves fast food as much as the average person. And he certainly understands the risks that arise from our cravings, including obesity and diabetes. But he also finds in his own reactions, and ours, a broad research agenda for uncovering why modern life has become so frenetic. He worries about even more than the weight gain, insulin resistance, and other public health hazards associated with fast food, which have been so well documented during the previous decade, beginning most prominently with Eric Schlosser's 2001 book *Fast Food Nation*. DeVoe's intriguing hypothesis is that the environmental cues from fast food, which we see every day, have speeded up the pace of life. He told me, "The idea of researching fast food came from my own experience. I would go into a McDonald's and order a Quarter Pounder as a splurge, even though it is high in fat and high in calories. It's the kind of thing I knew I shouldn't be eating. But then, when I got it, I would become overwhelmed by my urges and just eat it immediately. I would eat it right that second. I wouldn't even savor it, which is what I should have been doing. And I thought, this is a really rich psychological phenomenon. There's a lot there."

DeVoe wondered if there might be a connection between time, impatience, and the effects of fast-food stimuli. Of course, not everyone craves fast food; many people despise it, particularly those who, like my twelve-year-old daughter, find meat revolting. Yet nearly everyone is exposed to fast-food logos and advertising, and many of us are eating faster than our parents and grandparents did—whatever it is we eat. Might DeVoe's urge to wolf down that Quarter Pounder be merely one example of a broader range of subconscious snap reactions to fast food? DeVoe began to wonder if McDonald's was making *him* faster, just as it has made food faster.

DeVoe and his colleague Chen-Bo Zhong, also at the University of Toronto, decided to study the effects of subliminal fast-food messages on a group of undergraduate students.[11] They sat the students at computer terminals and told them to focus on the center of the screen, where some exclamation points ("!!!!!!!!!!!!") would flash and then a word would pop up in the same spot. They were told to try to anticipate what the word might be and to ignore any flashing colorful squares that appeared in the corners of the screen. When all of the flashing stopped, the students were asked to read some brief instructions and a 320-word description of Toronto. There was no time pressure or test; they were simply asked to indicate when they had finished reading.

What the students didn't know was that, for half of them, the flashing objects in the corners weren't merely colorful squares. Instead, sandwiched between views of the squares were twelve-millisecond flashes of fast-food logos. The logos of six major fast-food restaurants were represented: McDonald's, KFC, Subway, Taco Bell, Burger King, and Wendy's. None of the students realized they had been exposed to these fast-food logos. Like the control group, they told DeVoe and Zhong they had seen only colored squares.

Normally, in this kind of an experiment, the objective would be to determine if the subliminal images made the students hungrier or more likely to eat fast food. But DeVoe and Zhong were after broader factors that related not to appetite or food but to speed. They wanted to test whether seeing the fast-food logos influenced how quickly the students read the description of Toronto. Could seeing a McDonald's image for twelve milliseconds make someone read faster?

That was precisely what they found. Although the control group took more than 84 seconds to read the passage about Toronto, the students who had been exposed to the fast-food logos did it in 69.5 seconds. We don't know whether they understood the passage as well; perhaps they didn't. But nevertheless, they finished reading about 20 percent faster. The findings suggest that if your goal is simply to cram, or finish a reading assignment faster, you should go to McDonald's.

In 1960 McDonald's operated 200 restaurants; now that number is 31,000. Today there are more than a quarter-million fast-food restaurants in America, and on any given day one in four Americans eats a meal at one of them. At the same time, the amount of time people spend reading has declined. On a typical weekday, Americans over age fourteen spend just twenty minutes reading. In a given year, one-quarter of Americans aged eighteen to twenty-four do not read any books for pleasure.[12] The median American will read just half a dozen books this year. Fast food both saves us time and speeds up our behavior. With more time and faster reading speeds, we could read more. Yet we read less.

DeVoe and his research team wondered whether fast food, by encouraging us to live faster, might be changing our perceptions in other ways and perhaps even spoiling how we experience the daily pleasures of life. Might the negative effects of fast food reach beyond physical well-being to emotional and mental health? Might reading be just one of many slices of culture that become less pleasurable because of fast-food stimuli? DeVoe's most recent experiments, with his Toronto colleagues Chen-Bo Zhong and Julian House, have yielded some startling results.[13]

DeVoe and his team showed a group of students flashing exclamation points, words, and squares, just as they had done in their study of reading speeds. But this time, instead of asking the students to read, they told them to take a break and look at three pleasant photos from *National Geographic* magazine. Immediately after participants viewed the photos, they rated how happy they felt at that moment.

Students who had been exposed to twelve-millisecond views of fast-food logos reported feeling significantly *less happy* after viewing the photos. It wasn't the fast-food images alone that made them less happy; DeVoe and his colleagues found that the happiness of students who saw only the fast-food logos, but not the photos, was essentially the same as the happiness of a control group of students who saw neither fast-food logos nor photos. The key was how the fast-food images interfered with the students' ability to enjoy the photos. Students exposed to fast-food logos alone were fast and happy; students exposed to both fast-food logos and attractive photos were fast and sad.

The researchers wanted to understand why fast-food stimuli would interfere with people's aesthetic experience, so they tried a similar experiment with music. The advantage of music over photos is that the experience is designed to occur during a fixed period of time—the duration of the sound. In this case, students listened to the first eighty-six seconds of "The Flower Duet" from the opera *Lakmé*.

As with the photos, those students who were exposed to fast-food logos and music were less happy. The logos interfered with their enjoyment. But the fact that the music lasted just eighty-six seconds gave DeVoe and his team another variable to test: impatience. To see if the students exposed to fast-food logos were more impatient, DeVoe and his team asked them to estimate how long the music had lasted. The students who saw the fast-food logos felt the music had taken longer. They scored higher on other tests of impatience as well. The fast-food stimuli warped these students' sense of time. Flashes of fast-food images made them unable to sit back and enjoy the music.

DeVoe sees the effects of fast food as a metaphor for the potential downsides of gaining speed and saving time. Fast food is a magnificent time-saving device, but in speeding us up as well as saving us time it can also make us less happy. We become less happy even if we are spending our extra time doing things—like looking at beautiful photos or listening to music—that ought to give us pleasure. People today read less, take fewer museum trips, and attend fewer concerts. Is that because these activities aren't as fun? The decline in the number and quality of our cultural experiences can be traced, at least in part, to unconscious stimuli that make us live faster. As DeVoe told me, "There are ironic consequences to time-saving devices. Fast food might save us time. But it also leads us away from the activities we might enjoy during the time we save. It stops us from smelling the roses."

And it isn't merely about aesthetics either. As we saw with high-frequency trading, good decision-making depends on timing and judgment about timing. Just as some trading strategies suffer because they are too fast, our decision-making more generally will suffer if it speeds up too much when we are bombarded by imagery on our television and computer screens. Perhaps our collective decisions to favor speed over high culture today are the right ones. But saving time is not always worth the cost, as we saw in the last chapter with technology firms, particularly in telecommunications. One lesson from the fast-food studies is that we should focus more on managing the delay in our own high-speed systems. An unwanted message might lead us to make a decision too quickly, even if we do not realize it.

———

Most of us don't want a subliminally flashed fast-food logo to speed us up or interfere with how we enjoy art and music or how we make decisions. We don't want a subliminally flashed penis in a movie to, well, do whatever a subliminally flashed penis might do. (Notwithstanding the popularity of *Fight Club,* there are no definitive studies answering this question.) In short, we typically don't want subliminal images to influence us at all. But how can we avoid their influence?

One strategy is for the government to regulate subliminal messages. An absolute ban would pose free speech concerns, but Congress might prohibit companies from using subliminal advertising in ways that have been proven to mislead customers. If regulators found an employer who had read DeVoe's studies and was flashing logos at employees to get them to work faster, they might shut down that practice. However, as with high-frequency trading, regulators are unlikely to be able to keep up with technology. We can't rely on regulators to prevent us from leading faster lives induced by subliminal messaging, any more than we can rely on them to stop people from trading stocks too frequently. Ultimately, the solution involves more self-help than law.

One approach is to try to be more aware of when we are vulnerable to being influenced by a subliminal message. For example, we are more susceptible to subliminal food and drink advertising when we are hungry or thirsty. If we drive by some fast-food restaurants, we might stare off into the distance for a few seconds after we arrive at our destination, just to clear our minds. Or, if we suspect we have been exposed to an unwanted image that will speed us up, we might try to counteract the stimulus by consciously slowing down our activities—we might read a bit more slowly, or pause before entering a museum or concert hall.

An even better strategy is simply to keep our brains active. Researchers at University College London's Institute of Cognitive Neuroscience cited *Fight Club* as an example in explaining their recent finding that subliminal images affect our behavior only when we have lots of unused brain capacity. In contrast, when our brains are busy (in their experiment, "busy" meant trying to find a blue *Z* or a white *N* amid a continuous stream of letters), the images don't affect us. If our brains are active, subliminal messages go unanswered.[14]

So, if we are watching *Fight Club* and we are engaged in the plot and puzzling through the final scenes, we are less likely to be influenced by that sexually explicit subliminal image. But if we are exposed to the image while our minds are inactive, perhaps because we aren't paying attention, then we might be in trouble (or, if we like the image, in luck). One way to be inoculated against a subliminal message is to be thinking when the message arrives. When users of Google's search engine reported a bug that allegedly caused subliminal flashes of hard-core pornography during certain online searches, there was understandable concern. Yet few people realized that, among those exposed to the images, the most vulnerable were those who were bored.[15]

—

Of course, salient images also can influence our reactions and decisions over longer periods than milliseconds, when we have enough time to be consciously aware that the images are there. People who look at fast-food logos or pornographic images for seconds or minutes are obviously affected. Conversely, we can become so accustomed to the presence of images that we become less consciously aware of their influences, as when our daily drive or walking path takes us past fast-food restaurants or photos of scantily clad models.

Now that we have explored the world of milliseconds from several different perspectives, we are going to telescope out from milliseconds to the world of seconds. For the slower-paced decisions we are about to examine, we have enough time to react both unconsciously and consciously. These decisions are fast, but not superfast, and that difference is a crucial one. Once we have a few seconds, we can think—and thought creates both opportunity and danger.

5 BAD CALL

Psychologists *often say* there are two systems of the mind: system 1, which is automatic and involuntary, and system 2, which is effortful and deliberative. They don't really mean there are two separate physical systems. As Nobel laureate Daniel Kahneman has written, "The two systems do not really exist in the brain or anywhere else."[1] But some scientists find this two-system idea to be a useful metaphor in describing our different mental approaches.

So far in this book, we have been looking at what a psychologist would refer to as system 1. As we have seen, timing and delay play an important role even for the kinds of superfast preconscious reactions that psychologists would label as automatic. Even during just a split-second, there is a lot of variability in heart rates, athletic responses, and subliminal reactions.

With this chapter, we begin looking at decisions that involve system 2 as well. Once we have at least half a second, we can engage in effortful, conscious thought, either to reinforce the automatic reactions of system 1 or to try to slow down or change them. When both systems are involved, we often get caught in an internal battle: intuition versus analysis, or instinctive emotion versus logical deliberation. With just a few seconds, we are capable of thinking through some judgments and choices, but probably not all of them. As we will see, both systems are prone to error, particularly under time pressure. System 2 has the capacity to correct system 1, but it also can magnify a mistaken snap reaction.

One of the most difficult tasks when we enter the conscious world of seconds is to know when we are an expert who can safely go with a snap decision, and when we are a novice who needs to step back and take more time. An expert generally won't need to delay a decision, but a novice generally should delay, as much as possible. The toughest part of the expert-novice distinction is that we can be experts in an area, with years of seemingly relevant experience, but then be confronted in the same area with a new twist on a decision that turns us into a novice. Not very many experts will admit, or even see, when they are novices.

—

It is Sunday, November 19, 1978, another dark fall afternoon for Bob Gibson, the offensive coordinator of the New York Giants football team. Historically, the Giants have been a powerhouse, from the 1927 team that won the franchise's first title to the 1950s "all-decade" team led by Frank Gifford, the popular running back (and later television commentator). But memories of those glory days at the Polo Grounds and Yankee Stadium are fading. It has been fifteen years since the team made the playoffs, and the owners have been unable to resuscitate the franchise, even with new players and a state-of-the-art new stadium next to the Meadowlands racetrack.

Hope is fading this season as well. The Giants have lost three road games in a row. Now, with a record of 5–6, the team desperately needs a win at home against the Philadelphia Eagles, who lead by one game in their division. The pressure is on Coach Gibson to design and implement an offensive package to take out the tough, defense-minded Eagles.

Joe Pisarcik, the Giants' second-year quarterback, begins the game brilliantly, with two touchdown passes in the first quarter.[2] But then Coach Gibson's plans falter, and the Eagles take control. Late in the fourth quarter, the Eagles trail by just five points, and the crowd at Giants Stadium is on edge. Ron Jaworski, the Eagles' star quarterback, is known for leading game-winning drives: he did so in each of his four seasons as a starter, twice in the previous month alone.[3] As the Eagles march closer to the end zone, it seems inevitable that Jaworski will throw a last-second touchdown pass, ruining the Giants' playoff chances. Giants fans appear to be on the brink of a losing season. Again.

Then suddenly, miraculously, the clouds break. Odis McKinney, a rookie defensive back for the Giants, intercepts what might have been a touchdown pass from Jaworski. The beer-soaked crowd cheers as the game clock ticks under a minute. They sense a pivotal moment. Finally, after so many losing years, the Giants seem back on track. All Coach Gibson needs to do is call three quick plays and the Giants will win. Pisarcik and Larry Csonka, his All-Pro running back, are about to celebrate a season-changing victory.

On first down, Coach Gibson calls a running play, which leads to a short gain. With thirty-one seconds remaining, the standard coaching wisdom is to tell his quarterback Pisarcik simply to yell "hike," grab the ball from between the legs of his center, and fall down on top of the ball. Once a defender touches him, that play will be over,[*] and the Eagles will call their last time-out. Then Pisarcik will repeat his actions on third down. The clock will run down to zero, and the Giants will have won the game.

On second down, Coach Gibson follows the standard wisdom. He calls for Pisarcik to fall on the ball.

In this type of end-of-game scenario, the team playing defense typically concedes defeat. But the Eagles and Giants are archrivals, even archene-mies. Instead of accepting a loss when the ball is hiked, Frank LeMaster, a massive Eagles inside linebacker, barrels through the middle of the sur-prised Giants' linemen. He falls on and nearly injures Pisarcik, who is face down on the turf. A fight breaks out, and LeMaster gets up swinging his fists.

The Giants fans are too sloshed and elated even to notice LeMaster. They already have recorded the game as a win and are heading for their cars. On the television broadcast, CBS scrolls credits in yellow block letters as announcer Don Criqui thanks everyone from the producer and director to the crew and statisticians. The Eagles call their last time-out, and Criqui pronounces the team dead for the season.

The game has ended for just about everyone. Except Coach Gibson, who still has to make his final, crucial decision. The pressure is on, as it has been all day, from every direction: the high stakes of the game, the roller-coaster scoring, the surprise fight. Gibson is still angry with Pisarcik from the previous week's game, when the quarterback had disobeyed an

---

[*] The National Football League later changed this "touch" rule, to protect quarterbacks. Today it is not necessary to wait for a defender to touch the quarterback in order for the play to end. Instead, the play ends the moment the quarterback kneels down to the ground.

order and changed one of Gibson's calls during the huddle. But Gibson has to put aside those feelings and protect his quarterback from another last-second threat from the Eagles defense. For the Giants to have a chance at the playoffs, they need Pisarcik to be healthy.

Gibson knows the standard wisdom is still to call for Pisarcik to fall on the ball, just as he has already done. But is this scenario standard? LeMaster wasn't supposed to violate the unwritten end-of-game rule that defensive players should stay away from prone quarterbacks. If LeMaster did it once, he might do it again, alone or with others. Danger is in the air as the Eagles defense assembles for the next play. Both of Gibson's decision systems are firing: his system 1 is automatically reacting to the threat to an important member of his team, and his system 2 is consciously considering his choices. Should he tell Pisarcik to fall on the ball again on third down and risk exposing him to another onslaught? Or should he choose a play designed to keep his quarterback safe?

He has just a few seconds to make the call.

————

A football coach lives in a slower world than the hitters in the games of tennis, baseball, and cricket. His predicament is more like that of an emergency room nurse or a firefighter or a military first responder. Life moves fast for these people, and a large part of their decision-making is unconscious. However, with a few seconds, they also have a little bit of time to think. The trick in this slower time frame is to tap into cognition when it helps and to shut it off when it doesn't.

In superfast sports, there isn't time for our networks of glands and hormones to react. But in a slower situation, like the end of a football game, there are several seconds. During this longer period, experienced players often benefit from not thinking about what to do and avoiding thoughts that pop up as their biological networks respond, especially as the pressure mounts. At the end of a basketball game, Michael Jordan could calmly stretch time—even while he was in the air. Jack Nicklaus might not have been able to take just thirty strokes to finish the back nine holes and win the 1986 Masters at the age of forty-six if he had consciously focused on his swing. These athletes showed grace under pressure by burying their thoughts. Instead of overthinking, they relied on years of training to respond naturally and automatically.

A few seconds isn't long enough for system 2 to map out every possibility, but it is long enough for a coach's biological systems to kick in and interfere with his ability to deliberate. The noise from these physical reactions can lead to mistakes from both systems 1 and 2.

Antonio Damasio, one of the world's leading neuroscientists, has written extensively about how our drives and instincts induce physiological states that lead us to behave in particular ways.[4] He has found that, although our neurons fire instantaneously, within a few milliseconds, the biological changes instructed by these neural responses happen more slowly, sometimes much more slowly: "Neural signals give rise to chemical signals, which give rise to other chemical signals, which can alter the function of many cells and tissues (including those in the brain), and alter the regulatory circuits that initiated the cycle itself."[5] In other words, a part of our brain reacts right away, but the rest of our body's reaction takes longer.

Why might our physiological responses occur within seconds rather than split-seconds? One explanation is evolutionary. Imagine two of our hunter-gatherer ancestors out on the savanna a million years ago. One person's heart races instantaneously anytime he spots a predator. The other's heart beats normally at first, but then races after a few seconds if the circumstances suggest real danger. There's a trade-off here: quick reaction time versus cardiac wear and tear. The person with the immediately racing heart might not survive long. According to Damasio, "Life depends on those biochemical processes being kept within a suitable range, since excessive departures from that range . . . may result in disease or death."[6] In other words, stability mattered to our evolution. Our ancestors needed to outrun predators, but they also needed to preserve their bodies for the longer haul. The apparent result: people with instantaneous biological responses died out, and ours have some brief, hardwired delay.

Coach Gibson's body is bursting with biological responses as he decides which play to call during the Eagles' final time-out. The primary actor is his adrenal medulla, located on the top section of the kidneys—right smack in the middle of what we think of as the gut. As Gibson perceives danger, neurons fire in the basal ganglia region of his brain, telling his adrenal medulla to pump fight-or-flight hormones, particularly adrenaline, throughout his body. The adrenaline rush causes his blood pressure to rise. His adrenal cortex releases cortisol, a stress hormone, which makes his blood sugar increase too. His appetite and libido shut down. The blood flow to his stomach drops. His saliva dries up. Physically, he is a mess.

Mentally, he is a mess too. Much of the executive function of his brain, in the cerebral and prefrontal cortices, shuts down and is overruled by the amygdalae, two almond-shaped nuclei that help process emotional reactions from deep within the brain's lobes. The amygdalae release a flood of noradrenaline, a stress hormone that increases his reception to stimulus, making it difficult to figure out priorities. His decision-making becomes intensely focused on safety. His brain is scrambling as if he is being attacked, tapping the survival instinct that helped our hunter-gatherer ancestors stay alive. He is under so much stress that he cannot filter what is important. He appears more reckless and flighty than usual, perhaps even scatterbrained.[7] As his conscious system 2 breaks down—not immediately, but over the course of a few seconds—he defaults to his unconscious system 1.

When our brains are loaded with stimulus, it is more difficult for our conscious processes to work. As the load on our brains increases, we rely more on our unconscious processes. That is what is happening to Coach Gibson. As the seconds tick, he is moving away from control toward automaticity. He is flooded with stimulus. His brain is full.

A full brain is not necessarily a problem for a highly skilled expert, such as a professional football coach. In fact, one major advantage experts have over novices is a capacity to make good decisions even when they are loaded with stimulus. Experts can turn off the tap of their conscious minds and still react beautifully based on experience and intuition.

No one understands experts facing time pressure better than Gary Klein. Since 1985, Klein, a research psychologist, has conducted fieldwork studying experts in real-life settings to see how they make time-pressured decisions. His first major project, for the US Army, became one of the definitive studies of expert decision-making. It tells us a lot about Coach Gibson's predicament.

During the 1970s and early 1980s, military researchers spent millions of dollars trying to understand how people make decisions. They developed expensive decision aids for officers in the field, flow charts that showed how people react in various scenarios. However, as Klein explains, "no one would use them. After ten years of research and considerable expense, they were not much further along than when they had begun."[8]

Klein proposed to the US Army Research Institute for the Behavioral and Social Sciences that he could help the military by conducting a study, not of its own officers, but of fireground commanders, the people who decide how to attack fires. These people are highly experienced and work under intense time pressure. Klein said fireground commanders and military commanders should use the same strategies. The army's program directors had seen more traditional approaches fail, so they decided to roll the dice with Klein, a newcomer to military research. He won the project.

Klein began by having background conversations with several fireground commanders to discuss the standard model of decision-making taught at all of the leading business and management schools. This model supported a conscious "rational choice" strategy: identify, evaluate, and weigh all of the options, and then pick the one with the highest score.

But the fireground commanders didn't understand the model. It made no sense to them. When Klein asked about decisions and options and weighing, they didn't know what he was talking about. One experienced commander said, "I don't make decisions. I don't remember when I've ever made a decision."[9]

Instead, the commanders relied on their experience. When they saw a particular kind of fire, they knew just what to do. There was no conscious appraisal leading to a decision, just action. If it was a vertical fire, one that would spread straight up, they sprayed water down from above. If the fire had spread too far, they would conduct a search and rescue to get everyone out. Each situation was a prototype, and each prototype had a solution. There were no options. As Klein concluded, the fireground commanders were such experts that their first reaction was the right one: "They knew the typical course of action right away . . . so they did not bother thinking of others."[10]

Klein's study was a huge success, and he reached similar conclusions about how experts behave under time pressure in areas ranging from military strategy to emergency medicine to high-speed chess. One decision

Klein studied was made in April 1988 by Captain William C. Rogers III, who elected not to shoot at two Iranian F-4s that had used their radar to lock onto his ship, the USS *Vincennes*. Even though the Iran-Iraq War was ongoing, Captain Rogers knew from experience that pilots make idle threats during military exercises. He didn't need a complex decision matrix of pros and cons. He simply could not imagine how two Iranian pilots realistically would be preparing to attack him under the circumstances. Rogers was correct. He quickly decided not to fire, and the F-4s flew away, without incident.[11]

In addition to his fieldwork, Klein conducted several experiments to compare how experts and novices make decisions in a few seconds. In one study, a group of paramedics and CPR instructors watched a brief video of six people performing CPR and then chose which of the six people they would want to perform CPR on them in an emergency. Only one of the six people in the video was an actual paramedic.

Ninety percent of the paramedics chose the actual paramedic. When asked why they made this choice, they couldn't point to anything specific that the paramedic did. They just said that, in a general sense, "he seemed to know what he was doing."[12] But only 30 percent of the CPR instructors chose the actual paramedic. Instead, the instructors criticized him for not precisely following the rules they had taught, such as carefully measuring where to put his hands. The instructors might have been certified to teach CPR, but they were novices when quickly judging it in real life.

Another of Klein's experiments involved blitz chess, a variation of chess in which each player has only three to five minutes to play the entire game. On average, that is about six seconds per move, barely long enough to find a piece and pick it up. The opening moves, which are essentially formulaic, learned behavior, are even faster. In blitz chess, there is no time to generate options and analyze them. Players just have to react and then hit a button on the clock, so that their opponent's time starts ticking away instead of their own.

Expert chess players cope well with this kind of intense time pressure. Klein found that when grand masters play blitz chess, the quality of their moves hardly deteriorates at all.[13] They instinctively pick the best move, right away.[14] But when novices play blitz chess, it is a disaster. Either they tap their conscious system and use up too much time thinking about the next move, or they make quick, bad moves. Either way, their systems overload and they lose.

Klein concluded that experts in numerous areas are like grand masters playing blitz chess. They perform well under time pressure, when they shut down their conscious system and trust their gut. And the converse is true: novices perform horrifically under time pressure because they take too long and their gut is wrong. The message is clear: if you only have a few seconds to make a decision, you had better be an expert.

———

Just three months after Captain Rogers demonstrated his expertise by deciding not to fire on the two Iranian F-4s, he confronted a more complex, high-pressure situation and had to make a decision that is among the most studied in modern military history.[15] At 10:22 AM on July 3, 1998, crew members on the USS *Vincennes* reported to Rogers that an aircraft they had been tracking for five minutes was now within air-to-surface missile range. The crew in the ship's Combat Information Center believed the plane was an Iranian F-14 Tomcat fighter.

At least one other crew member thought the plane was a commercial airliner. The crew had sent several emergency radio warnings, but the plane had not responded. The air manifest showed that a commercial flight had been scheduled to depart from nearby Bandar Abbas Airport in Iran thirty-two minutes earlier. If that plane had departed on time, it already would have been at or near Dubai, its destination, and nowhere near the *Vincennes.* The commercial flight plan was just a twenty-minute hop across the Strait of Hormuz. But it was unclear whether the plane had departed on time.

The crucial factor was the plane's altitude. A commercial flight would have been ascending as it overflew the *Vincennes,* whereas an attacking Iranian F-14 would have been descending. If Captain Rogers knew the plane was descending, he should fire his missiles. But the ship's controls did not indicate whether the plane's altitude was changing. Instead, the crew had to keep track of altitude numbers as they flashed on a small computer screen and then infer the altitude trend from any changes in those numbers. Captain Rogers reported later that this was a rapid process that took "perhaps five to ten seconds." Several crew members performed the calculations, but they reached opposite conclusions. The crowded control room was noisy, and there was confusion about the flight's tracking number, which the computer system apparently had switched. Meanwhile, the plane was getting closer.

By 10:24 AM, there wasn't enough time left to conclude definitively whether the plane was going up or down. If Captain Rogers waited even a few more seconds, the plane would be too close, and the *Vincennes*'s weapons would be ineffective. Rogers decided to fire. He launched two SM-2MR surface-to-air missiles. Both of them hit, destroying the target.

The crew and captain quickly learned to their dismay that the plane had not been an Iranian F-14 Tomcat fighter. It was an Airbus A300B2-203, operated by Iran Air. The plane was gaining altitude, as planned, when it approached the *Vincennes* on its routine flight path to Dubai. All 290 passengers and crew were killed, including 66 children. It was the seventh-highest death toll from any aviation incident in history. The plane had left Bandar Abbas twenty-seven minutes late.

By all accounts, Captain Rogers was an experienced officer. Since being commissioned twenty-three years earlier, he had been on numerous tours, ranging from a Gearing-class destroyer in Japan to two Spruance-class destroyers in the Middle East to the *Vincennes*. But this was a new scenario for Captain Rogers: an imminent threat, a disagreement among the crew about the target's altitude, a commercial flight whose departure time was unknown, and a lack of response to emergency radio warnings. Just three months earlier, Rogers had demonstrated his expertise during the incident involving the Iranian F-4s. But this time, in a new scenario under intense time pressure, he was a novice.

———

When we are not experts and we don't have time to compare and choose rationally among options, the best choice is often to do nothing. Because novices are prone to make the wrong move, the right move is often no move at all.

Even the world's leading experts are novices some of the time, and when that happens they often should do nothing. Sometimes you might believe you know exactly what to do and yet be better off acting as if you were overwhelmed with indecision and unable to move. Studies of penalty kicks at the end of elite professional soccer matches, when the goalkeeper faces one opposing player at close range, show that although goalkeepers usually jump left or right the optimal strategy is to remain in the center of the goal.[16] Similarly, a common adage among top doctors, which I learned from Justin Graham, an infectious disease specialist, is "Don't just do something. Stand there."

When a small-town fire commander in Gary Klein's study responded to a massive fire at an oil tank farm, he saw a one-hundred-foot wall of flames, bigger and hotter than any fire he'd ever encountered. Most of the time, the commander was an expert, but here he was a novice. Fortunately, he recognized that. His men were just as bewildered, and no one had any idea what to do. Normally, they would have rushed in and turned the hoses on the flames. But they didn't. Reflecting on the incident, the commander said, "Our heads turned to stone." The firefighters didn't make a decision. They didn't do anything. They watched the fire burn.

It was a fortunate nondecision. If they had tried to put out this fire, they would have failed and might have died. Instead, the fire burned on as the commander and crew tried to figure out why the flames continued to blaze so intensely. Finally, after two days, they uncovered a twenty-two-inch pipe that was pumping fresh oil directly into one of the burning tanks. They shut off that pipe and let the fire burn out.[17]

If we are novices, by the time we have only seconds left to make a decision, it is often too late. The best decisions made in time-pressured situations are those we have prepared for in advance. The real challenge is to anticipate those situations in which we, as experts, might suddenly become novices, and then train for those scenarios. Klein suggests that people prepare by doing a "premortem." Whereas a *post*mortem reviews lessons learned after a decision, a *pre*mortem imagines that a future decision has failed and asks why. Assume we lost the game, shot the wrong plane, or died in the fire. Why? Which assumptions were wrong? Were we biased? Were we working with flawed data? Premortems take longer than seconds. They should be done early, before a time-pressured crisis hits.

Unfortunately, if you haven't done a premortem and you aren't an expert, these insights aren't likely to be very helpful. If you can't take a time-out or ask for help, and you haven't already thought through the precise scenario you face, you are most likely headed for a bad decision. Novices who wrongly believe they are experts are doomed. They don't realize their predicament until it is too late. Which takes us back to Bob Gibson.

—

Even in the heat of the moment, the Giants players are assuming Coach Gibson will tell Pisarcik to fall on the ball. That is what an expert coach automatically would do. And after all, who is more of an expert than Gibson? He was the quarterback at Youngstown State University during the 1940s, and he had a distinguished college coaching career during the 1950s and 1960s. As head coach at Bowling Green University, he won more than two-thirds of his games, including the Mid-American Conference title. By the time he joined the New York Giants, he had more than twenty years of coaching experience. As of November 1978, Gibson had made thousands of high-pressure coaching decisions. Anyone would rightly conclude that Bob Gibson is a football expert. In most football scenarios, he is.

However, on third down, with seconds left to play during the game against the Eagles, Coach Gibson is a novice. He has never seen anything like LeMaster's attack on Pisarcik. No one has. Gibson is like Captain Will Rogers III trying to decide whether to shoot down a plane without knowing for sure whether it is gaining or losing altitude.

When Gibson calls the final play—"Pro 65 Up," a handoff to Csonka— the Giants players are stunned. In the huddle, Csonka tells Pisarcik, "Don't give me the ball." But Pisarcik remembers how angry Gibson was when he disobeyed instructions a week before. The players are disorganized as they line up. They are arguing. One says, "Joe, just fall on the damn ball."[18]

Don Criqui, the CBS announcer, his voice initially pattering with the certainty of a veteran who knows the game is over, describes what happens next: "As the clock winds out on the Philadelphia Eagles in a game they thought would project them into a possible wildcard position . . . but a late interception by the Giants will preserve a Giant victory, an upset win as the Giants lead 17 to 12. And we are inside of 30 seconds."[19]

Then, as Criqui casually notes that "the Eagles have no time-outs," Pisarcik loses control of the snap. He spins clockwise, looking for Csonka, who is barreling forward on Pisarcik's left as he turns. Pisarcik tries to tighten his grip, but now Csonka is too far away and he shoves the ball into Csonka's hip instead of his hands. The ball falls to the ground, bouncing on the Astroturf twenty-seven yards from the Giants' end zone. Criqui shouts, *"Wait a minute, here's a free flah— . . . I don't believe it, the Eagles pick it up and Herman Edwards runs it in for a touchdown. An incredible development. . . . This is the most astounding development . . . absolutely unbelievable . . . unbelievable . . . unbelievable."*

Tom Curry, a Giants fan for fifty years, described the scene: "We were leaving, I was six steps up the walkway. All of a sudden we hear this roar. I turned around and saw Herman Edwards running into the end zone. I said, 'You gotta be kidding me.'"[20] With that touchdown, the Eagles won the game, 19–17. The Eagles went on to make the playoffs for the first time in eighteen years; the Giants did not. The play became legend, known as the "Miracle at the Meadowlands."

Gibson was fired the next morning and never worked in football again. He opened up a bait shop and general store on Florida's Sanibel Island. Unfortunately for scientists who study decision-making, he has never said whether he called the play more as an automatic response or whether his decision was based on some quick deliberation. To this day he refuses to talk about the fumble or its consequences. He says he "hasn't in 30 years and is not going to start now."[21]

—

After the Giants-Eagles debacle, football coaches everywhere recognized that they couldn't put themselves in Gibson's position at the end of a game. They needed to use a time-out or ask for help. They needed to be aware of how their biological reactions to pressure could change their decision-making. They needed a premortem.

Teams created new "victory formations" designed to protect both the quarterback and the ball. They practiced these formations repeatedly so everyone on the team, including the coaches, would be an expert during a game's final seconds. They implemented fail-safe systems so an offensive coach could and would check with the head coach before calling a new last-second play in an unanticipated situation.

Dick Vermeil, who coached several professional football teams, said Gibson's decision "embedded a memory in every coach that you don't take something like that for granted. You don't assume anything." Herm Edwards, the defensive player who scooped up Pisarcik's fumble, remembered having a similar reaction: "I can remember the next week we had an extra guy back there just in case something happened. Even now, that's one of the formations we walk through on Saturday."[22]

Today, good coaches anticipate what might happen late in a game, and they practice it constantly, just in case. In basketball, coaches simulate late-game situations when the team has no time-outs remaining so players will know not to call one (which would result in a turnover). In baseball, coaches consult statistics so they will know when to call for a bunt or replace a pitcher. In football, everyone remembers Coach Gibson.

Near the end of a November 2009 game against the Indianapolis Colts, Bill Belichick, the coach of the New England Patriots, decided to attempt a pass on fourth down instead of punting the ball to the Colts. The play failed. The Colts took possession of the ball near the Patriots' end zone and scored a last-second, game-winning touchdown. Many people criticized Belichick's decision, arguing that a punt would have put the Colts farther away from the end zone, reducing the likelihood they would score. A few angry Patriots fans even compared the call to the Miracle at the Meadowlands.

But Belichick's decision differed from Gibson's in one crucial way: Belichick was an expert at fourth-down attempts.[*] He had been an assistant coach in the National Football League for fifteen years, and a head coach for eighteen more. He had studied and experienced the precise scenario that arose during the game. He had even read and considered the academic literature on fourth downs (yes, there is such a literature), which shows that teams punt too often and that the right decision under the circumstances is to attempt a play instead.[23]

Belichick knew the numbers favored going for it on fourth down, by a large margin. He knew he might lose the game, but going for it was clearly the right call. His body and brain were under tremendous stress during the final seconds, but as an expert he could see there was only one choice. His intuition, backed by decades of experience and a mountain of statistical data, told him what to do. He didn't need time to weigh the pros and cons. He had been doing that for more than two decades.

---

[*] Likewise, near the end of the 2012 Super Bowl, Belichick told the Patriots defenders to allow the New York Giants to score a touchdown, because he knew the probability of the Giants winning the game with a last-second chip-shot field goal was greater than the probability of them defending against a last-minute drive by quarterback Tom Brady. Again, Belichick was an expert. But again, the Patriots nevertheless lost.

6 A SLICE
TOO THIN

***D**octors generally don't seem racist.* They swear an oath to treat patients equally, and most try hard to do so. Even as medicine has become more business-focused, students overwhelmingly choose medical practice because they want to help people, regardless of race. When doctors of all kinds are quizzed about racial stereotypes, they score high for tolerance and low for bigotry.

Yet more than one hundred studies have shown that bias and prejudice among doctors leads them to treat patients differently based on race.[1] Doctors are more likely to refer a patient suffering chronic renal failure for a kidney transplant if he is white than if he is black. Doctors treating heart attacks are up to twice as likely to administer a thrombolytic drug meant to break up clots in the coronary arteries if the patient is white than if he is black. In general, doctors are more likely to provide treatment and medication—whether for psychiatric illness, cancer, or broken bones— for whites than for blacks.

In one recent study, a group of seven researchers presented several hundred resident physicians at four academic medical centers in Boston and Atlanta with a hypothetical scenario in which a fifty-year-old male patient named Mr. Thompson shows up at an emergency room with chest pain ("sharp, like being stabbed with a knife"). The researchers gave the doctors a photograph of the man, along with details about his medical condition. To test how the patient's race might influence the doctors' answers, the researchers randomly varied the race of the man in the photograph. As a result, some doctors thought Mr. Thompson was white; others thought he was black. The researchers then asked whether the doctors would prescribe thrombolysis, a blood-clotting procedure.[2] The researchers also asked the doctors about their racial views.

Sure enough, the researchers reconfirmed the puzzle of previous studies: although the doctors said they had no explicit racial bias, they were significantly more likely to prescribe thrombolysis for a white patient than a black one.[3] The doctors didn't appear racist, yet they treated blacks differently (by undertreating them)—the very definition of racism.

To try to resolve this contradiction, the researchers administered a series of tests designed to determine whether doctors *implicitly,* or unconsciously, favored whites over blacks. These tests were customized versions of the Implicit Association Test, or IAT, a widely used computerized test for measuring unconscious bias.* The IATs revealed, as expected, that the doctors unconsciously viewed whites more positively than blacks. IATs have demonstrated this kind of bias in millions of people, including doctors. No surprise there.

But the IATs also led to a new finding, and the answer to the puzzle: there was a strong association between the doctors' IAT scores and their decision to give thrombolysis to white versus black patients. Simply put, doctors who unconsciously favored whites over blacks gave whites more treatment than blacks. The study concluded, "As the degree of antiblack bias on the race preference IAT increased, recommendations for thrombolysis for black patients decreased." Doctors undertreated blacks, not because of *conscious* racism, but because of *unconscious* racial preferences.

The researchers said their findings "suggest that physicians, like others, may harbor unconscious preferences and stereotypes that influence clinical decisions." Doctors might insist they are unbiased as to race, but all you have to do to get them to undertreat a black patient is show them the color of the patient's skin.

Why is unconscious prejudice winning out over conscious tolerance? Research into the implicit racial preferences of doctors revealed a further dimension of the problem. The implicit, unconscious form of racism detected in the doctor study appears to be contagious.

Dana Carney, one of the seven researchers on the doctor study, and Greg Willard, a postdoctoral fellow at Harvard University, demonstrated

---

* The IAT calculates implicit racism or other bias based on how quickly we can label stereotyped photographs and concepts. For example, an IAT designed to test racial preferences might ask you to put labels into one of two columns. One time the columns might be "White/Good" and "Black/Bad"; the next time the columns might be "Black/Good" and "White/Bad." The theory is that if it takes you a lot longer to put labels such as "evil" in the "White/Bad" column than the "Black/Bad" column, you have an unconscious preference for whites over blacks. In fact, more than 80 percent of people have pro-white associations, including many blacks. That doesn't mean those people are racist. But preferences do carry the potential to change our behavior based on race.

this contagion by asking students of various races to watch brief videos of a white person and a black person interacting. The black person's behavior was constant in all of the videos, but the white person's behavior varied in ways that studies have shown are consistent with racial prejudice (fewer smiles and laughs, certain physical movements, less overall warmth).[4]

All of the students had similar feelings about the white person, regardless of which videos they watched. But students who watched the "prejudice" video formed a more negative impression of the black person and demonstrated a higher degree of racial prejudice. These results held even when the black person was cut out of the videos and participants were merely shown a photograph of who was interacting offscreen with the white person. Once the students saw the white person's prejudice, they became prejudiced too.

The term "institutional racism" was coined by Stokely Carmichael, the Black Power advocate, to describe government agencies, corporations, and schools where racism is pervasive. The idea isn't limited to explicitly racist institutions, such as the Ku Klux Klan or the white supremacy movement. Institutional racism is broader and can encompass an entire social institution, such as educational testing or the media. For example, a late 1990s inquiry into the murder of Stephen Lawrence, a black teenager from southeast London, led to a public report condemning the British Metropolitan Police Service as institutionally racist. The study by Dana Carney and Greg Willard offers a simple explanation as to how racism can arise within an organization whose focus, unlike that of the KKK, is not directly related to race, and whose members might not even have conscious racial biases: the organization's members have unconscious implicit racial preferences, and they see each other a lot.

We know that hospitals and doctors' offices can be dangerous places. There are viruses and bacteria everywhere, moving from infected patients to doctors and back again. But now we also know that one of the diseases being spread there—and indeed everywhere—is unconscious racism. It comes from our turbo-charged brains. And you can catch it in a few seconds, just by glancing at a face.

The expression "thin slicing" was coined in a 1992 article published by Nalini Ambady and Robert Rosenthal in the *Psychological Bulletin*.[5] They used the term to describe people's ability to detect patterns in an event even if they experience only a narrow portion of that event. In particular, they focused on what people can glean from brief, silent video clips. And their answer was: a lot.

Their best-known finding, from a 1993 follow-up study, was that people who watched a series of brief, silent videos of a teacher reached similar judgments about the teacher as did students and supervisors who sat through the teacher's class for months. The study has been widely cited as an example of the power of our unconscious system. Its subtitle says it all: "Predicting Teacher Evaluations from Thin Slices of Nonverbal Behavior and Physical Attractiveness."[6]

The concept of thin slicing dates back at least to the 1930s, when psychologist Gordon Allport claimed people can make broad generalizations about the personalities of others based on limited exposure.[7] During the following decades, a few psychologists suggested that people form accurate impressions of each other merely from a glance, but these views were controversial and largely unsupported. Most researchers remained skeptical, and until recently the popular view was that our first impressions of strangers are often wrong and rarely useful.

That changed in 2005 when author Malcolm Gladwell published *Blink,* a brilliant and accessible book that introduced thin slicing research by Ambady, Rosenthal, and others to a broad audience. Gladwell begins with an example of thin slicing extraordinaire, a story about whether a marble statue purchased by the J. Paul Getty Museum in California was a fake. He describes four experts who saw the statue and were instantly repulsed. He then introduces his book as follows: "In the first two seconds of looking—in a single glance—they were able to understand more about the essence of that statute than the team at the Getty was able to understand after fourteen months."[8]

It was tempting for readers to draw a simple message from such a story: tap into the power of thin slicing, master those first two seconds, and you too can be an expert, not just with videos and art but in every aspect of life. Thin slicing became the rage as more and more people latched on to the apparent magic of the first two seconds.[*] Enter that term in a search engine today and you will get more than four million results. Gardner Resources Consulting in Wellesley, Massachusetts, will help you "thin slice your way to better hiring decisions."[9] Virtulink LLC has developed "procedure thin-slicing," a consulting methodology to help companies streamline performance.[10]

The two-second time interval became a popular mantra for thin slicing. Suddenly, everyone was talking about two seconds. This comment from

---

[*] Malcolm Gladwell recognizes many of the dangers of thin slicing in *Blink*. He discusses racism by New York City police officers in the shooting of Amadou Diallo, an unarmed Guinean immigrant, and explains how music auditions are biased based on gender. But even though *Blink* covers the downsides of thin slicing, the public seized on the pros more than the cons, either because that was where public opinion was inclined to go, or because readers didn't make it to (or focus on) the final third of Gladwell's book.

The Lit Show, a Chicago radio program, was typical: "In the first two seconds we meet a new person or challenge, our unconscious naturally sifts through the stimuli and keys in on the important details."[11] Malcolm Gladwell reinforced the importance of the two-second interval in talks, on his website, and within *Blink,* which he summed up as "a book about those first two seconds."[12]

Stop for a moment now—for longer than two seconds please—and think about the idea of "thin slicing." When we thin-slice, we detect patterns in an event even if we see only a narrow portion of that event. The key to the concept is that we reach a conclusion even though we don't have the full picture. Thin slicing is driven by the unconscious system because it takes the lead over the conscious system in decision-making during such a short period.

But thin slicing is almost *never* about just two seconds. In fact, not even the titles of the leading articles on thin slicing are about two seconds. The revolutionary paper by Ambady and Rosenthal is entitled "Half a Minute." John Gottman's coauthored study of videotapes of couples (which *Blink* describes as his "thinnest slice") is called "Predicting Divorce Among Newlyweds from the First Three Minutes of a Marital Conflict Discussion." *Minutes,* not seconds.

Neither of those studies found that anything close to two seconds was the optimal thin slice. To the contrary, Ambady and Rosenthal found that although students who watched three two-second videos (six seconds total) of a teacher did pretty well in matching the evaluations of people who sat through the entire semester, students who watched ten-second-long videos did better. More recently, Ambady and other coauthors defined a thin slice as "any excerpt of dynamic information less than 5 min long."[13]

Perhaps the most famous thin-slicers of all are John and Julie Gottman, cofounders of the Gottman Relationship Institute, which advertises:

"We're able to quickly determine a great deal of information about a couple from analyzing a very thin slice of data collected in one short lab session."[14] In *Blink*, Gladwell marvels at John Gottman's snap assessments of married couples and relies on Gottman's research in concluding that "thin slicing often delivers a better answer than more deliberate and exhaustive ways of thinking."[15]

But we don't know how well participants in the Gottman study would do during two seconds because they examined intervals that were 180 times longer than that. Indeed, although John Gottman is good at making snap judgments about couples, he recommends gathering information over a much longer time period: two days, not two seconds.*

So how thin should a thin slice be? The answer is rarely two seconds. If we are judging whether someone is dangerous, our brains and bodies are wired to react very quickly, within milliseconds. We assess race, gender, and age in a fraction of a second. We aren't as good at guessing sexual orientation, but, to the extent we see it, we see it right away: when students are shown a photo of a man and asked if he is gay, they are about as accurate within one hundred milliseconds as they are after longer periods.[16] For these reactions, we don't need anything close to two seconds.

But for other questions, two seconds isn't nearly long enough. If we are asked to tell whether someone is friendly or dangerous, we do better with

---

* The Gottman Institute's "Art and Science of Love" workshop lasts two days, as does "Deepening the Gottman Method." Other multi-day programs include: "Private Couples Retreats," "Marathon Couples' Therapy" (at the Gottmans' private island home), and "Premarital Preparation" (this one makes a great wedding gift!). The Gottmans do not offer a two-second therapy session. See http://www.gottman.com. And recall from Chapter 1 that Gottman also is not opposed to using much thinner slices than two seconds when appropriate, as he did with the studies of young children's milliseconds-long cardiac reactions to their parents.

more time. To accurately assess whether someone is sociable, we need at least a minute, preferably five.[17] The same is true if we are judging complex aspects of personality, such as neuroticism or open-mindedness.[18] For these decisions, our impressions during the first two seconds fail us. We need more time.

For many judgments, thin slicing has a kind of learning curve, steep at first as we quickly gather information about what we are watching and then flatter as we process that information. Although some people describe thin slicing as a snap judgment, it is really more of an acceleration than a snap, more like a car climbing a hill than a lightbulb going on. Sometimes we do reasonably well within a few seconds, but we often do better with a minute or longer. It depends on the difficulty of the assessment—the steepness of the hill. Usually thin slicing isn't as easy as flipping a switch.

As we examine decisions that take at least a few seconds, we will see that our ability to gather and process information can vary widely during different time intervals. The research on thin slicing demonstrates that we can be fast, but it also shows that even a little bit of extra time can often help us make better decisions. One slice does not fit all, and there is nothing magical about two seconds. Instead, how long we should thin-slice depends on what we are slicing.

———

In addition, thin slicing, at whatever speed, is not necessarily good. We like to believe we are experts about people, in the way Gary Klein's fireground commanders are experts about fires. We marvel at how we tap our unconscious system to fill gaps in what we see. But while our automatic processing is powerful, it is dangerous, too. We are hardwired to make judgments we might prefer not to make.

Psychologists, particularly Paul Ekman, have shown that the face is filled with instant, reliable information. Particular facial expressions are associated directly with specific basic emotions. Many of these simple expressions are universal, regardless of culture. Most humans can detect anger, disgust, fear, joy, sadness, and surprise right away, without thinking, just by looking at a face. We have an instant biological reaction to these expressions, and for basic emotions our quick impressions are reasonably accurate.[19]

We have an almost magical ability to gather information about people just by looking at their faces. Besides gender, race, and age, we pick up on more ambiguous qualities as well. Experiments show that people are reasonably good at discerning Democrats from Republicans just by looking at faces. We can tell good salespeople from bad ones just by their faces. We can even draw conclusions about organizations based on photos of their people. We can tell which law firms make higher profits by looking at the partners' decades-old college yearbook photos, from before they even attended law school.[20] We can predict which companies will have the highest profits from photos of their chief executive officers.[21]

But by thin-slicing faces, we also can deceive ourselves. Our automatic reaction to facial expressions can lead us astray. We prefer certain consumer products or housing options when they are associated with happy faces, which is why good salespeople and real estate agents are always smiling. We have the opposite reaction to sad or angry faces, even if they are selling something of high quality that we want. Although some experts can reliably tell when someone is lying, most people cannot.

We judge people with physically attractive faces, often quite erroneously, to be more trustworthy, intelligent, sensitive, kind, modest, outgoing, altruistic, and cooperative—they seem just plain happier too.[22] Attractive politicians win more votes.[23] Attractive employees are paid better and are promoted faster and more frequently.[24] Attractive lawyers bill at higher rates.[25] Attractive waitresses receive higher tips.[26] There is an extensive scientific literature on sex signals, intended and not, but if you've ever been to a bar, or a high school, you probably understand the basic idea.[27] Faces (and bodies) that we find sexually attractive skew our judgment.

Physical appearance can be even more important in our business lives than it is in our personal lives. Consider, for example, how we judge the faces of business leaders. In one experiment, Nalini Ambady and Nicholas Rule asked 170 undergraduate students to judge the personality traits and leadership skills of several dozen chief executive officers, not by assessing their decisions or their companies' performance, but by simply looking at their faces for a few seconds. They didn't tell the students anything about the people they were seeing, or even that they were CEOs. Their first study was of white male CEOs because they wanted to try to isolate facial features unrelated to race and gender. They found a strong relationship between subjective judgments about the CEOs' faces and their companies' profitability. The study concluded that "the judgments of naïve, uninformed college students (regardless of their gender) predicted the success of Fortune 1,000 companies from just the faces of their CEOs."[28]

Next, Ambady and Rule decided to test whether we perceive female CEOs differently. This wasn't an easy task. They scoured the Fortune 1,000 list of companies for female chief executives and found just twenty. Then they ran the same experiment they had run with male CEOs. They flashed the CEOs' faces on a computer screen in random order and asked people to rank them on a seven-point scale for competence, dominance, likability, maturity, trustworthiness, and leadership. Participants were told to make their judgments as quickly as possible.

Our reactions to photos of female CEOs demonstrate the double-edge of thin slicing. In general, we judge attractive people more favorably. But when it comes to our female leaders, the opposite is true. Although we find women who are more feminine-looking to be more attractive, we also find them to be worse leaders. Instead, we view anyone with a masculine appearance, male or female, as a more competent leader, as more powerful, and as more likely to be a good financial provider. Women with more attractive female features might be perceived more favorably in all kinds of ways that are crucial to social relationships, including finding a spouse. But to be seen as a better leader, a woman should look more like a man.

Similar conclusions hold at lower levels of the workplace, where being physically attractive typically helps men, but can be disastrous for women. In late 2010, Bradley Ruffle and Ze'ev Shtudiner published a comprehensive study of responses to several thousand advertised job postings in Israel.[29] They chose Israel because it is neither taboo nor a social norm there to embed a head shot of oneself in the top corner of a résumé. Half of the applications they sent to employers contained such a head shot. A panel of judges rated the photos, of both men and women, as either attractive or plain.

Prospective employers punished attractive women. Whereas attractive men were twice as likely to be called back for an interview as plain men, attractive women were less likely to be called back than plain women. Men who submitted no photo got fewer callbacks than attractive men who did, but women who submitted no photo got more callbacks than attractive women who did. Attractive men raised their chances of getting the job by including a picture; attractive women lowered theirs.

Ruffle and Shtudiner considered and rejected several possible explanations for why attractive women were punished, including the nature of the job sought and the "dumb blonde" hypothesis that attractive women appear less intelligent. (In fact, perception of attractiveness and intelligence are correlated.) Then they noticed that being attractive was negative for women only when the companies themselves screened applicants for interviews, not when outside employment agencies did the screening. Screeners outside the company treated attractive women about the same as plain women, whereas screeners inside the company favored plain women over attractive ones.

Ruffle and Shtudiner also noticed that the vast majority of screeners were women, so they asked whether female screeners inside companies might be threatened by attractive women in ways female screeners at outside employment agencies were not. If a company hires an attractive woman, the screener at the employment agency will never see her again. But the company's screener will see her at work, perhaps every day.

Why might internal female screeners refuse to grant interviews to attractive women while granting interviews to plain women, or women with no photo? Ruffle and Shtudiner suggested jealousy as a possible answer. Female screeners inside companies might not give attractive women interviews because they implicitly, or unconsciously, prefer to have plain women, but not attractive women, around the workplace. As they explained, "Females in charge of hiring at companies themselves may well be jealous of prospective female employees who are attractive and thus may compete with them for mates or at least the attention of male coworkers."[30] Although there is some research supporting this explanation, the question remains open and controversial.[31]

We like to believe everyone would be gender-neutral in their decisions, just as we like to believe doctors wouldn't favor whites over blacks. And our society has eradicated many forms of conscious discrimination based on gender and race. But we might only have scratched the surface of unconscious discrimination, where the culprit seems to be one of our most remarkable skills. We thin-slice brilliantly. We learn a lot about people just by glancing at their faces. We instantly spot who we prefer. But we also instantly spot people we don't prefer. And when we unconsciously react with bias, we treat those less-preferred people unfairly, even if we don't realize it.

———

Dana Carney, one of the coauthors of the doctor racism study, is a rising star of social judgment research. She is among the leaders of a new movement that wants to rethink decision-making. During the past few years, she and a handful of colleagues and co-researchers have uncovered new ways to study, and influence, the double-edged aspects of thin slicing. Carney's pathbreaking experiments are a long, long way from traditional decision research, which emphasizes alternatives and probabilities.

The most striking way to demonstrate this is to try to find her lab at Columbia Business School, as I did one rainy Friday fall afternoon in New York.* First, I walked up the steps of Uris Hall, the business school's nine-story building, entered the spacious lobby, and saw Columbia's dean, Glenn Hubbard, a former chairman of President George Bush's Council of Economic Advisers, who had just grabbed a sandwich for lunch. I then took the elevator to the seventh floor, where the management faculty have window offices and graduate students are stuffed into cubicles stacked high with boxes and paper. Reprints of peer-reviewed articles from leading journals were scattered everywhere. Carney wasn't there, so I called her cell phone. When I told her I couldn't find her lab on the seventh floor, she laughed.

---

* Since my 2010 visit, Carney has moved to the Haas School of Business at the University of California, Berkeley, where she is easier to find.

To reach the lab, I had to go back outside, circle around Uris Hall, walk under a set of staircases, find a hidden subterranean door, and then follow a passage back underneath the building. By the time I found the entrance, I was soaked and felt curiously like I was going down Alice's rabbit hole. What I saw inside was just as strange.

Carney had arranged for a representative from BioPac Systems, Inc., a scientific research company, to demonstrate some new physio-measurement equipment for several students and colleagues. She brought me into a white, windowless room where one graduate student was being outfitted with sensors to measure his heart rhythm, blood flow, and skin conduction. A dozen researchers, mostly women, eagerly watched four pulsating lines of color as they streamed across a flat-panel monitor.

As Carney explained the meaning of each trace line, I took in how different this scene was from the business classes I attended at Yale during the early 1990s. Faculties then were overwhelmingly male, with a focus on math and finance, not biology. My most interesting class—on the differential equations used in derivatives pricing—was taught by a man in a suit from J. P. Morgan. If you had shown me a classroom with an attractive blond woman hooking electrodes up to an unshaven man, I'd have assumed it was a film shoot, not a business school seminar.

As Carney is the first to point out, she doesn't look or act like a buttoned-down business school professor. For the BioPac demonstration, she was wearing all black, with fashionably shiny black boots. She's naturally exuberant; in a movie, she could be played by Renee Zellweger. Carney was focused on the spikes and dips in the green line, which measured galvanic skin response, or GSR. She explained the essence of it: "GSR shows a skin conductance response to autonomic arousal. It's amorphous. If the subject receives a stimulus, it will shock him. It doesn't have to be physical. I don't have to touch him. If I just scare him, the green line will spike. If he feels pain, fear, or anticipatory stress, we'll see it move up."

I understood what she meant when she asked us to shout and clap at the graduate student. The physical response depicted by the green line was automatic. But it wasn't instantaneous. Instead, it took the skin one to three seconds to react. Clap-pause-spike. Yell-pause-spike.

Carney compared the green line to the other lines, which recorded stimuli from other electrodes connected to the student. The GSR reaction was slow compared to the brain's immediate response, but fast compared to a conscious reaction. Carney explained how GSR was used in the so-called Iowa gambling task, in which a subject's galvanic skin response reflected the anticipated stress of having made a bad bet before the subject consciously understood the bet was bad. Our skin tells us we are about to lose money before we consciously understand it.

Carney explained how different kinds of stimuli cause different kinds of physical reactions, starting with our brains and spreading throughout our bodies. When we tested the graduate student's responses, we saw his physical responses clearly reflected on the screen: brain waves, changes in pulse and blood pressure, and variance in skin conductance. But he didn't perceive those changes, at least not right away. (I imagined that Coach Bob Gibson's GSR measurements must have been off the charts near the end of his last game coaching football, but he probably didn't perceive the changes either.)

If thin slicing is a series of physiological responses, as Carney was demonstrating, it should, in theory, be possible to adjust them, in the same way we control other parts of our biology.[32] The responses are measured in seconds. They are relatively slow and often controllable. Indeed, after a few minutes of being yelled and clapped at, the graduate student who was wired with BioPac sensors was able to dampen his own physical reactions to us. He was becoming accustomed to the test and was no longer shocked by it. Put another way, he was becoming more expert in being shocked and was therefore able to control his body's reaction to the shock. The last time I screamed at him, the green line barely moved.

———

During a break from Carney's lab demonstrations at Columbia, I asked her whether it was possible to counter the problems that arise from thin slicing. How might we influence our biological reactions, or those of others? Instead of directly answering my question, she abruptly sat down, leaned way back in the chair, put her hands behind her head, and propped her boots on a table in front of me so I was looking at the soles. It was the kind of "I've got it made" pose I had become accustomed to seeing among my colleagues at Morgan Stanley when I worked on Wall Street during the 1990s.

She then asked me, "Okay, in the last few seconds, how have I changed? Biologically, how am I different?" When I joked that she looked more like an investment banker now, she immediately released the pose and lunged forward. "Exactly right. You could feel the testosterone coming. That was a high-power pose."

She then explained a recent experiment she had conducted with Amy Cuddy of Harvard and Andy Yap of Columbia.[33] They had forty-two students assume what she calls high-power and low-power poses. High-power is either the "I've got it made" pose she showed me or a pose standing up with legs spread and hands forward on a table. Low-power is either sitting with hands in lap and shoulders hunched or standing slumped with arms crossed. The students were told to hold each of these poses for sixty seconds.

The researchers took saliva samples before and after the poses to measure biological changes in testosterone (a hormone associated with dominance and status) and cortisol (a hormone associated with stress and weakness). The relative differences were remarkable. The high-power posing students had significantly more testosterone and less cortisol. They reported feeling more "powerful" and "in charge." On standard financial tests, they were more likely to take risks. The opposite was true of the low-power posers.

As Carney and her coauthors concluded, "The implications of this result for everyday life are substantial."[34] Just by high-power posing, we can increase the flow of testosterone to make us act stronger or more dominant. Alternatively, if we are worried about being too aggressive, we can add some cortisol by slumping. We can adjust our hormonal levels in either direction before an important meeting or presentation.

Because these hormonal changes persist over time—for at least seventeen minutes according to Carney—we can pose earlier, in private, and still benefit from the jolt of testosterone later on. Look at boxers in their locker rooms before a fight. They are power posing in the extreme, loading their bodies with testosterone before they enter the ring. We might prepare for work in the same way, in a boardroom instead of a locker room. Just stand at the table, arms extended and legs spread, leaning forward—and wait for the hormones to flow.

With further advances, we might be able to counter some of our negative thin slicing responses simply by posing and then waiting. Not surprisingly, the posing experiment has generated a fair amount of popular interest, but the experiment illustrates a deeper insight that we have not yet begun to explore beyond the surface: once we better understand how our biology affects our decisions, we might be able to harness that power.

When Dana Carney and her colleagues conducted the doctor racism experiment, they were worried that some participants might figure out that the study was designed to test implicit racism and thereby skew the results. So they asked the doctors to say what they thought the purpose of the study was. That question inadvertently revealed a possible solution to the problem of implicit racism.

Doctors are smart and perceptive, and the IAT is well known at medical schools. Some of them wondered why the researchers would include a photograph of Mr. Thompson. About one-quarter of the doctors surmised that the study was designed to test racial bias, even before the researchers asked any questions.

The researchers excluded those doctors from their main results, but also saw this subgroup as an opportunity. They separately checked to see if these doctors recommended different treatment than the others. They did. Although this "aware" subgroup, like their peers, showed an implicit preference for whites over blacks on the IAT, they actually prescribed *more,* not less, thrombolysis for black patients. In other words, once the doctors understood that race was an issue, race was no longer an issue. They counterbalanced their implicit bias, like a driver adjusting to a misaligned steering wheel.

A few seconds of glancing at the photograph of Mr. Thompson changed the way some doctors treated him based on his race. But a few seconds of awareness that race was an issue reversed that change for other doctors. The implication is that if you have implicit racial preferences, you should know that fact and think about it. Doctors who pause to consider their IAT scores when they see a black patient have some protection against their own unconscious racial preferences. They are like people who have been subliminally exposed to a fast-food logo or a split-second pornographic image: just a little bit of conscious thought goes a long way toward correcting any snap bias.

It is difficult, perhaps impossible, to obliterate implicit racial preferences. But we can take the time to become aware of them, by taking IATs or similar tests, and then we can pause before reaching judgments when we think our implicit racial preferences might be implicated. We can reinforce positive stereotypes and ignore negative ones. We can counter unconscious racial favoritism with conscious racial awareness.

In general, if we are aware of the dangers of thin slicing, we can prepare to overcome those dangers. If we know, as Dana Carney has shown, that for some judgments a few minutes is better than a few seconds, we can wait longer before making those judgments. If we want to become better thin-slicers, we can prepare in advance and make snap conclusions only when we know they are sufficiently well grounded. As John Gottman, the marriage guru, explains, "The reason our swift analysis works is because each thin slice of data is actually grounded in a tremendous amount of 'thick slicing'—i.e., huge volumes of data that we've been collecting and validating on thousands of other couples for more than thirty years."[35]

It turns out that a doctor glancing at a photograph of a black patient and a student watching a two-second video of a teacher are performing similar tasks. So is a young American woman looking at images of terrorist cells in the Middle East, or a young man in the Middle East looking at images of ostentatious wealth in America. Or any number of people everywhere who judge others based on first impressions. When we thin-slice, we reach powerful unconscious conclusions about others in seconds. Unfortunately, they are often wrong. Fortunately, they can be consciously unwound.

Even contagious beliefs can reverse their spread. The authors of the racial contagion study worried about what happens when "a child feels her father grip her hand a little more tightly as they pass a black man on the street; or a little boy views his mother speak less and make less eye contact than usual while transacting with a black cashier at the supermarket."[36] But they also concluded, more hopefully, that "the flip side of these results, of course, is that acts of genuine egalitarianism can also shape racial attitudes toward equality."[37]

Substitute any stereotyped group into the above passages and you have an apt description of many of the world's problems. And, perhaps, a partial solution.

7 DON'T PANIC

The writer *Douglas Adams* used the phrase "DON'T PANIC" prominently and often: in the novel *Hitchhiker's Guide to the Galaxy,* in the *Hitchhiker* television series, on a badge that was packaged with a video game he cowrote, and even on a towel. Arthur C. Clarke said Adams's phrase was the best advice ever given to humanity.[1]

One of the main reasons why "DON'T PANIC" is such valuable guidance is that the sudden onslaught of fear we label panic can seriously interfere with our ability to decide on the best course of action. Panic makes it difficult for us to use logic or reason. Panic shuts down our conscious system 2 and leads us to rely on our primal and automatic system 1. Relying on system 1 is not necessarily a bad thing, especially if we are experts.

But panic can turn experts into amateurs. It ended the career of football coach Bob Gibson. It has resulted in military and police officers shooting civilians. And it can lead all of us to make bad decisions.

One problem with panic has to do with our perception of time. How we experience time varies depending on our environment, even when we aren't stressed or afraid. As consumers, we react more quickly to cheap prices and bright lighting, which is why there are so many sale prices at stores and why the lighting is usually so good. If you live in a city with a population of over one million, a pause will seem twice as long as it does to someone who lives on a farm or in a small town.[2] Try having someone time you trying to hold up your hand for precisely one minute. Put your hand down when you think the time is up. It probably will take about forty seconds. Or try pausing for a full minute during a conversation, or a speech. You probably won't make it. Instead, after ten or twenty seconds, you will break down and speak.

When we are panicking, this time warping gets much worse. People who have panic attacks or related mental disorders often experience time dramatically slowing down or speeding up.[3] For children, intensely emotional experiences, such as a scary Halloween carnival or a funeral, seem to last longer than they really do. If you have been in a car accident or a high-speed chase, you probably felt time expand. It can happen on the way to the hospital or in a race.

Neuroscientists David Eagleman, Chess Stetson, and Matthew Fiesta tested the effects of panic on time perception by strapping people into a harness, hoisting them up 150 feet above the ground, and then dropping them into a safety net. The pure terror of this free fall lasted three seconds. But when these people were asked to reimagine the fall immediately afterward and use a stopwatch to time how long they thought it had lasted, they believed that the drop took four seconds—one-third longer than it actually did.[4]

What is happening? Our brains are making time elastic. Time itself isn't stretched, but our perception of it is. Under extreme stress we are hyper-attuned to the moment. Surges of adrenaline warp how we experience time under pressure, fooling our judgment. After the fact, the culprit is the intensity of our memories. Because memories are carved more deeply into our brains during high stimulation, the event seems to have taken longer in retrospect.[5] Eagleman explains the idea this way: "In a dire situation, your brain may lay down memories in a way that makes them 'stick' better. Upon replay, the higher density of data would make the event appear to last longer."[6]

Time warping can happen in real time as well as in retrospect. We understand this idea from the movies. In *The Matrix,* time slows down for the hero, Neo, and he dodges bullets in slow motion. Or as Max Payne says in *Max Payne 2: The Fall of Max Payne—A Film Noir Love Story,* "When you're looking down the barrel of a gun, time slows down. Your whole life flashes by, heartbreak and scars. Stay with it, and you could live a lifetime in that split second."

Professional athletes do something like what Neo and Max Payne do: they take charge of time when they need their brains to slow down the action so they can see what to do. Think of Michael Jordan suspended in midair. Or race car drivers, who are probably the best examples. Here is former Grand Prix champion Jackie Stewart describing a turn: "The corner can be taken at a hundred and seventy-three mph. At a hundred and ninety-five mph you should still have a very clear vision, almost in slow motion, of going through that corner—so that you have time to brake, time to line the car up, time to recognize the amount of drift, and then you've hit the apex, given it a bit of a tweak, hit the exit and are out at a hundred and seventy-three mph."[7] If Jackie Stewart's brain ran at normal speed, he might misjudge the turn and crash.

Because of how panic influences our perception of time, it magnifies the difference between experts and novices. Experts understand the downside of panicking, but they also use time warping to their advantage by stretching every second to maximum effect. Novices are more vulnerable. Their world speeds up and slows down, whether they want it to or not.

In the previous two chapters, we explored some of our instant conscious responses in the world of seconds. We focused on people's actions: choosing the correct football play, putting out a fire, or diagnosing a medical condition. In this chapter, we are going to stay in the world of seconds, but we are going to look at words instead of actions. Panic and the perception of time are massive topics that easily could fill a book on their own, so we are going to focus on how panic and time warping affect one particular aspect of decision-making: the timing of our communications with each other. We are going to look not merely at which words we use when we are talking, but *when* we say those words. In both our work and personal lives, choosing when to speak is one of the most important decisions we make.

Panic leads us to act unnaturally when we are talking to other people. And perhaps most importantly, as Douglas Adams and his fellow comedians have understood better than anyone, panic makes it harder for us to be funny.

Carol Burnett, one of the greatest comedians ever, loves the old saw, "Comedy is tragedy plus time." So does Woody Allen, who used it in

Crimes and Misdemeanors, his 1989 film in which Alan Alda, playing a crass television producer, remarks, "The night Lincoln was shot, you couldn't joke about it, you just couldn't do it . . . but now time has gone by, and it's fair game."

Timing is central to comedy. As Jack Benny and Victor Borge showed millions of fans, how funny a joke is depends largely on pacing. They developed the concept of "extended beats," sometimes called "pregnant pauses," when the delay becomes even funnier than the punch line.

Beats are important, not only because they create suspense, but because they give the listener more time to process information about the joke.* Choosing when to tell the punch line differs from preconscious reactions, such as hitting a ball, but these two share some of the same timing elements. Too early and you'll manage a glancing blow at best. Too late and the opportunity has flown by. But when you get the timing right, a joke is effortless and powerful, a thing of beauty.

When a master comedian is on, he or she creates a new and warped world of time. The greatest comedians are masters of delay. They can make us feel a pregnant pause with the same intensity a race car driver feels while powering through a high-speed turn. Time expands.

Jon Stewart, the host of *The Daily Show,* is an expert at extended beats. Watch what he does after he shows a video clip of a public figure saying something foolish: *nothing.* He waits, and he waits, and he waits, sometimes

---

* The same is true of music. Songwriter Paul Simon says: "I try to leave a space after a difficult line—either silence or a lyrical cliché that gives the ear a chance to 'catch up' with the song before the next thought arrives and the listener is lost." Musical theater composers cater to our limited attention spans and memories by using pauses after rhymes to remind us what we've just heard. Some of the most recognizable songs include such pauses as well: just before the climax of Handel's *Messiah,* or after each "Happy Birthday to You" or "He's a Jolly Good Fellow." And catchy pop songs typically pause at the end of lines (think about the Beatles' "Yesterday" or Gino Vannelli's "I Just Wanna Stop"). See Paul Simon, "Isn't It Rich," *New York Times Book Review,* October 31, 2010; Jan Swafford, "Silence Is Golden," *Slate,* August 31, 2009.

for five or ten seconds. Then, finally, when the tension is peaking and he has squeezed those seconds as hard as he possibly can, he senses it is time for a release and he delivers a line.

On March 29, 2011, Stewart showed a clip of former Alaska governor Sarah Palin discussing the limited use of American military force in Libya. Revolution was spreading throughout the Middle East, from Tunisia to Egypt and finally to Libya. Palin was skeptical about what President Obama was doing. She said, "I haven't heard the president state that we're at war. That's why I too am not knowing—do we use the term 'intervention'? Do we use 'war'? Do we use 'squirmish'? What is it?"

When we see this clip, we know immediately that the target of Stewart's derision is going to be Palin's use of the nonword "squirmish."

But we don't laugh right away at the video. Nor does he. He could have told a joke that second or even just repeated the word ("squirmish?") and gotten a pretty good laugh. But instead, Stewart says nothing. He delays. He looks forward and cocks his head to the right for four seconds, blinking at the camera in apparent disbelief, neither laughing nor speaking. Then, head still cocked, he begins fiddling with a pencil. Another four seconds pass. Next, he turns his head left and stares into the distance again, for four more seconds. Still there is not a word, or even a smile.

Next, he raises an eyebrow, gives a skeptical look, suppresses a laugh, and looks down briefly. Finally, he seems ready to speak. But still he doesn't. The delay is becoming excruciating. We think that, finally, he must be about to say something. Indeed, he raises his finger, poised to deliver a line. But instead of speaking, he just raises his finger still higher. For a full second, he holds it there.

Now the delay really is painful. We can't take any more. We are dying to laugh. (*Squirmish! She said "squirmish"! Now say something!*) Yet even then, Stewart waits another four seconds. One last time, he appears as if he's about to speak, but instead raises his finger yet once more, higher than before, wringing yet another dramatic second out of the silence before he finally brings down his finger and—a full twenty seconds after the audience heard Sarah Palin say the nonword—delivers just two words of his own: "Nailed it!" The crowd erupts in riotous laughter. Afterwards, if we were asked to time what Stewart just did, using a stopwatch, we would insist it took him even longer to speak.

Finally, as his coup de grâce, Stewart waits two more full seconds to deliver the punch line: "Squirmish, huh? That's either some sophisticated foreign policy analysis or what happens when worms get into a fight." By this time, it doesn't even matter whether the audience hears him. No one cares what the words are. It really doesn't even matter whether the line is funny. We aren't laughing because of the "worms in a fight" metaphor. We are already in tears, not because of what Stewart said, but because of how long he waited before saying it.

If Stewart had simply shown the clip and delivered the punch line, it would have been mildly humorous. But by pausing, stretching out the moment, delaying our anticipation of the line, he created a belly-laugh resolution. Had he just done a quick line about fighting worms, it would have been a foul ball. But after twenty seconds, the joke was a home run.

—

Walker Clark is something of a renaissance man. An actor, instructor, coach, writer, and amateur philosopher, he grew up in upstate New York, where he was a skilled hockey player and pole vaulter. After graduating from Duke University, Clark studied theater, worked in finance, and then moved to Hollywood, where he landed numerous acting roles. During the first few seconds after I met him, his face cycled through several genuine emotions: delight, then seriousness, then concern, then delight again. He is as magnetic in person as he is on television, where you might have seen him in *Veronica Mars, Justice,* or *ER.*

Clark is obsessed with panic. Before high school, his coaches thought he was bound for the U.S. Olympic hockey team. He played with unbelievable ease and seemed to be in a "flow" state every time he hit the ice.[8] But then, almost overnight, he started to panic and choke.* As he explained it to me, "For years and years, I never thought about anything when I played hockey. I was just having fun. But then they got me to analyze my game, so I would get even better. I started thinking. And thinking about hockey caused me to panic, to worry about what I might be doing wrong. Once that started, it was all over."

The same thing happened with pole vaulting. He became the top-ranked vaulter in the state of New York, easily clearing sixteen feet in practice. But under pressure at a meet, he would often "no height"—he would miss all three of his chances at the lowest bar. As he explained, "I would panic right when I grabbed the pole. Anything could psych me out, the idea of being in the air, even the wind. There was a lot of choking." To this day Clark is terrified of heights.

Fortunately, acting was different. He still panicked, but he understood how to deal with it. He learned from failing, succeeding, asking why and how, and watching. He joined a group of actors in New York who got together every Monday to improve their craft. The idea was that a different

---

* Clark and I both use the words "choke" and "panic" interchangeably. There has been some debate about the distinction between these terms. As Malcolm Gladwell has explained, choking is about "thinking too much . . . and the loss of instinct," whereas panicking is about "thinking too little . . . and the reversion to instinct." See Malcolm Gladwell, "The Art of Failure," *The New Yorker,* August 21 and 28, 2000. This is an important distinction, so, to be clear, what Clark and I (and most performers, I think) mean when we use *either* term is a failure to perform effectively due to nervous agitation or tension. In other words, in this context, either "choke" or "panic" means thinking too much.

person would teach the others each week, but pretty quickly everyone agreed that Clark should teach all of the classes.

He thought about acting all the time, though rarely while he was doing it. He had a knack for understanding the strengths and weaknesses of fellow actors. He told me, "If we walk into a room full of actors, I can pick out the best one right away, the one who will move the world. And I can see who is too self-conscious as a human being."

This self-consciousness is a central problem for decision-making in the relatively quick time period of several seconds. Unlike superfast decisions, merely fast decisions that take seconds have both unconscious and deliberative elements. We have time to become aware of what our instant reactions tend to be; we can even watch our snap reactions on videotape if we want, and then we can adjust them if necessary. But this extra time also can lead us to interfere with our unconscious reactions even if they are perfect. Sometimes having an understanding of precisely what we are doing unconsciously can kill the natural spontaneity. If we are too self-conscious, we will impede our instincts when we need them. Yet if we aren't self-conscious at all, we will never improve on our instincts. The challenge during a period of seconds is to be aware of the factors that go into our decisions (should I raise my finger while making an important point?), but not to be so aware of them that they are stilted and ineffectual (look, everyone, now I'm raising my finger to make an important point).

Clark developed a theory of acting based on hockey, pole vaulting, and a simple observation: the best actors are the ones who don't panic. Even the slightest panic leads actors to think about what they are doing, and actors who are thinking cannot act. When they panic, they speak too quickly. They jump the beat. Instead, actors need to bypass their thoughts and wait for situations to come to them. Once they are in a "flow" state, they will naturally interact with the other actors and the camera or audience. As

Clark explains his theory, "Acting is not doing. Acting is not reacting. Acting is access to your true emotions. Once you have access, acting becomes interaction. Then it's not acting. It's *inter*acting."

The simplest way to explain Clark's approach is to look at how he welcomes a new teenage student to his workshop. He introduces the new student to a group of a dozen other teenagers standing in a circle (it could just as easily be a group of adults) by telling her to join the circle and announcing that they are going to play "the clap game."

"Okay, it starts with me. I have the clap. No pun intended." He claps his hands and raises his eyebrows while the kids snicker, even if they don't get the joke. "I can pass it to my right or left by pointing at a person at my side and clapping. Then that person has the clap and can pass it either way. You decide where the clap goes next. Then we just keep going. It's fun. Everybody ready? Let's do a practice round." And then they start. Clark claps; the others clap. It's easy for everyone, even for the new kid. No one forgets to point or clap. No one panics.

After a minute or two, Clark says, "Okay, now we'll have the elimination round. This is for real. If you make a mistake, you are out. You'll leave the circle and sit down against the wall. The last one standing wins the best acting award, and I'll give that person a free coaching session." Given Clark's hourly rates, he now has everyone's attention.

Suddenly, the room is filled with tension. Many of the students, even the veterans, are uneasy. Everyone is thinking about their actions now. The new kid looks terrified. Should she send the clap right or left? How quickly should she react? What if she forgets to clap or point? When Clark starts the game by clapping, he is smiling. But the new kid is not. You can see in her eyes that she will be the first one out. And she is.

Clark explains what happens. "Inevitably, every time, the new person screws up first. I tell him or her, 'Okay, go sit down. You lost. Now tell us why.' I keep asking questions until everyone sees that the culprit was panic and thinking. Conscious thought made you screw up. The clapping game is like acting. If you were playing a role and you were thinking, you wouldn't have been truthful. The techniques I teach are tips for bypassing your mind, for figuring out how not to think while you are on stage or on camera. Because if you cannot bypass your conscious thought, you cannot be truthful in a scene."

Clark's goal is to get clients to produce a spontaneous truthful performance. He sounds a lot like Gary Klein talking about a paramedic. If you are an expert, you can tap your unconscious and do the right thing. You don't panic. You don't react too quickly or too slowly. You are making a confident decision based on experience and expertise. If you are Jon Stewart, you unconsciously understand exactly how long to wait before speaking. Time naturally stretches before you, and you don't think about it. You just know.

The veteran students in Clark's group have become comfortable enough with the clap game that they can access their instincts instantly and reliably. They have learned through deliberation how to respond quickly and effortlessly, without panicking. The new kids are self-conscious at first, until they understand how to harness their natural instincts. It takes some thinking at first, because no one instinctively understands that they should point and clap during the game. You have to figure out how to internalize these new kinds of responses, so you don't need to think about them later. This is the key difference between the clap game and superfast reactions: we need to use both our automatic and deliberative systems, first system 2 and then system 1.

When I asked Walker Clark about the "squirmish" joke, he practically jumped out of his chair with excitement. "Jon Stewart is just like Johnny Carson. Look at all the deadpan. There's not a lot of activity. One specific look, a raised eyebrow, maybe a smirk. If he did more or moved around, we would lose it. He's telling us, 'I'm going to let you have this moment,' and we have faith. We know he won't take too long. He hits it and hits it, and then, just before we are about to lull, he gives it to us. Kaboom! It's not that it wouldn't be funny a beat earlier. It would. But we love the ride he's taking us on, building it up and up. And then finally he delivers, at the last possible moment."

What Clark is talking about, and Stewart is doing, is acting at a very high level, but there are lessons here for everyday communication. We constantly face some kind of an audience, whether it is one person or a group. Although we don't usually think about delay thresholds when we are having conversations, they are there. Some of us are better at talking than others, and a lot of the reason for that has to do with panic and pauses. If we don't pause enough, we lack drama. If we pause too much, we sound boring or fake. The best storytellers naturally pull people along with their words and the spaces between their words.

According to Jose Benki, a speech scientist at the University of Michigan, speakers who use frequent short pauses are more persuasive than speakers who are perfectly fluent.[9] The reason is that pausing four or five times per minute sounds most natural to most people. If you barrel through those pauses, you sound too scripted and your audience doesn't have time to think or react.

The best radio announcers and interviewers (Larry King, Vin Scully, Terry Gross) pause several times per minute. The best orators (Martin Luther King Jr., Ronald Reagan, Bill Clinton) use even longer and more dramatic breaks. Colin Firth's portrayal of the stuttering King George VI in *The King's Speech* won our emotions and an Academy Award, not for the words, but for the silence between the words.

Part of the genius of these communicators derives from deliberative thought, at least at some early stage in their lives when they internalized the specifics of how long they should delay at different times. Some of this might have happened when they were young or as they became more experienced and learned which pauses worked best when. But once they came to understand their own timing, performance became effortless. First, Colin Firth had to think about how to stammer. Then, he had to do it un-self-consciously. What is so remarkable about his performance is that he appears so naturally to confront and overcome the panic arising from a speech defect that he does not have.

Great communicators naturally understand how long a speech should be: as long as possible, but not a millisecond longer. As Dorothy Sarnoff, the actor, singer, and speech trainer, advised, "Make sure you have finished speaking before your audience has finished listening." At some point, you must stop and not say another word. No one understands this idea better than my best friend from high school, an expert salesman who uses long pauses to persuade his customers to buy. He delivers his closing line and then falls silent, convinced that the next person who speaks will lose. One evening several years ago, when he was selling water purification systems, he sat on a sofa staring at an elderly couple in silence for an hour before they finally relented and spoke. And then they bought.

Effective communication is about silence, or delayed talk, as much as it is about talk. The amount of silence or delay depends on context. An hour is obviously extreme. During the 1920s, when Ivar Kreuger, the infamous "Match King," was regarded as one of the world's most effective speakers, his audiences could handle a one-minute pause. Today, on television, even five seconds is a lot. With a less engaged audience, Jon Stewart might have waited only a second or two before delivering his punch line. For some jokes, he doesn't pause much at all. And off camera, Stewart has the same speech patterns as any normal person. In casual conversation, he doesn't cock his head and wait for four seconds.

We can and should emulate these delay masters. For most of us, that means pausing more and panicking less. As a professor, I have learned to use longer pauses when I teach a large class than I do in a small seminar. Depending on the feel of the room, I sometimes can get away with a pause of ten seconds or so after an especially dramatic point. But in this era of instant gratification, I have to be careful. If I wait too long, my students will get up and leave.

Our days are filled with opportunities to delay when we speak. Most of the time, especially when we are under stress, we blow through these opportunities and instead rely on our untrained instincts. Our automatic response is to fill silence with speech. But we could decide to manage the timing of our words more effectively. It would require conscious effort and even some practice, and we certainly would feel self-conscious and awkward at first. But most of us could become better communicators without changing a word we say—just by saying some of those words a little bit later.

When we are in a state of panic, our speech isn't the only thing that comes too fast. Panic generally leads us to respond too quickly, to rush through the beat. This kind of instant reaction can be helpful when we are in danger. But in modern life, panic can warp our perception of time and lead us to make quick decisions we later regret. If we can control our tendency to panic, we can slow down our actions, avoid some of our animal instincts, and make better decisions. We might even get a few laughs.

8 **FIRST DATES AND FIGHTER PILOTS**

Dr. Iannis, a character in *Captain Corelli's Mandolin*, has this to say about love: "When you fall in love, it is a temporary madness. It erupts like an earth-quake, and then it subsides. And when it subsides, you have to make a de-cision."[1] The doctor, though unlicensed, is right: when we first meet someone, we have plenty of superfast and fast reactions. We are attracted, or not, right away. But then, over the course of several minutes or longer, we learn more about the person. We have time to think and deliberate about them, and we might change our minds.

Irene LaCota is one of the world's leading experts on first dates. As the longtime president of It's Just Lunch, the international dating network, she has closely studied first dates since her last first date, a group event two decades ago, with her husband. LaCota helped build It's Just Lunch from a tiny office in 1991 to a global dating service for professionals, with offices in more than one hundred cities worldwide, from Alabama to Singapore.

When I met LaCota, it wasn't for lunch but for happy hour at a fashionable restaurant. I hoped we might observe some dating couples in the wild. As she looked around for people who might be on a first date, I asked why so many smart lawyers, doctors, and businesspeople were willing to pay thousands of dollars to It's Just Lunch when online dating sites charged less than $50.[2] As she explained it, part of the reason is service: with an online site you have to find and arrange your own dates, whereas It's Just Lunch arranges them for you.

But LaCota's research points to two other factors that matter much more than convenience. These factors account for much of her firm's success.

"First," she explained, "we don't show people photos. We won't do it, ever. Our clients ask for photos all the time, especially guys, and they get mad when we say no. 'What do you mean you won't show me?' But you can't tell anything worthwhile from a photo. The two most important elements of a relationship are chemistry and compatibility, and a photo won't help you with either. You need to smell and sense the person, live, or you won't get an accurate idea of what really matters. Besides, people doctor their photos. In person, they look completely different."

If you sign up for an online dating service such as Match.com or Zoosk or JDate, you will find lots of information about potential dates. But what's really striking about these websites is the sheer volume of visuals. The very first thing you see at Match.com, where each online profile can include up to twenty-six photos, is a large green "View Photos" tab. Even if you spent every waking moment for an entire year on that website, you couldn't view all of the photos. Likewise, Zooskers proudly feature their primary photos on everything from date cards to Zoosk Desktops to Facebook tie-ins. An adviser on the blog for JDate, the Jewish dating service, suggests that subscribers follow the five F's in choosing which photos to post: Face, Full body, Fun, Friends, and Family, in that order.[3]

LaCota sees this focus on photos as counterproductive. She is trying to stop people from jumping to conclusions based on first impressions. She says, "We're trying to get people away from the snap decisions they make with photos." LaCota understands the research on thin slicing and how it can be both useful and counterproductive. She sees that, when it comes to dating, one of the best ways she can help her clients is by deliberately pre-empting their inclination to thin-slice.

Although It's Just Lunch uses analytical surveys and questionnaires, LaCota avoids the mechanized approach of the many online dating sites that match people based on their responses to multiple-choice questions. The online approach has some obvious advantages in addition to cost, including a huge pool of potential dates. Online survey data can be especially useful if your primary goal is sex. (The question "Do you like the taste of beer?" is the best predictor of whether someone will have sex with you on a first date; correct answer: "Yes.")[4] It's Just Lunch cannot compete in these ways, and doesn't try.

Instead, It's Just Lunch employees conduct extensive interviews to get to know clients and potential matches, so they can pair them just as a real yenta would, based on a combination of intuition and analysis. As in *Fiddler on the Roof*, LaCota's challenge is to get beyond searching for a mere marriage of convenience to find a pairing based on true love. A dating website might have suggested the arranged match between Tevye's eldest daughter, Tzeitel, and the widower Lazar Wolf. But the younger daughter, Chava, would never have met the Russian soldier Fyedka online.

The second important factor at It's Just Lunch is more obvious than avoiding photos. It *is* just lunch. As LaCota explains, "We focus on lunch because our research shows that's about the right amount of time for a first date. Dinner is too long. If they want to go for a drink after work instead of lunch, that's probably okay. But not dinner. Absolutely not dinner. That's way too involved, way too much time. And don't extend a lunch date either, even if it's going great and you think you have fallen in love with each other. You'll have plenty of time later for that." LaCota advises that this kind of delay, and willingness to trust in the future, is the essence of relationship building.

—

Daniel Gilbert launched the modern happiness movement in 2006 with his pathbreaking book *Stumbling on Happiness*. Gilbert, a Harvard psychology professor, already had won numerous teaching and research awards, but his book was so comprehensive and engaging that it reoriented thinking about what makes us happy and created a surge of new interest in an old but fundamental idea.

Today happiness research is so mainstream and pervasive that it is easy to forget where Gilbert started, at the beginning of his first chapter, with what he called "The Sentence." He joked that it is a rite of passage for psychology professors that they must publish a book making the case that "*The human is the only animal that. . . .*" This is the first part of The Sentence. A professor's job is to finish it.

How did Gilbert finish The Sentence? What did he say is the defining feature of our humanity, the personal characteristic at the center of our ability to be happy? *"The human being is the only animal that thinks about the future."* Gilbert argued that thinking about the future is the key to understanding what makes us happy—and unhappy. It is what distinguishes us as human beings. Throughout his book, Gilbert focuses on time and delay, on our capacity to consider and imagine future events, countered by our tendency to misremember, misproject, and live too much in the present. It is easy to remember that Gilbert was writing about happiness. It is easy to forget that he was focused on time.

In this book, we are exploring human decision-making by looking through several different time lenses. With that goal in mind, I would like to offer a friendly amendment to Daniel Gilbert's version of The Sentence. Here it is, with my italics: "The human being is the only animal that thinks *very far* into the future."

I am adding "very far" because recent research shows, as we saw with dogs in the introduction, that many animals can think ahead for at least several minutes, though not for a full day. The precise timing varies by animal, but two conclusions are apparent based on new experiments: (1) animals can think about the future, and (2) humans can think about the future better, and for longer, than animals. The words "very far" remind us that we can be similar to animals in the short term and that our relative advantage depends on how far into the future we are looking. During milliseconds and seconds, we sometimes aren't much better than animals. It is only as our thinking stretches beyond that we distinguish ourselves as human beings. As much as I love him, my dog Fletch can't do lunch.

Back in the early chapters of this book, you might have caught yourself thinking that human snap responses are not so different from animal snap responses. In a half-second or less, just about every animal, even a worm, can "think" unconsciously about its immediate future. Animals don't return tennis serves or hit baseballs, but they can perform remarkable acts in a few hundred milliseconds. Nature programs on television use slow-motion video for good reason: to show how an animal stretches time as it considers and plans a strike. Whether it is a mongoose attacking a cobra, or a cobra attacking a mouse, the animals' responses resemble those of human professional athletes. In the world of milliseconds, humans aren't the only animals that think about the future.

The same is true to a lesser extent of decisions that take seconds or minutes. Recent research shows that in this relatively short-term world of seconds or minutes many species, particularly apes, can match humans in forward thinking. Animals can't put out fires or diagnose medical conditions or use humor, and in many ways animals are almost always in the kind of panic that prevents them from anticipating the future. But scholars are finding that animals can anticipate future risks and benefits over periods of seconds and even minutes, especially when food or reproduction is involved.[5] Chimpanzees collect tools they don't need immediately but might need soon.[6] Monkeys, rats, and pigeons* choose large delayed rewards over small current ones.[7] Scrub jays store food in breakfast-unfriendly locations where they might have to spend the evening but won't be able to get food in the morning. Birds build nests. Beavers build dams. And so on. Recall from the introduction that some dogs will wait more than ten minutes for a bigger chicken chew treat.

Not all of this animal behavior is really thinking in the way we typically understand it. Still, many animals can "contemplate" the future about as

* Pigeons are a surprisingly popular subject for scientists who study thinking about the future. We will learn more about pigeon decision-making when we eventually get to procrastination, in Chapter 10. For now, I just want to note that although pigeons can't outsmart a monkey or outpace a rodent racing through a maze to find drugs, they can wait several seconds for food. The next time you see a person sitting on a park bench mindlessly tossing bread crumbs to a pigeon, watch both of them closely. It isn't clear which one is thinking further into the future.

well as young kids do. As one study found, "Chimpanzees appreciate the time dimension for a time period exceeding that of other tested animals, and their performance resembles that of children."[8] Young kids typically don't differentiate the timing of future events until about age five. Even at kindergarten age, they don't think very far ahead. It's called a "children's garden" for good reason, because that school year is focused on in-the-moment play, tending the garden now, not thinking about the future. A four-year-old child who can wait fifteen minutes for a second marshmallow has about the same sense of the importance of patience and self-control as does a bonobo.[9]

As humans mature, we are able to think about the future for a lot longer than animals can. The average adult spends 12 percent of the day thinking about the future, roughly one of every eight hours.[10] We can imagine events years into the future, well beyond the abilities of any nonhuman. If more than several minutes are involved, no animal can keep up with us.

And this is the key point about personal daily decisions and happiness. What makes us uniquely human is our ability to think about the future for longer than animals can. That doesn't mean we always do, just that we can. We might want to behave like animals throughout the day, moving through a series of short-term, unconnected acts. We might prefer to stay focused on the present (as in meditation and yoga) or the immediate future (as in eating and entertainment). One wealthy executive told a family member of mine when he retired that he would devote most of his remaining days to bowling, because it was totally mindless.

But we often benefit from thinking forward, as only humans can. It is true not only of mundane tasks (even apes cannot plan a visit to the grocery store) but also of personal interactions and relationships. Our happiness often depends on holding off animal-like short-term reactions in favor of future-oriented behavior that is in our longer-term interests.

Sometimes we want to react like an animal. But often we don't. As Robert Browning wrote, "What's time? Leave Now for dogs and apes! Man has forever."[11]

———

What does all of this animal research have to do with first dates? The answer depends on what you think of the idea of love at first sight. Snap love is a powerful trope with romantic appeal, but it can be disastrous too. The Greeks wisely labeled passionate love "madness from the Gods," which is what Louis de Bernières's Dr. Iannis remembers.

Humans certainly possess some animal-like brain circuitry for instant affection. As we already have seen, people can identify the attractiveness of a face in a split-second. Men instantly favor women with a waist-to-hip ratio of 0.7. Anyone who has been at a bar at closing time can attest that both men and women are good (or perhaps I should say bad) at making these kinds of quick decisions.

The scientific community is still split about whether animals feel romantic love, as Charles Darwin believed.[12] It certainly is the case that what animals do when they fall in love—or whatever you would call it—doesn't take very long. It is a snap reaction based on first impressions. Some animals, most notably the prairie vole, a small rodent, form an instant, monogamous bond, and then they generally stick together.[13] Prairie voles spend the equivalent of just a lunch together, and thereafter they remain satisfied and rarely stray. But not many animals are like prairie voles.

One key to a first date, according to LaCota, is being more human than animal, or at least more prairie vole than rabbit. During lunch we can get some perspective. We can try to imagine what a second date would be like.

We can observe the other person, orient ourselves to their reactions, decide what we think of them, and finally act by asking them out again—or not.

This sequence of behavior—observe, orient, decide, and act—is recommended in an area of decisions where the rules of engagement are much more confrontational than in first dates. These are battles of a different kind.

———

Military strategist John Boyd is arguably the greatest fighter pilot in American history. Boyd advocated lightweight maneuverable aircraft, such as the F-16 Fighting Falcon, because they could be used like a switchblade in a knife fight. A pilot could pump the control stick back and forth, force the adversary to overshoot, and then flick through buttonhook turns to gain a tactical advantage. Boyd could outmaneuver his opponent, not by acting first, but by waiting for his opponent to act first. Boyd saw these pilot tactics as a metaphor for military strategy more generally.

Boyd said what matters in battle is not merely speed. He cited Germany's blitzkrieg attack against France and Israel's raid at Entebbe Airport as examples where the crucial question was not just how fast to attack but when to strike. Boyd developed a time-based theory of conflict, derived from Sun Tzu, in which the crucial insights for a fighter come in stages: first, *observe* the rapidly changing environment; second, *orient* yourself based on these observations, process the disorder, and understand when and how your opponent might become confused; third, *decide* what to do; and finally, *act* quickly at just the right moment, when your opponent is most vulnerable. Boyd spoke of operating "inside" your adversary's time cycle: once your opponent moves, gauge his degree of overaction or underaction and swoop in accordingly. This four-step process has become known as OODA (observe-orient-decide-act), or, when repeated in a cycle, the "OODA Loop." The ultimate goal of OODA is to act fast, but not necessarily first.[14]

The central insights of OODA apply to much of what all humans do, the lesson being that we make better decisions if we can minimize the time it takes to decide and act so we can spend more time observing and orienting. As with hitting a ball, the faster we can draft a memo or assemble a spreadsheet or prepare a speech, the more time we free up to understand the task, gather information, and analyze the issues. If we require too much time to decide or act, we are forced to finish observing and orienting earlier. And if we act too quickly, we might respond to a problem that changes or even goes away before the deadline.

Boyd's OODA framework is similar to the decision processes we have explored in superfast sports, high-frequency trading, and comedy. In responding to a tennis serve, a professional observes the speed and trajectory of the ball, processes that information to determine where the ball will land and how it will bounce, and finally acts by swinging the racquet. The UNX computers acted like high-speed fencers, letting UNX's competitors go first and then placing stock trades with a delay of just a few dozen milliseconds. Likewise, Jon Stewart gauges the responsiveness of his audience and then delivers punch lines as late as he possibly can.

What Boyd did was to frame the different stages of decisions very specifically in the context of battle so that fighter pilots would first consciously think through and train themselves how to observe, orient, decide, and act and then later be confident that they could automatically and effortlessly follow these steps in the heat of battle. Some of Boyd's suggestions for aerial combat require the kind of split-second reactions made by superfast athletes and high-speed computers. But most of his strategies are designed for longer time periods—minutes rather than milliseconds. In many ways, OODA is simply a longer-term version of "see-prepare-hit," the strategy in which professional athletes get faster at returning tennis serves and batting balls so they have more time to judge the ball's spin and trajectory.

What Boyd is saying about the decision process isn't unique to the military or sports or comedy or stock trading. The framework remains the same. First you gather information, then you process it, and finally you act. The main difference is that whereas a baseball hitter gathers information for just a split-second as the ball is hurtling toward him, a fighter pilot gathers information for much longer as he watches his opponent zig and zag. The genius of Boyd's formulation is that whether we look from the perspective of milliseconds or minutes, with a narrow time lens or a wide one, we see the same steps.

Although Boyd's OODA insights are most frequently applied to military tactics, they are equally applicable to dating. A military battle often unfolds at about the same pace as a relationship. And a first date can feel like engaging with an F-16.

—

On an ideal first date, we harness our ability to think about the future in order to decide whether the person we are meeting is friend or foe. When LaCota assesses a couple at a bar, as she did when we met, she makes the same kinds of observations that John Gottman, the psychologist, does in assessing married couples: this guy isn't paying attention; that woman looks defensive. LaCota looks for cues about each person's emotions, particularly negative ones. People who have just met typically don't show contempt for each other in the way couples in bad marriages do. But LaCota is good at picking up on the kinds of signals and behaviors that will lead to problems later. Her observations are tests, revealing the couple's strengths and weaknesses.

To help her clients observe and orient, and to give them a framework for assessing their reactions, LaCota tells them to think about what a second date might be like. The key question is: "What will I think about this person when the date is over?" As LaCota explained to me, "We tell clients their only objective for the first date is to decide if they want to see this person again. That's it. And they should wait until the end of lunch to decide whether they want another date. Don't make up your mind right away. The only thing that should go through your mind on a first date should be 'Do I want a second date?' You should cycle through that question as lunch moves along, but you should wait until the end to answer it. Keep your mind open until lunch is over. Then, if looking back you felt comfortable being yourself throughout the meal, you are ready for a second date."

It takes years of training to develop LaCota's expertise, and some people—like me—will never get it. But even people who are prone to making terrible snap decisions about relationships will do much better if they listen to her two key pieces of first-date advice. First, don't make any decisions until after lunch. And second, when lunch is over ask yourself one simple question: should we meet again? This question is designed to harness the best of both our automatic system 1 and deliberative system 2 responses. We allow enough time to gather and consciously process information about the date, but ultimately we go with our gut response. Then we can try another lunch. And then perhaps dinner. And then who knows?[15]

LaCota's first-date "dos and don'ts" resemble military strategist John Boyd's OODA framework. Don't assume lunch should last a particular amount of time. Instead, take as long as you need to carefully observe the other person. Be flexible. Orient yourself toward focusing on how you feel about another date, without being distracted. Don't react too quickly. Give the other person time to demonstrate his or her strengths and weaknesses. In the end, when it is time to consider a second date, don't revisit every detail of the lunch. Be decisive. If you've given yourself enough time, there's no need to second-guess. Just act: either ask your companion out again or, in the nicest possible way, shoot them down.

9 WHEN TO EAT CROW

On the morning of October 8, 1997, with President Clinton's approval ratings near record highs, Republican senator Fred Thompson thought he'd found a smoking gun. His staff discovered records from June showing that two Clinton fund-raisers had entered the White House with a former Teamsters consultant for a private meeting with the president. The consultant already had pled guilty to arranging an illegal swap of political contributions. The crime was a simple kickback scheme: the Teamsters gave money to the Democratic National Committee, and the DNC promised a similar amount to the campaign of the Teamsters president, Ron Carey. The newly discovered records suggested to Thompson that Clinton might be part of the conspiracy.

Initially, this story resembled an explosive one from Thompson's own past. As minority counsel on the Senate Watergate Committee, he had been a key player in the televised collapse of Richard Nixon's presidency. He was one of the first people to learn that Nixon had tape-recorded conversations at the White House, and on July 16, 1973, Thompson shocked the public by asking a former Nixon aide, "Were you aware of the existence of any listening devices in the Oval Office of the President?" That question triggered the events—a subpoena from special prosecutor Archibald Cox, Nixon's "Saturday Night Massacre" search for someone to fire Cox, and the Supreme Court case ordering the release of the tapes—that ultimately led Nixon to resign.

Might the Teamsters meeting records become Clinton's Watergate? Thompson saw the possibility, and he pounced. At the opening of that morning's Senate hearing into fund-raising abuses, he connected Clinton to the Teamsters indictment, noting that the "meeting with the President occurred only four days before the date when, according to the indictment, the Teamsters determined they would indeed send $236,000 to state Democratic parties as part of the contribution swap scheme."[1] Thompson emphasized that this was a private meeting with the president, implying that the parties had discussed the illegal deal with Clinton behind closed doors.

However, this time Thompson had reacted too quickly, and the gun wasn't smoking. Within an hour, a lawyer for the Senate committee holding the hearings countered Thompson. He produced documents showing that what Thompson had called a "private meeting" actually was a lunch attended by half a dozen other people. The documents explained what was discussed at lunch, and there was nothing suggesting Clinton was involved in the illegal contribution scheme. The lawyer said Thompson had been "disingenuous" to suggest otherwise.

Thompson was proved wrong, and now he faced a quandary. He needed to apologize. But should he do so immediately, during the hearing? Or later? If later, when? He knew the aphorism from Harry Truman's vice president, Alben W. Barkley, who said of political apologies, "If you have to eat crow, eat it while it's hot." Many people agree with Barkley that when you are caught in a mistake you should express regret immediately, as soon as you possibly can. Get it over with, show your contrition, minimize the damage, and move on.

But Thompson didn't apologize right away. Instead, the hearings continued and more evidence emerged during the following hours. White House officials confirmed that the meeting was public. Witnesses who attended the lunch said no one had discussed swapping political contributions. Democrats vented at Thompson for wrongly implicating Clinton in the crime.

When the hearings ended, Thompson conferred with his staff. Finally, that night, several hours after his mistake, he made an announcement. He apologized for "leaving the wrong impression." He admitted that "I should have taken a little more time to explore some of these avenues before I left that implication."

Thompson is a man who chooses his words carefully, and as I know from personal experience, he is not afraid to correct himself immediately, even during a televised Senate hearing.[2] He has degrees in philosophy and political science and a law degree from Vanderbilt. He was a successful lawyer and lobbyist. He is credited with writing the question his mentor, Howard Baker, famously asked during the Watergate hearings: "What did the President know and when did he know it?"[3]

So it is worth listening carefully to what Thompson said when he finally apologized for his Clinton gaffe. In the southern drawl he made famous on television and as an actor in several films, he concluded by paraphrasing, but not precisely quoting, Barkley. Thompson said, "If you have to eat crow, or maybe half a crow, it's better to eat it warm than cold."[4] Barkley had said "hot." But Thompson said "warm."

Thompson understood how to manage the timing of his apology. He knew not to apologize right away, in the heat of the moment, because a snap apology would have seemed thoughtless and would have reinforced the notion that his quick accusation that morning had been impulsive and rash. He needed to let the explanation of why he had been wrong percolate, to be sure all the information was out and to make it clear that he understood the facts. Thompson postponed an announcement for hours, and when he finally apologized he tweaked Barkley's language to match his delayed approach. He didn't want to wait too long to say he was sorry. But he wasn't going to say it too early either. Instead, Thompson favored a Goldilocks-like tactic—apologizing not when the reaction to his offense was too hot or too cold, but when it was just right.

——

When is the ideal moment to apologize? This question, like many of the decisions we are examining in this book, is more complicated than it appears at first, though it has some of the same elements. If you accidentally spill a drink on someone or step on a stranger's toe, a quick apology is expected and appropriate. When the offense is unintentional or impersonal, if you wait too long, even more than a few seconds, an apology will seem insincere. You should tap your automatic system 1 response: there is no need to observe or orient or deliberate. In these circumstances, you should say you are sorry right away.

In other situations, a snap apology can be less effective or even disingenuous; it might even suggest panic or fear. For Senator Thompson, it was important to apologize later, with a more deliberative system 2 response. When the offense is more intentional and personal, as was his accusation of President Clinton, a degree of delay permits the apology to be more sincere. If we take some time before apologizing—if we can enter the longer-term world of hours, or even days—we show that we have considered the feelings of the wronged person, something we could not have done had we apologized right away. By waiting, we can employ John Boyd's OODA framework, taking some time to observe and orient to the person we have wronged before saying we are sorry. The decision to apologize presents some of the same opportunities and challenges related to delay that we have been exploring in other decisions.*

In his book *On Apology,* psychiatry professor Aaron Lazare says that when he first asks students when they should apologize, most reply that sorry should come immediately. After all, that's what we are taught as kids. But after some discussion, students see the drawbacks of quick apologies. According to Lazare, most students conclude that "timing is an important and complex ingredient in delivering effective apologies."[5] The students come to understand that the first decision they must make when it becomes clear that they owe someone an apology is not whether, but when.

The topic that helps students understand the importance of timing in apologizing is not spilling a drink or stepping on someone's toe. It is infidelity.

During one of Lazare's classes, as his students were debating the timing of apologies, one student admitted he had been caught cheating on his girlfriend. He explained his thinking when she confronted him: "Right away I told her we would talk about it; but I did not apologize to her at

---

* The timing of "I forgive you" isn't easy either.

that moment."[6] The other students were appalled at first. The cheater's behavior seemed sleazy and coldly calculating. Shouldn't he have apologized right away?

There are two good reasons to wait. One is that a snap apology can prevent the offended party from expressing how he or she feels, especially after a serious personal transgression. A quick apology might not give the victim enough time to go through the natural emotional response, to understand what the wrongdoer might have been thinking, and to express his or her feelings. If a stranger bumps into you, it takes just a split-second to understand it was an accident. But if your partner admits to cheating, you will want to think and vent—for a while. Time gives victims a chance to use their conscious system, and most crucially their voice.

A second reason to delay an apology is that letting some time pass allows for more information to bubble up around the wrongful act. The victim can learn more about who, what, why, where, and when. Was the affair a one-night stand or a longer-term relationship? When did it start? Why did it happen? The additional information helps put the apology in context and shows not just that the apologizer was wrong, but why. Thus, a later apology can be more credible and informed and therefore more satisfying. Time gives victims a chance to understand.

Apologies for infidelity are important. According to the General Social Survey, about 10 percent of spouses admit to cheating every year. The numbers are higher for unmarried couples. A large percentage of people reading this book will be caught cheating and will need to apologize. Obviously, it goes without saying that you shouldn't cheat. But if you do, and you're caught doing it, you need to apologize as effectively as possible.

—

In 2005, Cynthia McPherson Frantz and Courtney Bennigson published the first formal academic paper on the role of timing in apologies.[7] Their hypothesis was that victims feel more satisfied when apologies are delayed, because the additional time gives them a chance to express themselves and to feel they have been heard and understood. Frantz and Bennigson tested this theory by conducting two studies of undergraduate students at Amherst College and Williams College, their respective alma maters.

The first study asked several questions about recent conflicts in which the students had been involved. First, the students listed the order of events during the conflict, including any apology. Then they ranked how well they thought the conflict had been resolved, how angry they remained, and how much they had forgiven the offender. They also rated how much they had felt heard and understood. The students did not know that the purpose of the study was to test the importance of timing in apologies.

The results were stark: "Apology timing was positively correlated with outcome satisfaction; when the apology came later in the conflict, participants reported greater satisfaction."[8] Statistical tests showed that, the greater the delay, the more a victim felt heard and understood. With more time, there was more opportunity for voice and understanding.

In the second study, students rated their emotional responses to a hypothetical situation in which they and a friend had arranged to get together one evening but the friend never showed up and instead went out with others. Then the students randomly were given three alternative descriptions of a phone call with the friend the next day. In the first, the friend apologized at the beginning of the conversation. In the second, the friend apologized at the end. In the third, the friend did not apologize at all. Finally, the students re-rated their emotional responses.

Not surprisingly, the students felt most negatively in the "no apology" situation. Saying you are sorry is always better than not apologizing at all.

But as with the first study, the students felt better about a delayed apology: "Improvement in the late apology condition was significantly greater than improvement in the early apology condition."[9] In fact, a statistically significant improvement in the students' reactions occurred only in the late apology condition, when there was a chance for them to discuss what had happened and why.[10] Overall, these studies suggest that the relationship between apologies and timing follows a "bell curve" distribution: effectiveness is low at first, then rises, peaks, and ultimately declines.

During class discussion, Lazare's cheating student explained that he didn't apologize right away because "I needed to give her enough time to get the anger out of her system. Many days later, I apologized and everything came back to normal."[11] Perhaps the relationship should never have gone back to normal. But not apologizing, or apologizing right away, probably would have killed it.

The timing of apologies is more art than science. There is no formula for determining exactly when to apologize. Still, we can use some tools to help us gauge timing and to make sure we wait long enough. We can observe and process information before apologizing. Aaron Lazare devotes two full chapters of *On Apology* and much of his subsequent research to questions of timing and delay. He finds that effective apologies typically contain four parts:

1. Acknowledge that you did it.
2. Explain what happened.
3. Express remorse.
4. Repair the damage, as much as you can.[12]

This checklist has two important functions. First, it sets out the important elements of an apology so that we cover each one, in order. Second, it cues us to pause before each element, so we don't speed through an explanation of what we did wrong. Lazare's student acknowledged that he had cheated. Then he took a minute before he explained what happened. Then he paused again, this time for several days. Finally, he apologized. And after that, he spent yet more time—perhaps years—on the last part, trying to repair the damage.

———

It isn't easy to follow this apology checklist, and it doesn't guarantee success. It won't undo hurtful actions or words. But as some public figures have shown, if we use the right apology strategy, we can prevent a bad situation from getting worse.

On June 3, 2011, comedian Tracy Morgan told several inappropriate gay jokes at a nightclub in Nashville, at one point even saying he would stab his son if he were gay. As news spread about the remarks, it became obvious that Morgan needed to apologize. He did so perfectly, step by step.

First, after he gave the public a few days to react to his comments, Morgan acknowledged that the performance "went too far." Next, he admitted that the act "was not funny in any context." He sent a statement to several gay rights groups apologizing for his choice of words. That covered the first three items on the checklist: acknowledgement, explanation, remorse.

Then, after a few days had passed, Morgan met with homeless gay teens at the Ali Forney Center in New York. He spoke to a woman whose son was killed in a recent antigay hate crime. He returned to Nashville to apologize to leaders of the Gay and Lesbian Alliance Against Defamation in person and to film a public service announcement for GLAAD.[13] He went back over parts 2 and 3 above, like a fighter pilot cycling through John Boyd's OODA Loop.

Morgan's apology didn't persuade Tina Fey, his friend, boss, and costar in the television show *30 Rock,* or Bob Greenblatt, head of entertainment at NBC, which airs *30 Rock.* They both criticized Morgan even after his apology, at one point saying they could never accept him again (though they later did). But the public accepted Morgan's apology. People wanted acknowledgment, explanation, remorse, and repair, in that order, and that is what Morgan gave them. His apology reminded them that his numerous previous gay spoofs had been funny, insightful, and obviously ironic—not malicious. No one who watches *Saturday Night Live* thought Morgan really would need to wolf down the drug Homocil to cope with having a son who likes to bake crème brûlée. By the end of June, Morgan was back onstage, even telling gay jokes: "I'm 42, man, and now all of a sudden I'm homophobic? My father was the lead singer in the Village People . . . I was sitting right there when he wrote the song, my daddy. The Indian was my godfather."[14] Morgan's decision to take time and care with his apology paid off.

In contrast, consider Mel Gibson's botched apology after he was arrested for drunken driving late one summer evening in Malibu in 2006 and launched into a profanity-laced anti-Semitic rant, railing against "fucking Jews" and proclaiming that "the Jews are responsible for all the wars in the world." As news spread about his tirade, the event provoked intense reactions. Rightly or wrongly, many people already had believed Gibson held anti-Semitic views based on the selective reading of the Gospels in *The Passion of the Christ,* a movie he had directed, produced, and cowritten two years earlier.

Given the amount of public anger, Gibson needed to take special care in timing the steps of his apology and give the public time to get its anger out. Although the media was clamoring for an immediate statement, Gibson should have waited for the public to fully express its reaction, however long that took, and then given a full acknowledgment of what he had done wrong.

Instead, Gibson's first apology was immediate, and it was a disaster. The day after his arrest, Gibson acted like a businessman efficiently processing a complaint against his company. His publicist issued a press release framed in generalities, apologizing but not directly addressing claims that Gibson had made anti-Semitic remarks. The lack of substance in the press release generated renewed howls of protest. A popular cartoon video on YouTube caricatured Gibson's apology as follows: "I'm really, really sorry about your big noses. I'm really sorry about how greedy you are. But most of all I'm really sorry about your dirty, underhanded, backstabbing ways. Your number one dirty Jew fan, Mel Gibson."

Gibson's initial press release was so widely regarded as ineffective that he had to issue a second press release, which was not much better. When both apologies failed to move public opinion, Gibson sat for an interview with Diane Sawyer of ABC News to try to explain himself. When that interview aired, it also was viciously parodied online. Gibson's apology became the canonical example of what not to do. He should have taken more time to formulate a complete acknowledgment and explanation, and he should not have moved on until the public was ready for his apology.

Gibson's mistake was failing to figure out the maximum amount of delay—the most time he could possibly spend until acknowledging what he had done and explaining what had happened. It is counterintuitive, but we actually want to drag the apology process out for as long as we possibly can, until our audience is finally ready to hear us. An apology is kind of like delivering the punch line of a joke—except that it isn't funny.

You might imagine that politicians would understand all of this, as Senator Thompson did. You might think they would have learned from all of the transgressions and apologies that have come before them. But if you do, you would be wrong.

—

On May 27, 2011, Representative Anthony Weiner, a six-term congressman from New York, sent a twenty-one-year-old woman who had been "following" him on Twitter a link to a close-up photograph of gray underpants concealing an erect penis. The image was quickly removed. But not quickly enough. Conservative blogger Andrew Breitbart obtained a copy and published it on his website the next day.

Four days later, Weiner gave a series of interviews about the photo. He denied sending it. He suggested someone had hacked into his Twitter account. He said the photo might have been altered. In a cryptic double negative, he said he could not say "with certitude" that it was not him. Weiner's statements during these interviews were raw meat for television commentators, news programs, and bloggers, who devoured the story. Then, on June 6, Weiner called a press conference and tearfully admitted that he had lied. He apologized. In the aftermath, as more photos emerged, Weiner held another press conference, apologized again, and resigned.

Weiner's apology was a catastrophe—first, because he denied the misdeed; second, because his apology was incomplete; and third, because by the time he finally admitted everything he was an emotional mess and the process was out of his control. He'd become a national joke. Instead of using observe-process-act, he ducked, wavered, and crumpled.

There is no science dictating when politicians should apologize for sexual transgressions. The timing is a function of the type of the offense, the evidence, and the politician's reputation. Still, there have been so many of this category of apology that we can assemble a kind of elected-official-sexual-transgression-apology playbook. Good apologies generally follow observe-process-act. And bad ones don't.

Many politicians confronted with sexual transgressions have timed their apologies poorly: John Ensign, Newt Gingrich, Gary Hart, and Mark Sanford, to name a few. In 2008, Senator John Edwards admitted to an affair but denied having an out-of-wedlock daughter; two years later, just before a book covering the details was to be released, he admitted to paternity. Senator Larry Craig, caught soliciting an undercover police officer in an airport men's restroom, refused to apologize, later announced a plan to resign, and then waffled, serving out his Senate term in dispute and disgrace.

Some politicians have done better. Representative Chris Lee, caught sending a shirtless picture to a male-to-female transsexual on the Craigslist network, saw and analyzed the evidence and then apologized and resigned the day after the news broke. He is now a successful businessman. When the *New York Times* reported that Governor Eliot Spitzer of New York had patronized Emperors Club VIP, a prostitution service, Spitzer gave the media and public two days to react and then quickly apologized and resigned. Within months, he reemerged as a commentator and consultant. Governor Arnold Schwarzenegger was about as effective as a secret politician-father could be, under the circumstances, when he waited until after the end of his gubernatorial term to confirm rumors that he had fathered a son with a household employee fourteen years earlier, while he was married to Maria Shriver.

President Bill Clinton's belated apology about White House intern Monica Lewinsky deserves its own category. After wagging his finger at the camera and denying "sexual relations with that woman, Miss Lewinsky," Clinton waited eight months—until he was forced to testify before a grand jury—before he quickly covered all four elements of the apology checklist. It isn't clear how much Clinton observed and processed during those eight months, and people disagree about how effective it was. Most of us already thought he *had* had sexual relations with that woman, especially after Lewinsky credibly claimed she had performed oral sex on Clinton nine times. But he survived the scandal.

Of all these political mea culpas, Anthony Weiner's was the least effective. It is hard to imagine Anthony Weiner reemerging as a credible public figure. Even Weiner's colleagues and supporters concluded that, whatever one might think of his behavior, he could no longer be trusted. And yet, was Weiner's behavior really worse than that of others on our elected-official-sexual-transgression-apology list? He never even met the six women he texted and emailed. He didn't inseminate or impregnate anyone. His fatal mistake was to appear ridiculous in his underpants and then woefully mismanage his apology. He reacted too early and then apologized too late.

It shouldn't be surprising that elected politicians, with their healthy egos, would be poster children for bad apologies. As Oliver Wendell Holmes noted, an apology is only egotism wrong side out.

———

A late apology is better than none at all, but apologies that come too late tend to lose their effectiveness. Secretary of Defense Robert McNamara's apology for misjudgments he and others made about the war in Vietnam would have meant more had it come a decade or two earlier. Muhammad Ali's apology to George Frazier for calling him an Uncle Tom and a gorilla didn't carry as much weight thirty years after their historic fights, and when Frazier died in 2011 the feud was remembered, to Ali's detriment.

The art of the apology centers on the management of delay. For most of us, the lesson is that the next time we do something wrong to a close friend or family member, or say something at work we wish we could take back, we should try to imagine how the victim might react to an apology tomorrow instead of today, or in a few hours instead of right now. If delay will give a friend or relative or coworker a chance to react, to voice a response and prepare themselves to hear our regret, the apology will mean more later than right away.

If our transgression is sufficiently serious, we likely will have to apologize several times, which will make the choices about delay even more challenging. We will have to orient ourselves to our victim and observe his or her reaction after each apology; then we can decide how long to wait before we undertake yet another act of apology. The cycle of delay in an ongoing apology resembles the OODA Loop of an aerial dogfight.

For any apology, instead of doing it immediately, most people should think for a minute first about when to apologize. Admit the wrong, and then listen. Stop and consider how and when to take the next step and explain what happened. Take plenty of time. And then, at the last possible moment, say you are sorry and begin trying to pick up the pieces. As Fred Thompson put it: eat crow not when it is hot or cold, but when it is warm.

10 AT LAST, PROCRASTINATION

When does putting off something we don't want to do, such as apologizing, become procrastination? If Fred Thompson waits several hours before he admits it was wrong to implicate President Clinton in a kickback scheme, that is good strategy. But if he puts off his apology day after day, the delay becomes a problem. It makes good sense to wait until the end of lunch to decide whether to ask someone on a second date. But what if you are still putting off the decision a month later? Where is the line between good delay and bad delay?

The economist George Akerlof was spending a year in India after graduate school, and his good friend and fellow economist Joseph Stiglitz visited him there. (This was decades ago, before both men won the Nobel Prize.[1]) Stiglitz had purchased many souvenirs and clothes during his trip. On his return, when a customs official at check-in told Stiglitz he had too many bags and would have to leave one behind, Stiglitz put the extra ornaments and clothes in a cardboard box and asked Akerlof to ship it back to the United States. Then Stiglitz flew home. Neither of them imagined that this box would form the basis of one of the most important theories in behavioral economics.

Akerlof is charming and mild-mannered, a rigorous and focused scholar who has written dozens of important articles and several books. Recently, I asked him if he is a procrastinator, and he answered, "Absolutely not. I'm the opposite. I take care of the important things right away." But when I mentioned Stiglitz's box, he hesitated. Then he asked, "Well, what do you do when you're supposed to send a box from India?"

———

Our society is obsessed with productivity and efficiency, and we despise procrastination. The early Americans imported the Earl of Chesterfield's admonition: "No idleness, no laziness, no procrastination: never put off till tomorrow what you can do today."[2] They read Jonathan Edwards's sermon "Procrastination, or The Sin and Folly of Depending on Future Time." They built on the Puritan work ethic, which wasn't much fun, but became a major part of American culture. Over time, the admonitions from Chesterfield and Edwards seeped into everyday life, along with the biblical references that Edwards peppered throughout his speech, especially Proverbs 27:1, which advises, "Boast not thyself of tomorrow; for thou knowest not what a day may bring forth."

And then, beginning in the 1970s, the do-it-now anti-procrastination industry burst onto the scene. Managers began following Peter Drucker, the consultant, who advised, "First things first; second things not at all."[3] Jane Burka and Lenora Yuen wrote a best seller about how to avoid procrastinating, and their "Procrastination Workshops" became popular.[4] Self-help guru Stephen Covey told us that highly effective people do "first things first."[5] David Allen coached us to "Get Things Done."[6]

Over time we began to feel terribly guilty about procrastinating, yet we did it even more. The percentage of people who say they procrastinate "often" has increased sixfold since 1978.[7] Students report spending over one-third of their time procrastinating.[8] According to some studies, nearly one in five adults is a "chronic" procrastinator. [9] Our focus on procrastination is relentless. America really has become a "Procrasti-Nation."[10]

But it wasn't always so. In ancient Egypt and Rome, procrastination was thought to be useful and wise. Only a handful of early writers, such as Cicero and Thucydides, admonished people not to delay. Until the mid-eighteenth century, procrastination-hating was a minority view.[11]

Many iconic figures have been inveterate procrastinators, from St. Augustine to Leonardo da Vinci to Duke Ellington to Agatha Christie to John Huston to Bill Clinton. Like many of my colleagues and friends, I tend to procrastinate, and I've always bristled at being told that was bad. To the extent I have creative breakthroughs (and they don't come often), it is because I put something off, not because I meet a deadline. Recent procrastination research suggests I am not alone. Studies find that although procrastination is problematic for some people, others can procrastinate but still get plenty done without stress, coping problems, or low self-esteem.[12]

When the *Wall Street Journal* recently reported on some "fans of procrastination," several psychologists who research procrastination shot back. They fumed at the notion that Paul Kedrosky, a successful entrepreneur, would, as he said, "circle topics like a dog trying to tromp down a nice place to sleep." Joseph Ferrari, a psychology professor at DePaul University, retorted, "The misperception of our culture is that it's OK to procrastinate. A bigger misperception is that it isn't a serious problem." Jane Burka, the psychologist and author, joined Ferrari, saying procrastinators are people who fear failure, success, or being controlled: "It's a way of protecting yourself from having your true abilities evaluated." Kedrosky, however, seemed bemused by this criticism, citing the "nagging suspicion that a lot of the things that I get asked to do I don't actually have to do."[13]

Academics who study procrastination fall into camps with about as much in common as the tribes of Afghanistan. Many psychologists follow a definition from Piers Steel, a leading researcher, that procrastination is "irrational" delay—in other words, we procrastinate when we know we are acting against our own best interests.[14] However, psychologists don't agree about what causes our irrationality. Is it dark thoughts, behaviors, and personality traits? Compulsiveness? Is it "unconscious death anxiety"? Rebellion at the finality of existence? Some say the cause is overly indulgent parenting, while others claim it is overly demanding parenting.[15]

Another group of psychologists gives procrastination a more positive spin, depending in large part on the amount of energy the procrastinator expends.[16] So-called active procrastination is smart: it simply means managing delay, putting off projects that really don't need to be done right away. In contrast, passive procrastination is dumb, equivalent to laziness. This group says procrastination might be good or bad, depending on how much effort we put into it.

Economists approach procrastination in yet another way. One group observes how common it is, and asks—using the standard classical economics move—how something can be irrational if it is so widespread.

Why would human beings engage in procrastination if it weren't some-how making them better off? Carolyn Fischer, a public finance and natural resources economist, developed a clever mathematical model to show how procrastination can be in our best interests.[17]

A second strand of economics, the one originated by George Akerlof,[18] laid the groundwork for Piers Steel and dozens of other prominent econ-omists and psychologists who see procrastination as closely tied to im-patience. Procrastination has become a hot subfield in economics, but if we asked three economists about procrastination, we might get five dif-ferent opinions.

There are also camps of historians with diametrically opposed views. One group points to evidence that procrastination has been around for-ever and views it as a deeply entrenched phenomenon at the core of human nature, at least since St. Augustine's proclamation: "Please, Lord, make me chaste, just not today!" Another group sees procrastination as a relatively recent phenomenon driven by technology, urbanization, and the temptations of modern life.[19]

Neuroscientists are also investigating: recent fMRI studies have helped scholars map some of our procrastination-related reactions to different regions of the brain. Other disciplines now cite these multicolor brain scans, which look much cooler than anything a psychologist or economist or historian might do. There are burgeoning combo-disciplines, including neuroeconomics and neurofinance, each of which points to parts of the brain that might be the source of our irrational delay.[20]

On one thing nearly everyone agrees: virtually all of us, at least some of the time, feel the urge to procrastinate. And there is wisdom in each camp.[21] Paul Kedrosky's bemused skepticism about what he supposedly needs to get done works well for creative, outside-the-box thinkers. The psychologists Joseph Ferrari, Jane Burka, and Piers Steel help chronic procrastinators who suffer from paralyzing stress and negative self-esteem. The various perspectives from economics and history are enlightening, too, like different views of a cathedral. Yet notwithstanding all of the books, websites, and self-help courses on the topic, there is no grand unified theory of procrastination.[22] The closest we have is George Akerlof.

———

In 1991, twenty-five years after his postgraduate year in India, Akerlof was invited to give a lecture at the 103rd meeting of the American Economics Association. By this time, he had developed an economic model to explain why humans procrastinate. He began his lecture, entitled "Procrastination and Obedience," by telling the crowd about Stiglitz's box.[23]

The heart of classical economics is the assumption that human beings are rational and forward-looking. Essentially, economists assume that people use a simple tool—multiplication—to make decisions in two different ways. First, economic models assume people multiply the probability of each possible outcome of a decision by how desirable that outcome would be, and then choose the decision with the highest total "expected" value. For example, we would rather have $100 with certainty than a chance at $150 on a coin flip, because the coin flip is expected to be worth, on average, just $75 ($150 multiplied by one-half). However, we'd take the coin flip over a certain $100 if the coin flip paid $250—that chance is worth, on average, $125. According to this theory, we would almost never buy a lottery ticket, because its "expected" value is usually negative: the cost of the ticket is more than the tiny probability of winning multiplied by the payoff (except when the Mega Millions jackpot reached $390 million in 2007 and the odds of winning were a mere 175 million to one). The assumption that we make these kinds of calculations might seem implausible, but it held up pretty well for more than two centuries after mathematician Daniel Bernoulli first proposed it in 1738.

The second assumption is that people use multiplication to "discount" the value of payments to be made in the future. The basic idea of discounting is straightforward: a dollar tomorrow is worth less than a dollar today. Most of us naturally would prefer to pay someone $100 in one year instead of $100 today. Conversely, we would prefer receiving $100 today to $100 in one year. Classical economists assume that the way people decide between money today versus tomorrow is by multiplying any future payment by a discount factor, which we calculate based on the amount of time and risk involved (adjusted for inflation). For example, if you are assessing a promise from me that I will pay you $100 in a year, you might discount it by multiplying it by nine-tenths. In other words, in today's terms, my $100 promise would be worth just $90. When interest rates and risk are low, we don't discount future payments very much, but when they are high we discount them a lot.

If these two assumptions hold, and people are multiplying correctly, there can be no such thing as procrastination. Instead, if someone is delaying a decision, it must be because they have calculated the probabilities and discounted the future costs and benefits correctly, and then determined that it simply is not worth it to act today. (As a child who liked math, I made a similar argument when my parents told me to make my bed. The probability of a guest coming over and looking at my room was low; it would occur, if at all, in the future and therefore should be discounted. Making my bed was costly and had no current benefit—why should I do it now?)

Consistent with the classical economic model, the economists listening to Akerlof's talk assumed he had acted rationally in shipping the box back to Stiglitz. After all, the cost of sending it was relatively low, and the benefit to Stiglitz, who presumably wanted the contents he had recently paid for, was relatively high. There also was a benefit to Akerlof, from the happy feelings he would derive from helping his good friend.[24] If Akerlof multiplied properly, using the right probabilities and discounting the future correctly, he would choose to send the box quickly, perhaps even the next day. Naturally, the audience assumed this was what Akerlof had done.

Yet, as Akerlof revealed, he didn't. Not that day, or the next. Or the one after that. To the horror of the economists in the crowd,[25] Akerlof confessed how long he had taken to ship the box, and how he had decided each day not to ship it: "Each morning for over eight months I woke up and decided that the next morning would be the day to send the Stiglitz box." Eight months? This wasn't just rude to young Stiglitz. It was a slap across the face of classical economics.[26]

Akerlof claimed that, although people are not irrational in general, we are prone to small repeated errors of judgment "due to unwarranted salience of some costs and benefits relative to others." The mere mention of this unwarranted "salience" froze the roomful of economists, rationalists to a man or woman. Akerlof was suggesting that human beings are irrational. And he was saying it using *math*. Akerlof described an algebraic model of his decision, which included the cost of sending the box, the value of the clothes to Stiglitz, and a new factor related to the vividness of the activity he might do each morning instead of navigating Indian shipping regulations. Using math to describe human behavior is at the core of economics, but mathematizing the problem didn't comfort the economists, and it didn't hide Akerlof's radical conclusion: people make bad short-term decisions even when they understand the long-term consequences.

Worst of all, Akerlof had understood his mistaken thinking about "salience" even as he continued to postpone shipping the box. He knew he'd get up each morning, smell the hot sambar and coffee, think about the nightmare that was Indian bureaucracy, and put off sending Stiglitz his box for yet another day. Akerlof knew the benefits of sending the box outweighed the immediate costs. He knew the probabilities and the discount factors indicated he should send it. He did the multiplication. Yet he still didn't send the box. For economists who believed in rationality as an article of faith, this was heresy.

In his talk, Akerlof compared his decision to other bad short-term decisions with long-term consequences, ranging from alcoholism to dieting to the savings habits of elderly retirees. His audience was full of old, overweight, boozing economists. Didn't they understand the long-term costs of *that* kind of behavior? Akerlof suggested that these behaviors are closely related to procrastination in that all of them involve too much focus on today. People aren't doing the math in the way economists thought: they don't factor in the probability of negative long-term consequences and they discount the future too much (as in, "I won't get liver or heart disease," or, "I'm not worried about retirement"). Akerlof's point hit too close to home: classical economists aren't rational either.

Today most of us aren't surprised by Akerlof's insight. We know we might delay finishing a household chore or studying for an exam or replying to email because the cost of acting today seems unduly high. If we could see through the fog and understand that the cost of future action will be just as high, or higher, we might act now. But we cannot see. We cannot understand. As Mark Twain quipped, "Never put off till tomorrow what you can do the day after tomorrow."

The tricky part about all of this is that often we really *should* put off costly activities until tomorrow. When we have a choice between paying someone $100 today and $100 in one year, we generally should choose to wait to pay the money in one year. The reason is that, from today's perspective, paying $100 today costs more than paying $100 a year from now. If our bank pays interest (admittedly, a rarity today), we can put the $100 in the bank, make the $100 payment in a year, and then pocket the interest.[27]

It is easy to choose between paying a set amount today and the same amount in the future. It is tougher to choose when the future payment is higher. If the choice is between paying $100 today and $115 in one year, we might choose to pay $100 today. But if the choice is between paying $100 today and just $105 in one year, we might choose to pay the $105 later. At some future payment amount we become indifferent about paying today versus paying in one year. If we view $100 today versus $110 in one year as basically the same, economists would say we are using a 10 percent "discount rate." At a 10 percent discount rate, $110 in one year is essentially the same to us as $100 today.

We often decide to pay more money in the future instead of paying less money today. Sometimes that is by choice. Sometimes we make this choice because we don't have enough money today. But this kind of delay isn't necessarily bad: we often quite rationally prefer to pay later. This is why we have credit cards and home mortgage loans. It is why businesses have accounts payable. It is why governments take on debt. Of course, we often make mistakes and borrow too much. But the discounted cost of future payments is at the heart of many of our decisions, and we don't always call these decisions to delay payment procrastination.

The key to thinking about future payments is the discount rate. For most of the twentieth century, economists assumed that people discount the future at a consistent rate for both the short term and the long term.[28] If our discount rate is 10 percent, they assumed, we use that same rate regardless of when we owe money—in a day, a month, or a year.[29] Economists also assumed we use the same rate regardless of our level of wealth, or whether we owe or are owed money. The standard economic model assumed that people think about these factors and are consistent about risk and time.

Then, in 1979, psychologists began dropping bombs on these assumptions. Daniel Kahneman and Amos Tversky published an article in *Econometrica,* a prestigious economics journal, arguing that the standard economic model of decisions was wrong. A few economists, particularly Richard Thaler, showed that people's discount rates vary dramatically depending on how far into the future they are discounting. In 1981 Thaler reported the results of an experiment designed to test what people's discount rates actually were for different periods of time by asking them a series of questions about whether they would prefer money today or in the future. Thaler found that his subjects' discount rates were much higher in the short term and then declined over time. His subjects didn't have anything close to the same discount rate for different time periods. Instead, their discount rates were 345 percent for one month, 120 percent for one year, and 19 percent for ten years.[30] Discount rates were high at first and then fell precipitously.

Other scholars soon joined the criticism. Thaler and the economist George Loewenstein examined how inconsistent humans are about time.[31] The psychiatrist George Ainslie developed a model of impulsiveness that was closely related to Thaler's findings. Ainslie said humans use very high discount rates in the short term, meaning that when we want something today, we really want it and we don't think much about future costs.[32]

These researchers found that in the short term we are like the impatient four-year-old who cannot wait for a second marshmallow—we have high discount rates. Yet in the longer term, we are better at resisting the pull of temptation—we have lower discount rates. For example, if we are offered the choice of $50 today or $100 in a month, we might prefer to receive $50 today. But if we are offered the choice of $50 in a year or $100 in thirteen months, we almost certainly will choose to receive $100 thirteen months from now. The wait is a month in both instances, but our assessment of now is very different from our assessment of twelve months from now.

We anticipate that our one-month discount rate in a year will be a lot lower than it is today. But after a year passes, that one-month rate is high. Our preferences are not time-consistent: we think that in a year we will be more than happy to wait a month to double our money, but when you ask us right now, we'd rather take the fifty bucks. Researchers have found that we have similar time inconsistencies with addictive behaviors: we say we'll quit smoking or drinking or gambling in a year, but after a year passes, we don't want to quit.

Time inconsistency is important in distinguishing between good and bad delay. If we are consistent about time and we use an appropriate discount rate, there is nothing wrong with putting off a decision. I put off doing my taxes until the second week of April for the same reason I pay my credit card bill at the last minute. My time and money are more valuable to me today than in the future. Problems arise not when I decide to put off some costly act but when I am mistaken about the benefits of doing so.

Until recently, economists didn't have a good model that captured the relationship between discount rates and procrastination. George Akerlof got them started, but even he wasn't aware of some of the research about time inconsistency when he gave his 1991 procrastination talk to the American Economics Association, or a decade later when he gave his Nobel lecture that tied research by Loewenstein, Thaler, Ainslie, and others into his economic model of procrastination.[33]

In fact, economists and psychologists didn't figure out how to think about procrastination and its close relative, impatience, until they stopped focusing exclusively on human beings and started thinking more about animals. The breakthrough came, surprisingly enough, when they discovered what James Mazur, a professor of psychology at Southern Connecticut State University, had been doing with pigeons.

———

In the early 1980s, many scientists were skeptical about whether any animals think about the future. Even people who thought chimps might be able to think about the future didn't imagine anything useful might come from experiments on pigeons.

But James Mazur did. He thought studying pigeons might yield insights about human impatience and the mistakes we make in assessing probabilities and discounting. In his early pigeon studies, he designed a set of meticulous tests in which he gave pigeons varying amounts of food at varying times, depending on whether they pecked a green or red key. Mazur found that pigeons could learn what each key meant: pecking the green key might get them a few morsels within one second, whereas pecking the red key got them twice as much food but with a delay of ten seconds.[34]

Richard Thaler had calculated people's discount rates for different time periods by asking them whether they preferred some money today or more money in the future. The pigeons obviously couldn't talk to Mazur about their preferences, but he could learn about those preferences by tracking which keys they pecked as he varied the amount of delay.

In a series of experiments, Mazur found the same pattern of results for pigeons that Thaler had found for humans: their discount rates were very high in the short term and then rapidly declined. The pigeons' timing was much faster than that of humans, seconds instead of months, but the insight was the same: just like the four-year-old child who grabs the marshmallow before fifteen minutes have elapsed, or the human adult who takes $50 today instead of $100 in a month, pigeons were very impatient in the short term.

Mazur's most significant insight came when he collated how the pigeons' discount rates varied over time. He found that they followed a curved "hyperbolic" shape: they were very high for short periods of time, but then declined rapidly and leveled off, like a steep roller-coaster drop.[35] It might seem implausible that pigeon preferences would follow an equation from high school trigonometry. But if hyperbolas show up in bridge suspension cables and tree trunks, why not in pigeon brains?

Over the years Mazur has shown in multiple experiments that pigeon discount rates consistently track this hyperbolic roller-coaster curve: high in the short term and then sliding steeply down. Pigeons want food right away, but they hate having to work for it. When Mazur requires them to peck more in order to get food, they will do everything they can to shift that pecking work into the future. Pigeons are so desperate to avoid the instant cost of immediate work that they are willing to peck four times more to get the same amount of food if they can put off that work until later.

These pigeons seem to be behaving irrationally. If they were willing to wait just a bit longer, they could get a lot more food. If they were willing to do just a bit of work right away, they could avoid doing much more of it in the future. These pigeons have the same time inconsistency problem we do. Mazur labels what they are doing procrastination.[36]

Economists, particularly David Laibson at Harvard, have cited Mazur's findings in developing new mathematical models to replace the classical models of human decision-making. Economists love math, so Mazur's claim that discount rates follow a hyperbolic curve had instant appeal. Laibson and others tweaked Mazur's hyperbolic equation to develop a "quasi-hyperbolic" mathematical model that does a reasonably good job of describing how people actually behave.[37] The key insight is that human beings, like pigeons, have high short-term discount rates and lower long-term discount rates.[38]

Today many economists use the term "present bias" to describe the fact that our immediate discount rates are so high: we prefer happiness today to happiness in the future.[39] Present bias models are complicated and controversial.[40] The math gets tricky, and no one seriously believes that people—even high school students who are taking trigonometry and can remember the equations for hyperbolas—actually use quasi-hyperbolic formulas while making decisions. Yet there is something fundamental and perhaps innate about rapidly declining discount rates. Why else would both pigeons and humans have discount rates that follow the same curve?[41]

The main difference between these new economic models and James Mazur's earlier findings, other than some technical tweaking, is that human beings' time frames are much longer. One second for a pigeon is like a day or so for us. Fifteen pigeon seconds is a human month. Beyond that, we are at the limit of the pigeon's attention span.

The parallels between pigeon and human discounting are another example of the connections we can make by looking at behavior through different time lenses. Humans and pigeons follow similar behavioral patterns, the main difference being that we take longer. There is a concept in mathematics called "self-similarity" in which some objects, especially shapes known as "fractals," look the same regardless of how much you magnify them. Mazur explains how the pigeon and human versions of procrastination are self-similar:

> The same thing happens with people, where there may be some small amount of work that we have to do right away such as get a small repair job done on our car and we're likely in many cases to procrastinate and in the end we are paying three or four times as much for a bigger repair job on the car. So I see that what I found with my pigeons in working for food is something that seems to be true with all of us. It may not be the same time scale but everybody seems to be in a position where they tend to postpone unpleasant tasks even if it costs them.[42]

There have been so many experiments about discount rates over the years that researchers now use standardized questionnaires to elicit people's rates. For example, in the Kirby Delay-Discounting Monetary Choice Questionnaire, subjects answer twenty-six questions, beginning with: "Would you prefer $54 today, or $55 in 117 days?" The amounts range from $11 to $85, and the timing ranges from 7 to 186 days. The questions usually reveal that people have a present bias: their discount rates are higher for one week than for six months. These tests confirm that the new economic models do a decent job of describing our behavior.

The tests also show that some people have higher discount rates than others overall. These people are in trouble.

Over and over, studies have shown that high discount rates correspond to bad behavior. People with high discount rates are generally less happy and less successful. They are fatter, have more debt and less savings, drink more alcohol, smoke more, exercise less, have lower-paying jobs, don't stay in a job for as long, and are more likely to be divorced.[43] If you have a sense of someone's discount rate, you know a lot about the kinds of problems they are likely to have.

In contrast, people with lower discount rates tend to think more about what they are doing and why. They have more moderate habits, they carry less credit card debt, and they consume and savor healthy foods.[44] While people with low discount rates are sipping their allotted glass of red wine per day, people with high discount rates are wolfing down a bacon double cheeseburger and guzzling beers at the racetrack.

The causes of high discount rates are hotly debated, and the environment certainly plays a significant role. For example, evidence suggests that poor people are especially prone to have high short-term discount rates.[45] They frame economic decisions in narrow terms, using blinders, which is one reason why so many poor people are trapped by crushing debt loads. Poor people are more likely to get "payday" loans—high-interest-rate advances on their next paycheck.[46] They are less likely to understand that the charges for payday loans are absurdly high, even compared to credit card rates. Or perhaps they do understand, but must have the money at once anyway. It remains unclear which way the causation runs: are people poor because they have high discount rates, or do they have high discount rates because they are poor?

Young people also tend to have high discount rates. If four-year-olds understood enough details about money to fill out the Kirby Questionnaire, we probably would find that the ones who grab marshmallows right away have higher discount rates. For older children, especially adolescents, we know from numerous studies that high discount rates are correlated with impulsive, self-destructive behavior.[47] Teenagers with higher discount rates do worse in school.[48] A study of eighth-grade students found that their discount rates mattered twice as much as IQ in predicting their grade point averages.[49]

———

With all of this research, we now have something approaching a general theory of procrastination, in two parts. First, our discount rates are the key variables. If they are reasonable and we delay some action, we really shouldn't call that procrastination, not in any pejorative sense. Instead, procrastination occurs when we use a discount rate that is too high, that is, when we discount the future too much. High discount rates are one of our biggest problems as decision-makers. High discount rates lead to the bad kind of procrastination.

Second, procrastination is closely related to impatience. Their kinship is based on discount rates and our bias toward the present over the future.[50] Both are examples of the human tendency to overdiscount future events. In both impatience and procrastination, we overweight the immediate. The main difference between the two is whether the immediate thing we are overweighting is a benefit or a cost. When what is immediate is a benefit, we are impatient gluttons, overindulging and consuming more than we should. But when what is immediate is a cost, we are procrastinators, putting off activities we should get done today.

Overindulgence and procrastination are two sides of the same coin. *Preproperation* is the term for acting when we should wait. *Procrastination* is the term for waiting when we should act. When scientists test preproperation and procrastination together, they find that both are associated with the same variable: high discount rates.[51]

Given what we now know about procrastination, what might we do about its evils? The answers are similar for all of our impatience problems:

find ways to reduce our short-term discount rates to levels that are both reasonable and closer to our long-term discount rates. Turn that roller-coaster drop into a low flat track. There are no simple fixes, but as with other areas of decision-making, simply being aware of our tendencies is a good place to start. For example, just as we can learn about our racial biases by taking an Implicit Association Test, we can learn about our time inconsistencies by taking a discounting questionnaire. Education is helpful: we can learn to make better trade-offs between today and tomorrow.

Some rules also can help, though we need the willpower to follow them.[52] We might tell ourselves that before we can put off a task, we must have a unique reason for why we aren't doing it today and we must commit to completing the task in the future by putting it on our calendar for a specified future date.[53] Web-based tools such as RescueTime.com can help us plan by keeping track of precisely how we fritter away time. Just as the best diet aids involve keeping track of what we eat, the best time management aids involve keeping track of what we do.

Borrowers can reduce their present biases by thinking more carefully about future costs, comparing the cost of a payday loan to the effective interest rate of a credit card, or looking at the estimated cost or savings for a year.[54] Employers can help us avoid our high short-term discount rates by automatically enrolling us in a savings plan unless we opt out.[55] For many straightforward tasks, it helps to impose strict deadlines.[56]

On the other hand, there can be real benefits from putting tasks off, and we should recognize those as well. Not every email requires an immediate response. Not every closet has to be cleaned every day. Two of the skills that many students develop in college are the ability to manage their time throughout a semester, and the ability to cram for an exam or quickly finish a term paper at the semester's end. Students who are required to finish an assignment every week might not develop these skills.

George Ainslie, the impatience scholar, has said procrastination is harder to quit than many other impatience-related problems, such as alcohol or drug addiction. One of the reasons roughly half of all alcoholics manage to quit drinking and a similar number of smokers eventually quit is that they can imagine a future world in which they no longer drink or smoke. There is an end in sight. But there's no such absolute condition for procrastination: we cannot do away with it altogether. It's inconceivable.

As Ainslie explains, we cannot imagine quitting doing stuff any more than we can imagine no longer eating. That is why quitting procrastination is so hard, more like sustaining a long-term diet than going without alcohol or cigarettes. Only 5 percent of overweight dieters achieve long-term weight reduction.[57] Of course, it is hard to quit drinking or smoking. But it is even harder to permanently lose weight.[58] One reason is that it is more difficult to imagine a future world with a lesser amount of eating—and it is impossible to imagine stopping eating entirely.

Procrastination is fundamental, like eating: when we look ahead to the future, we know we will have plenty of tasks that we won't be able to finish, just as we know we must eat. That is simply how life works. As Ainslie explains, the number of things we might do is potentially infinite: "It is literally impossible not to put off most of what you actually can do." Ainslie suggests that procrastination problems are simply part of the human condition: "While conspicuous temptations can be identified and subjected to personal rules, a preference for deferring effort, discomfort, or boredom can never be entirely controlled. It is as fundamental as the shape of time, and could well be called the basic impulse."[59]

Some people call procrastination a disease, a mental disorder related to attention deficit hyperactivity disorder, bipolar illness, obsessive-compulsive disorder, sleep problems, and brain and thyroid anomalies. Not surprisingly, if procrastination is viewed so negatively, treatments will be designed to eradicate its presence and influence. But we don't necessarily need to take such a draconian approach. If our problems are the result of high discount rates, so that we make decisions that leave us worse off, then procrastination is an evil and we should make every effort to stop. But often we use the term to describe behavior that is not so bad. Sometimes it is good to procrastinate.

In 2005, Paul Graham, a computer programmer, investor, writer, and painter, wrote an essay called "Good and Bad Procrastination." He opens by saying, "The most impressive people I know are all terrible procrastinators. So could it be that procrastination isn't always bad? Most people who write about procrastination write about how to cure it. But this is, strictly speaking, impossible."[60]

Graham notes that when we procrastinate we don't work on something. However, he says, we are *always* not working on *some*thing. In fact, whatever we are doing, we are by definition not working on everything else. For Graham, the issue is not how to stop procrastinating, since we will always be not working on something, and thus procrastinating. Instead, our real challenge is to figure out how to procrastinate well—how to work on something that is more important than the something we are not working on. In thinking about procrastination, Graham says what matters most is comparing what we are working on with what we aren't.

Francesco Guerrera, an editor at the *Wall Street Journal,* learned how to manage his time by procrastinating during college. Not only did he develop the ability to write quickly at the last minute, but he learned how to manage a list of priorities, a skill he uses constantly to this day: "Now, most of it happens naturally. I have a bunch of things I have to do. The list of what I have to do within a certain time sort of forms itself. The other stuff is procrastinated."

For projects that require different amounts of time, Guerrera makes separate lists. He describes a technique he and many other journalists use: "We have two sets of notebooks, a small one and a big one. The small one is for immediate day-to-day stories, the work we have to do right away. The big one is for big thoughts, features and stories that have some time. There's an actual physical distinction between our immediate stories and the ones we can wait on. The physical form of two notebooks is our way of saying it's too overwhelming to do both at the same time."

Guerrera bristles at the suggestion that there is something wrong with his behavior. He told me he is really just managing delay: "This is not like traditional procrastination. It's a way we form our priorities. It's not that I'm delaying because I don't want to do something. I'm delaying because I can't. It's out of necessity." As Leonard Bernstein said, "To achieve great things, two things are needed: a plan, and not quite enough time."

If we aren't working at all, we are being slothful. If we are working on something unimportant, we are showing bad judgment. But if we are working on something important, then does it really make sense to judge us negatively for not working on something less important? If we put off errands because we are trying to cure cancer, are we really procrastinating? And if that is the meaning of procrastination, why is it so bad?

For Paul Graham, procrastination is all about trade-offs. We are constantly trading off what we are doing now against what we might do in the future. As long as we are doing that in a reasonable way, it doesn't matter that we are putting some things off.

In February 1996, John Perry, a philosophy professor at Stanford University, finally got around to writing an essay about procrastination for the *Chronicle of Higher Education*. He had been planning to do it for months, and he started writing, not because he had uncommitted time on his hands, but because he was looking for a way of *not* doing all the things he was supposed to be doing: grading papers, reviewing a grant proposal, and reading dissertation drafts. It is an avoidance strategy he calls "structured procrastination."[61]

By structured procrastination Perry means that we should structure, or plan, which items on our to-do list are the best candidates for being put off. He says structured procrastination can "convert procrastinators into effective human beings, respected and admired for all that they can accomplish and the good use they make of time."

As Perry explains it:

All procrastinators put off things they have to do. Structured procrastination is the art of making this bad trait work for you. The key idea is that procrastinating does not mean *doing absolutely nothing*. Procrastinators seldom do absolutely nothing; they do marginally useful things, such as gardening or sharpening pencils or making a diagram of how they will reorganize their files when they find the time. Why does the procrastinator do these things? Because accomplishing these tasks is a way of *not* doing something more important. If all the procrastinator had left to do was to sharpen some pencils, no force on earth could get him to do it. However, the procrastinator can be motivated to do difficult, timely, and important tasks, as long as these tasks are a way of *not* doing something more important.

Perry's advice is, first, to make a list of the things you have to do. Put a few important tasks at the top—these are the ones you will procrastinate. Then, below them, list some tasks that aren't as important but that you nevertheless need to do. According to Perry, doing these less important tasks "becomes a way of not doing the things higher on the list."

Perry says that procrastinators often follow exactly the wrong tack:

> They try to minimize their commitments, assuming that if they have only a few things to do, they will quit procrastinating and get them done. But this approach ignores the basic nature of the procrastinator and destroys his most important source of motivation. The few tasks on his list will be, by definition, the most important. And the only way to avoid doing them will be to do nothing. This is the way to become a couch potato, not an effective human being.

Perry admits there is a potential problem with the important tasks at the top of the list, because we aren't going to do them. So we have to fool ourselves—first by inflating the importance of the top items, and then by pretending that the lower-down items aren't as important. Perry puts finishing an essay for a volume on the philosophy of language at the top, along with the book-order forms for his next semester's classes. He finished his essay on procrastination long before the one on the philosophy of language, and before he had completed the book orders.[62]

So, was George Akerlof really procrastinating, in the most negative sense of the term? I asked him how hard it would have been to send a box from India. He described how he would have had to navigate the unruly bureaucracy there. He didn't know what to do, or even where to begin: "My real problem was I didn't know how to send it without wasting my whole day. This was India. It wasn't the United States."

When I asked Akerlof how important he thought the contents of the box were to Stiglitz, he told me, "Imagine the least practical clothes in the world—well, it was worse than that. There was a wedding costume from Nepal, for example. He didn't need these clothes right away. If Joe never saw the box again, it would have been a positive in his life."

In other words, Akerlof's immediate cost from sending the box, hanging around an Indian post office all day dealing with the bureaucracy, would have been significant. And there really wasn't much of a benefit to Stiglitz from receiving the box any sooner than eight months after he left India. As a young, untenured economics professor, Stiglitz probably wasn't planning to wear a Nepali wedding costume very often anyway.

So Akerlof's procrastination wasn't so irrational after all. He didn't suffer from self-control problems or impatience generally. He felt bad about not sending the box—we often feel bad about not doing things—but his behavior didn't suggest that his short-term discount rate was too high. The cost of sending the box was high, and the benefit was low.

The box was like one of Paul Graham's important tasks or John Perry's book-order forms. Akerlof was in India beginning work on a research program that would lead to dozens of articles, numerous influential books, and a Nobel Prize. For eight months, that box was at the top of Akerlof's to-do list, a salient task that he put off each day. He procrastinated, and at the same time he got a lot of other things done.

11 MASTER CLASS

The challenge of procrastination is figuring how to weigh immediate versus distant consequences. That same kind of now-versus-later evaluation is also at the core of professional expertise and judgment. We typically define professionals—lawyers, accountants, doctors, journalists, and financial advisers—as people who do high-quality work, have specialized knowledge, and follow high ethical standards. But professionals have another quality we might not notice as often: the ability to manage time.

The best lawyers and accountants are masters of delay. Litigators understand precisely how to allocate their time writing a brief or preparing for an argument or trial. Business lawyers develop an exact sense of the timing of deals and when negotiations should move forward or end. Experienced auditors can plan backward from a filing deadline to map out when work should be completed, hour by hour.

True professionals are able to act quickly, but are willing to go slow. They are comfortable using both intuition (from the automatic system 1) and analysis (from the deliberative system 2). They resist the fast-running herd and wait for the ideal time to make their move. That doesn't mean their decisions are slow; they can be faster than just about anyone when it matters. The best professionals understand how long they have available to make a decision, and then, given that time frame, they wait as long as they possibly can.

—

Jim Cramer's *Mad Money* attracts several hundred thousand viewers nightly during the coveted 6:00 PM Eastern Standard Time slot. During the show, Cramer shouts, gestures frantically, presses buttons that trigger dramatic sound effects, and tosses props, including plastic bulls and bears, as he recommends the purchase or sale of various publicly traded stocks. On a given night, Cramer might feature a "lightning round" of stock picks, a book promotion (often one of his own), some bobble-head dolls (often of himself), or a monkey named Ka-ching. *Mad Money* has been on air since 2005 and has been a huge commercial success for the cable network CNBC.

Cramer's nightly theatrics reverberate in the stock market the next morning. When Cramer recommends a stock, on average it opens for trading the next day 2.4 percent higher than the rest of the market. His average stock recommendation generates an instantaneous gain of $77.1 million. A lot of people are listening to Jim Cramer, and their demand causes prices to go up. It appears that if we knew in advance which stocks Cramer was going to recommend, we could make a fortune.

However, we don't know what Cramer will say in advance, and even if we did, it would be illegal for us to buy based on that knowledge. Instead, the people who follow Cramer's recommendations buy stock the next day at a higher price. They pay extra, reflecting the optimism Cramer generates among herds of investors about these companies.

According to a detailed analysis published in October 2010, viewers who bought the stocks Cramer recommended the previous night lost money relative to the market overall.[1] Even people who held those stocks for as long as fifty days lost an average of nearly 10 percent relative to the market. For those stocks with the highest overnight returns after Cramer's recommendations, the fifty-day performance was even worse: negative 29.54 percent for the top quintile. In other words, according to this study, if you watch *Mad Money* and follow Jim Cramer's top recommendations, you will lose almost one-third of your money in less than two months. Not very many people can afford to follow that kind of advice.

The study also found that an investment in the stocks Cramer recommended significantly underperformed the market over the longer term. Even if you had insider access to Cramer's recommendations and engaged in illegal insider trading, buying the stocks before Cramer recommended them, you still would not outperform the market in the long run. Jim Cramer has some interesting and useful things to say about investing in general. But he'd almost certainly be better at picking stocks if he did so less frequently and at a slower speed. The show *Mad Money* is entertaining, but its recommendations won't make you rich.

Behavioral finance is a relatively new area of research that combines psychology and conventional economics to try to explain why people make irrational financial decisions. It questions the long-held assumptions by financial economists that investors are rational and act in their self-interest, as well as the mathematical equations that purport to show how markets are largely predictable and efficient. A few economists, such as Eugene Fama, one of the founding fathers of efficient market theory, continue to cling to some of these assumptions. But many financial economists are jumping ship.

A wave of research, spurred on by Daniel Kahneman, Amos Tversky, and Richard Thaler, has demonstrated that investors have systematic biases. Numerous researchers have documented how we make mistakes in our financial decisions.[2] We anchor around certain numbers and concepts, we travel in herds, we overreact, we are overconfident, and we are very, very bad at assessing risk.[3] We trade too frequently. We pay too much for those trades. In short, we are unprofessional.

Much of Wall Street is even less professional. Bankers have their own set of self-control problems, which lead them to place spectacularly bad bets, such as those that nearly brought down the financial system in 2007–2008. Investment advisers take advantage of our mistakes by selling risky and inappropriate investments to us and to the mutual funds, pension funds, and insurance companies we rely on. Many brokers prey on our cognitive errors, particularly our overconfidence.[4] Financial advisers are supposed to have our interests in mind when they make recommendations, but we cannot always trust them, especially when their incentives are not aligned with ours, as when they profit from us trading frequently or buying risky securities.

There are still some reliable leaders in the financial business. Although investment banking has been vilified since the financial crisis, some investment banking firms, such as The Needham Group, Inc., have avoided the major losses and scandals that were so common at major Wall Street banks by focusing on the traditional business of advising companies about raising money, mergers, and strategy. Likewise, although most investors have fared poorly in recent years, others have done quite well. There is Warren Buffett, of course. Some investors, such as Wilbur L. Ross Jr. and Ralph Whitworth, have reliably made money by purchasing significant stakes in underperforming companies and turning them around. Several hedge fund managers, such as Bill Ackman and Ray Dalio, have remained successful before, during, and after the recent crisis.

These successful financial professionals are a diverse group, but they share one important characteristic: they are focused on the long term. Their investment horizon extends to years or even decades. They are capable of moving quickly, but they understand how to avoid dangerous short-term impulses.[5] They can do what some financial executives call "seeing around corners." They would never pick stocks during a lightning round. They do not respond to, or even watch, *Mad Money*.

Warren Buffett says one key to his success as an investor has been delaying decisions. He likens buying stocks to hitting a baseball—except without the strikes: "I call investing the greatest business in the world because you never have to swing. You stand at the plate, the pitcher throws you General Motors at 47! US Steel at 39! And nobody calls a strike on you. There's no penalty except opportunity lost. All day you wait for the pitch you like; then when the fielders are asleep, you step up and hit it."[6] As Buffett puts it, "We don't get paid for activity, just for being right. As to how long we'll wait, we'll wait indefinitely."[7]

Buffett isn't procrastinating. And although he has written that "lethargy bordering on sloth remains the cornerstone of our investment style," he certainly isn't lazy.[8] He works all the time, reading financial statements and reports, preparing for his next big trade. But although Buffett is constantly working, he is not constantly buying and selling. He does not respond to everything he sees. Instead, he delays his reactions as much as possible. His short-term discount rate is low. He is focused on the long haul.

Bill Ackman, the founder of the hedge fund Pershing Square Capital Management, is thirty-six years younger than Buffett, but he takes a similar approach. Ackman would be at the top of just about anyone's list of the best investors of the last two decades. He is often controversial, especially among the managers of companies he criticizes, but he has consistently earned high returns for his investors and he now manages almost $10 billion. Ackman is as slow as Cramer is fast, which is why he, not Cramer, is his generation's version of Warren Buffett.

Ackman explained to me that even top investment managers find it difficult to maintain Buffett's long-term perspective: "There's general institutional pressure to do something. You need to put the money to work. Most institutional managers can't afford to delay. Warren Buffett says that if you look at your investing track record, you get twenty fat pitches. That's it. You can't use them up again. That's why he says you want to wait. The problem with most institutional investors is that they can't wait."

On average, mutual fund managers hold stocks for less than a year. Pension fund managers aren't much more patient. And individual investors are the worst of all; they trade far more frequently than they should. Resisting this pressure, Ackman holds his investments for several years or longer. When his research uncovered problems at MBIA, an insurance firm, he took a short position, betting that the company would perform poorly. He held on to that position for seven years, in the face of intense skepticism and criticism from MBIA and Wall Street, until he was finally vindicated and made a fortune for his investors. (He set up a charitable foundation to give away the millions he personally made on the MBIA trade.) If he had been less patient and had unwound his MBIA trade within a year or two, he still would have been right, but he would not have made money.[9] He told me, "Unless something seems extremely opportune, we don't do anything. If we have a good investment, we can just watch it work."

The best financial professionals have this kind of discipline, and they create a work environment that reinforces their long-term philosophy. One hedge fund manager told me that he doesn't give his junior employees access to real-time price information because they would be glued to their trading screens, like teenagers playing video games. Instead, he sounds like an old-style parent: he wants his employees to read and think. It isn't easy to find investments that will generate high returns, and they typically don't pop up in the news. As he says, "If the goal is to get 20 percent per year, we shouldn't work on anything we'll hold less than six months." Perhaps surprisingly, the best high-frequency trading firms have low-frequency cultures: the firms' managers let their computers trade at light speed while they sit back and think strategically about the markets. Likewise, Julian Robertson, the founder of the Tiger investment funds, told employees that the best course of action is often to do nothing. The best traders I worked with at Morgan Stanley appeared to trade quickly, but those fast trades were often investments that they had pondered for months, until they finally could buy at a low enough price.

Most of us save in order to pay for something in the distant future: college for our children or retirement for ourselves. That means the core of our investing should be to buy some stocks and bonds and then simply leave them alone. The best investment strategies are those that harness the value of compounding returns, with the lowest possible fees. If we hire an investment "professional," we should be sure to understand how that person makes money, and we should try to minimize our trading and be as patient as Warren Buffett and Bill Ackman.

—

Since 2008, a group of master clinicians has held an annual conference on "Diagnostic Error in Medicine" (labeled DEM) to explore why doctors make mistakes and to try to improve medical decision-making generally. This new group of medical professionals is open to research and ideas that go well beyond traditional analytical thinking. The doctors who attend the DEM conferences talk about intuition and psychology. They compare expert physicians to chess masters: they "chunk" information into patterns based on their knowledge and experience and store "illness scripts" in their minds, the way good chess players store game strategies and openings.[10] Gary Klein, the field researcher who helped military officers understand the value of snap decisions by studying paramedics and chess masters, was a keynote speaker for the DEM conference in the fall of 2011. He entitled his address "What Physicians Can Learn from Firefighters."

The 2010 edition of *Learning Clinical Reasoning,* the classic book about how doctors think, also illustrates this new openness. It describes a process of medical decision-making that resembles observe-process-act from superfast sports and the military's OODA Loop: doctors should gather data, form a hypothesis about a patient's condition, refine the hypothesis using tests, decide on treatment, and confirm the effects of that treatment. The book also covers bias, poor memory, and other cognitive errors and includes more than sixty detailed case studies—with titles ranging from "A Serious Lack of Focus" to "Wrong Diagnosis, Wrong Tests, Wrong Treatment" to "Searching for a Pony"—that openly and colorfully recognize the errors doctors make.[11]

Gurpreet Dhaliwal, a medical professor and decision expert who is part of the DEM group, stresses the need for a flexible approach to medical decision-making. He told me, "Over the past three decades, there has been a heavy favoritism toward analysis over intuition to optimize doctor decision-making. I favor the opposite approach, which is to have individuals sharpen their intuition through experience and careful observation."

I spoke to Dhaliwal one morning before he began an emergency room shift. He talked to me about the time pressures he expected to face that day and how important it would be for him and his colleagues to take as long as they possibly could before making their diagnoses: "The amount of time we'll have for decisions will vary. There will be a minority of decisions that we will need to resolve in seconds. But a lot more things will need to be resolved over hours. And then more will unfold over days to weeks." Even in the ER, Dhaliwal is thinking about the future.

Most medical decisions are standard and can be made quickly. But Dhaliwal says that as many as 10 percent of cases are sufficiently complex that they do not fit routine patterns. For these harder cases, clinicians need to pair their analytical mode of thinking with their intuitive mode of thinking. According to Dhaliwal, those doctors who absorb lessons from their patients and case studies over the long term acquire a battery of knowledge that helps them spot nonroutine cases in the short term.

One of the biggest differences between financial and medical decisions is that doctors must swing at every pitch. Gurpreet Dhaliwal can't turn away those patients he doesn't quite understand. He can't wait for the easiest possible diagnosis. He is obligated to try to help everyone. He might see nine cases that are like routine fastballs. But he also has to be ready to hit the one curve.

—

In Atul Gawande's provocative and insightful book *The Checklist Manifesto,* he shows how doctors can use checklists to save lives by reducing mistakes in medical decision-making, particularly during hospital surgery.[12] He also advocates checklists for other nonmedical professionals, including airline pilots and financial professionals.

Checklists serve as a reminder when our memory fails and as a guard against cognitive mistakes. They provide a framework to make sure we pay attention to each step of a task. But there is an art to checklists. If they are too complex and cumbersome, they can be counterproductive. If a checklist includes too many steps or is inflexible, it will be inefficient or ignored. Good checklists streamline straightforward jobs. But bad checklists become logistical nightmares, the seeds of corporate and government bureaucracy. The ideal checklist is one page long, with not too many words on it.

Although Gawande is focused on the benefits of routinizing the straightforward parts of surgery, and he does not explicitly argue about delay, one of the overlooked reasons why checklists are so useful and important is that they force us to pause. A checklist adds a speed bump before a task, to force surgeons or builders or airline pilots or investors to stop and think through what they are about to do before they do it. A checklist is an example of how skilled professionals move back and forth between thinking about the present and the future.

Atul Gawande's surgery checklist includes three "pause points": before anesthesia, before incision, and before leaving the operating room. Each pause is designed to last no more than a minute—just long enough for members of the team to make basic checks (confirm the patient's identity at the beginning; check for all the needles and sponges at the end). It might not seem like something as simple as making sure everyone on the surgery team introduces themselves by name and role would matter. But the results are striking: even taking just a few extra seconds before the incision helps to slow down the tempo of a surgical procedure, and that slower tempo leads to better outcomes.

Starting in the spring of 2008, eight hospitals began using Gawande's checklist. Within months, the rate of major complications for surgical patients had fallen by 36 percent. Deaths fell 47 percent.[13] Now checklists are ubiquitous at hospitals. They aren't designed to anticipate every pitfall; a typical hospital checklist is only one page long. Pithy checklists work in part because they impose delay: people stop and think about what they are about to do.

Delay in superfast sports allows baseball batters a few extra milliseconds to better understand whether a pitch that initially looked like a fastball might actually be a curve. This insight is true in medicine as well, but at a longer time scale: minutes or days instead of milliseconds. Doctors have more time than superfast athletes, and more flexibility, because they can stretch out a decision. They have to react, but they don't always have to react right away.

Justin Graham—the infectious disease specialist who told me about the adage "Don't just do something. Stand there"—says even some of the most basic snap decisions by doctors in the ER, such as giving antibiotics, can have negative repercussions later. He told me, "Even a patient with a chronic bone infection can go several days without antibiotics if there are no signs of imminent disaster, such as septic shock. In that time, we can do the diagnostic tests that will help us determine the etiology of the infection and guide our therapeutic decisions. If a hasty emergency physician rushes to give antibiotics in the first thirty minutes, we can lose the chance of getting a meaningful culture result, leaving the treatment team flying blind for months."

—

Some doctors are becoming increasingly sophisticated about using delay and intuitive thinking as a tool outside the operating room, where much more time is available. When I asked Dhaliwal for an example of a diagnosis that improved because of delay, he immediately rattled off six. In each case, there was some wisdom in his initial snap reaction, but the decision improved with time. A patient taking blood thinners had pain on the outside of his chest, but nothing was visible and blood tests were normal; eventually, Dhaliwal found a hematoma in the patient's abdominal wall. Another patient had a severe burn, and the initial assumption was that the pain was causing his heart to race; instead, it turned out, an infection was causing the rapid heartbeat. A fisherman's legs gave out on a boat and he appeared to have been suddenly paralyzed; after several tests showed low levels of potassium, Dhaliwal determined that the patient had a thyroid problem.

Dhaliwal told me he figured out this last diagnosis after finally ordering a blood test for thyroid function on a hunch: "Thyroid problems usually don't cause patients to become paralyzed. Rather, they typically cause increases or decreases in energy, activity, and weight. That's what brings patients to the doctor. But in Asian men, an overactive thyroid gland can be the factor in sudden unexplained paralysis." Dhaliwal, who is Indian, is well aware of his own biases: he told me he'd read studies of doctor racism and had taken Implicit Association Tests. He understands how an instant racial assessment in milliseconds can lead to biased medical advice. But he also recognizes that race and epidemiology are deeply ingrained in medical training because thinking about those factors can improve results. A batter can't pause to take more time to see if the pitch is a curveball. But doctors, like coaches, live in a slower, more flexible world. They can take a diagnostic time-out,[14] to think about issues, including race, that might improve their accuracy. In the case of the fisherman, Dhaliwal says, "ethnicity was a trigger to make a link—severe weakness and hyperthyroidism—in this patient." He reached the right decision by pausing long enough to integrate race into his thinking.

As Dhaliwal rattled off these stories, he sounded like a chess master describing classic matches: "I feel like I'm building my database as I put more stories in my mind. The stories are there for the complicated cases, the ones where the diagnosis isn't clear. That's when you need judgment. I am building a set of scripts. It's a kind of mental training program. Some is from my experience. But not all. Either you have more experiences or you get more out of the experiences you have. That's where reading cases comes in. You can burn these cases into your mind so they are there in your mental system to give you feedback on your decisions." When Dhaliwal talks about past cases, he sounds a lot like Warren Buffett or Bill Ackman talking about past trades.[15]

Dhaliwal described one case in such vivid detail that I thought it must have been one of his recent patients: "A twenty-eight-year-old man presents with what at first appeared to be HIV. He had a depressed immune system and genital ulcerations. However, a doctor who understood standard diagnostic criteria would know that what appears to be HIV can instead be Behçet's disease, a rare immune disorder. In fact, this man's ulcers fit the classic three-pronged Behçet's pattern: he had them on his genitals, mouth, and eyes."

A snap diagnosis would have been HIV. A more considered diagnosis would have been Behçet's. But this patient didn't have Behçet's either.[16] As Dhaliwal explained, the doctors took a bit more time and noticed that although the patient's pattern of ulcers corresponded with the classic pattern of Behçet's, he also had some target-shaped lesions and splotches. The doctors waited for the patient's symptoms to develop. They ordered extra tests. They thought about the possibilities. Ultimately, they concluded that the patient had erythema multiforme, a skin condition that could be treated simply and effectively with steroids.[17] How did they figure this out? They used a combination of analytical and intuitive thinking. They watched the story unfold for a while and assessed the patient based on their experience.

I was surprised when Dhaliwal told me the patient was not his. Dhaliwal says the best medical decision-makers build diagnostic databases, not merely from their own patients, but from case studies in medical journals and stories from colleagues—the same way fireground commanders build expertise from experience as well as from stories they hear about fires. If the stories are specific and dramatic enough, when experts encounter a similar situation in real life, they will feel intuitively that they have seen it before. Although the modern health care system generates intense economic and time pressure, master clinicians can overcome this pressure by drawing on a stock of narratives.

Jeff Critchfield, the chief of hospital medicine at San Francisco General Hospital, confirms that time itself can be an important diagnostic tool, which is why doctors frequently order tests, wait, and then order more tests to see how the results have changed. The ideal amount of delay varies. For a surgeon about to cut someone open, a few seconds is about right. In non-emergencies, many doctors benefit from seeing a patient a second time, a day or two later, before they make a diagnosis. Specialists treating unusual conditions often wait weeks, months, or longer.

Critchfield told me that when he has to make a medical decision he imagines that a particular medical school professor he respected is right outside the door: "He told me I should assume I would always have to open the door and present my findings to him. I should have the discipline to act as if he is right there all the time." This is good advice for any professional, not just doctors: if we think about our decisions as stories we will have to tell an expert, we will be more likely to get our timing, and our decision, just right.

—

60 Minutes has been both hugely popular and critically acclaimed for more than four decades. Time has always been an important element of the show. It opens and closes with the dramatic ticking of an Aristo stopwatch. Each Sunday night's program is tightly scripted; every second is carefully planned. The reporters and producers are true professionals. They take months to develop stories, but work speedily at the last minute.

On Sunday, May 2, 2011, when Osama bin Laden was shot and killed inside a private residential compound in Abbottabad, Pakistan, Steve Kroft was in New York, working on a different story. He learned about bin Laden that evening, when all of us did, watching President Obama on television. Kroft and his colleagues immediately reached out to their contacts at the White House, hoping the president might do an interview in time for the next edition of *60 Minutes.*

Kroft already had interviewed Barack Obama on camera ten times, as candidate and president, and those interviews had been in the range of forty-five to sixty minutes. This time, though, the White House would only agree to a shorter interview, Wednesday morning from 11:00 AM to 11:35 AM. No longer. Kroft told me he tried to get more time: "I even asked the president as we sat down if we could have an extra ten minutes. He smiled, and admonished me, saying thirty-five minutes was plenty of time and promised to keep his answers short."

Having just thirty-five minutes of interview time obviously would be a problem for a program called *60 Minutes.* After allowing for advertising, lead-ins and takeaways, plus Andy Rooney, the amount of actual programming for the show was more like forty minutes than sixty (three segments of eleven to sixteen minutes each). Even if they used every second of the interview, there wouldn't be enough to fill three segments, and perhaps not even enough for two. As Kroft explained, "The president always tries hard to address the questions asked and can often be expansive in his answers. Interjecting or interrupting a sitting president is always a delicate matter. There was a lot of ground to cover in not a lot of time." To get enough material out of thirty-five minutes of interview time, every second would have to count.

Steve Kroft has been a correspondent for *60 Minutes* since 1989, and he has won nine Emmys and numerous other awards for his pathbreaking stories. He is what academics call a "traditional" professional journalist, a reporter who, in the spirit of Edward R. Murrow and Walter Cronkite, plays an active role in directing research and has a strong hand in writing his scripts and controlling his interviews.

Kroft worked as a reporter for the US Army during the Vietnam War and as a television reporter for three years after that. He then got a master's degree from Columbia's prestigious journalism school and continued as an investigative reporter in Florida until he joined CBS News in 1980, a year before Cronkite signed off for the last time. Like Murrow and Cronkite, Kroft has spent the bulk of his career at CBS.

After Kroft secured the Obama interview about bin Laden, his team came up with sixty possible questions and then they headed to Washington. At 9:00 PM Tuesday, the night before the interview, one of Kroft's producers, Maria Gavrilovic, gave him the final printed list of questions and left him alone to, as she put it, "hibernate."

People who work with Kroft speak with awe about what he is able to do at the last minute. James Jacoby, a *60 Minutes* producer, told me, "His gift is timing. Our stories are twelve minutes long. He knows what twelve minutes is better than anybody, in terms of fitting together how it's told. Going into an interview, he knows exactly what he needs and how long it must be."

Between 9:00 PM Tuesday night and the next morning, when the team met for coffee to run through the questions, Kroft had managed to completely rethink and reorder their plan. Kroft says he started revising at 5:00 AM, "eliminating questions that would lead to long answers."[18] He understandably didn't want to interrupt the president, so the direction of his questions was crucial—that would be his only chance to shape Obama's answers. According to Gavrilovic, "We met at 8:00 AM and had to be at the White House at 10:30 AM. At that point he already knew which questions he wanted to ask and where he was going to go. None of the rest of us knew until he started asking the questions and was skipping around."

———

Kroft looks smooth while interviewing Obama. There's no sign that he is straying from a predetermined script of questions, or even that he initially prepared a list.[19] We don't see his technique as unorthodox or novel. Yet Kroft is radically improvising during the interview, mustering all of his skill to ensure that every minute is compelling.

Kroft begins with a closed-ended, objective question: "Mr. President, was this the most satisfying week of your presidency?" This is the kind of question journalists typically use to elicit facts rather than opinions. The standard wisdom is that a closed-ended, objective question won't get you a vivid sound bite. Yet this one did. Kroft says he carefully chose this first question, specifically using the word *satisfying*. Obama repeats that word in his answer, which, though long, is both memorable and moving.

Well, it was certainly one of the most satisfying weeks not only for my presidency but I think for the United States since I've been president. Obviously, bin Laden had been not only a symbol of terrorism but a mass murderer who had eluded justice for so long, and so many families who have been affected I think had given up hope. And for us to be able to definitively say, "We got the man who caused thousands of deaths here in the United States," was something that I think all of us were profoundly grateful to be a part of.

Then, by keeping his questions closed and very short, Kroft elicits both medium-length answers in which Obama reveals his emotions and shorter-length answers in which Obama reveals new facts. When Obama finishes a long discussion of the raid on bin Laden's compound, Kroft asks simply, "Were you nervous?" When Obama responds by saying just one word—"Yes"—Kroft lets it hang there for a moment. Instead of hearing another question right away, we take in the silence. That pause says more than any words might have.

As the interview progresses, each question and answer becomes a miniature battle, like the jabs and parries of a fencing match. Obama orients to Kroft's short questions and responds with short answers. In turn, Kroft, aware of the ticking clock, asks even shorter questions. Both men are doing something like what military strategists call getting inside the enemy's OODA Loop, each side trying to obtain a slight edge by moving through the cycle of observe-orient-decide-act more quickly than the opponent.[20]

But the OODA Loop strategy works at slower speeds as well, a fact that some military strategists ignore but that in this interview Kroft and Obama did not. Sometimes there is an advantage to being faster than your opponent, but other times the advantage is in being slower, or at least in appearing to be slower, so your opponent wrongly comes to think he might gain an advantage by responding quickly. The notion of using timing to one's advantage by being both fast and slow is taken from *The Art of War* by Sun Tzu. It applies to just about any potentially adversarial situation—we saw it repeatedly in superfast sports and military decisions. In high-level journalism, it is verbal fencing.[21]

When Kroft asks, "Is this the first time that you've ever ordered someone killed?" he is going slow, setting Obama up for a quick yes or no, which might initially seem like the right move. But that kind of quick response would trap the president into admitting that this attack, or some previous one, was a potentially illegal assassination. Instead, Obama sees the ploy. He reorients and retreats, back to a more careful strategy of longer, broader responses:

> Well, keep in mind that, you know, every time I make a decision about launching a missile, every time I make a decision about sending troops into battle, you know, I understand that this will result in people being killed. And that is a sobering fact. But it is one that comes with the job.

Al Tompkins of the Poynter Institute, a distinguished journalism school, studied the bin Laden interview in detail, dissecting each question. He concluded that in mixing up so many different types of questions and approaches, Kroft "violated many of the guidelines that we teach about how to conduct an interview. Yet it worked."[22] The interview was a hard-fought battle between two expert communicators, but in the end both men won. It was a masterful piece of journalism, reflecting a full week of work and decades of expertise, and it showed President Obama combining thoughtfulness and decisiveness. The entire White House interview lasted thirty-four minutes and forty-eight seconds. But Kroft persuaded Obama to give him a few more minutes on camera later, after a ceremony for fire-fighters who lost their lives on 9/11, and that gave *60 Minutes* just enough material to fill all three of the show's segments.

———

Francesco Guerrera was born in Milan and has a first-class degree from City University in London. He has won numerous awards, including a For-eign Press Association Award for his investigation of "blood diamonds," an Overseas Press Award for his scoop on CNOOC's takeover bid for Un-ocal, and a SABEW Award for a video series on the collapse of Lehman Brothers.[23] He is widely considered one of the world's leading business re-porters and is editor of the *Wall Street Journal*'s respected "Money and In-vesting" section. He is twenty-eight years younger than Kroft.

When Guerrera began working as a journalist during the 1990s, tech-nology had not yet transformed journalism, but it was about to. As he de-scribed it, "There were no Blackberries or email, and the use of mobile phones was limited. For my first job, I got a beeper. Throughout the day, if I, or one of my sources, was out of the office, it took a long time to connect. There was a finite amount of work. I'd spend the morning on the phone, have lunch with a source, then work the phones some more. Each after-noon I'd hit a natural stopping point, usually around four or five PM, when there was no more reporting to be done. That was when I started writing."

Jonathan Glater, a former business reporter for the *New York Times,* recalled that when he covered the accounting firm Arthur Anderson as it was collapsing in 2002, he worked the phones frantically all day, but then stopped reporting every day at 5:00 PM and wrote up what he had learned for the next day's paper. Glater worked in repeated cycles of one-day loops: he took in as much information as he could, thought about it and talked to his editor throughout the day, and then, at the last possible moment, assembled the information in written form. He even considered what might go into a longer piece for the weekend. Until a few years ago, journalism tracked this relatively slow pace, even for reporters following the quickest stories.

Today most journalism is radically faster than it was a decade ago.[24] Guerrera explained: "I am always on deadline now. There are editions closing all the time. It used to be that when I got into work I had a full day before deadline. Now when I arrive Asia is going to close in two hours. Europe will close two hours after that. Something is always closing next. I can't block out separate time for news gathering versus writing. Because most of the time is spent either reporting or writing, I am forced to do my big-picture thinking in my spare time. The risk is that too often the pressure of the job makes it difficult for me and others in the media to gain an in-depth understanding of the situations we cover in the time we have before our first deadline."

Today's reporting tempo is fast. Technology has compressed journalism, and the convergence of television, print, and radio that academics predicted in the 1970s has fully arrived. Every major news organization responds instantly online with text, video, and sound—or else they risk becoming irrelevant and stale. Reporters face instant competition from bloggers covering events in real time. Stories no longer merely have a dateline; they are time-stamped, to the minute. News breaks instantly on television and reverberates through the Internet. Most journalists barely have time to breathe.

It would be easy to lament the changes, but Guerrera doesn't. He isn't wistful about the past, and he isn't pessimistic about the future. The breakneck pace of modern journalism is perfect for his skill set: a nimble mind, a lean writing style, an understanding of technology, and a fearlessness about hitting the Send button. When he says he doesn't have time to understand something in depth, he doesn't mean that he *can't* understand it in depth—he just means that his job requires him to move ahead before anyone, Guerrera included, is capable of doing so.

Several journalists have told me that when they are working on deadline at high speed they feel time slow down. They say it is a mind-bending kind of high, what Jackie Stewart felt while taking a high-speed turn in a Formula One race, or what Michael Jordan felt when going up for a dunk in the NBA finals. Some journalists are so quick at writing that it doesn't bother them to have only a short time to finish a story. They thrive playing a reporter's version of the game of chicken, waiting until the last possible moment before finally putting down the phone. A decade ago, when I received calls from reporters asking for comments on stories, they would say, "I'm on deadline for tomorrow," and I could sense the race against the clock. In late 2011, I got a call from a *Bloomberg* reporter who had just learned important breaking news about a bank. When I asked what his deadline was, he said, in an utterly calm tone, "Twenty-three minutes."

Steve Kroft also understands the importance of this kind of speed. He attributes his ability to shorten questions on the fly, as in his Obama interview about bin Laden, to being deeply involved in thinking about the interview throughout the week, writing the questions: "The good thing about writing your own questions is you know the material. I had to keep moving. I was so cognizant of the clock."[25] Few people could have matched the speed of his last-minute preparation for the Obama interview or his quick switching among the sixty questions he had planned.

But Kroft says a good journalist needs to be comfortable with a wide range of timelines. As he put it, "There are times when the situation dictates you get the story done and you have to be able to do it. You have to be able to hit both the changeup and the fastball. Any experienced journalist will tell you that they know how much work needs to be done, they know exactly how much time it will take to do it, and then that dictates what they will do and how they will accomplish it. You have this much time to screen the interview, edit. It all has to be thought out and planned from the beginning."[26]

When he was working for *CBS Evening News,* Kroft knew that it would take him an hour to write the script for a two-minute piece. If he had longer, he would take it. But he was confident that an hour would be enough and that the script would come together during the final minutes of that hour. He said, "Sometimes, just going over things in your head, you find things at the last minute. The longer you can wait, the more you feel like you have the most insight."

———

As schools introduce Internet-based journalism into their curricula, experts are polarized about whether the new programs will dilute the overall learning experience.[27] Critics are concerned about the quality of Internet-driven news sources. James Jacoby, the *60 Minutes* producer, is from the technology generation. He didn't receive the same kind of traditional training that Kroft did, so he worries about losing "news judgment"— knowing what's important about a story: "You've got such a panoply of information. A lot of things that aren't important get reported on, and a lot of things that are important get missed. What Steve Kroft's generation was able to do was have news judgment—that was everything." Jacoby continued: "Those of us who came up in the electronic era can't put the words down as easily. It's something that electronic journalists don't generally know, because they don't have as many constraints. The old model of journalism is that you have eight hundred words to tell your story or you have twelve minutes to tell your story—the skill that you develop is the skill of knowing time."

Knowing and managing time is unquestionably a skill. It's also a vital defense. Because if you don't know how to manage time, time can rule you like a tyrant. There is one dangerous piece of technology that leads us, even more than software or smart phones or the Internet or email, to focus too much on right now. It distorts our ability to make decisions and—tick, tick, tick—interferes with our thinking about those short-term versus long-term trade-offs that imperil not just professionals but all of us. It is, of course, the clock.

12 **GET OFF THE CLOCK**

Much human behavior is based on "clock time," which divides our day into quantifiable units, measured by an objective clock. In clock time, those units dictate when tasks begin and end.[1] Some of clock time is based on nature, but much of it is fabricated. A day is a natural length of time, determined by the rotation of the earth, and the rising and setting of the sun understandably drove our ancestors' living patterns, particularly in farming. The cycle of a day is physical and biological, and early calendars naturally followed days. Then, imprecisely, calendars evolved to include months and years, with leap periods added here and there to keep the whole thing roughly in line with the annual cycle of the seasons and the earth's orbit around the sun.

But the hour, sixty minutes, is an entirely arbitrary unit of time. It is an unnatural fraction of a day, a legacy of Babylonian culture, which was built around a base of sixty (sixty seconds in a minute; sixty minutes in an hour), and then of the Egyptians' derivative preference for counting in base twelve. If our ancestors had used base ten, as we do, an "hour" would be 20 percent longer (one-twentieth of a day instead of one-twenty-fourth). Yet the ancient practice of dividing up twelve hours of daytime and twelve hours of night has become the fundamental way we slice up our days. Clocks depict hours and fractions of hours. The hour is the time unit we use to schedule meetings and lunches and soccer practices. The hour is so fundamental to our daily lives that, if it didn't exist, we would have to invent it.

Clock time isn't the only way to organize behavior. A second approach is "event time." In event time, we continue doing something until we finish or some event occurs. Then we move on, regardless of whether it has taken ten minutes or a day. For example, you might start work, not at 9:00 AM (clock time), but whenever you finish breakfast (event time). You might stop practicing the piano, not after an hour, but once you can play the first section of a sonata perfectly three times in a row. Although clock time prevails today, especially in modern Western societies, event time has been and remains common in many cultures and circumstances.

To illustrate the differences between clock time and event time, imagine that you have five tasks to perform today. How would you organize them? One approach is to use a personal calendar, to plan each task for a specific time on the clock. Another is to use a to-do list, to plan to finish each task but not necessarily at a particular time. Which approach is better depends on your objective. In general, you should use a calendar when your primary concern is efficiency, getting tasks done as quickly as possible at the optimal times. In contrast, you should use a to-do list when your primary concern is effectiveness, making sure that the tasks are done, whenever that might be. Efficiency means going fast, within a set period of time; effectiveness means being complete, even if it takes longer. Efficiency goes with clock time; effectiveness goes with event time.

Our conscious system can help us determine whether to use clock time or event time. Ask yourself: do I care more about efficiency or effectiveness? If you have a legal brief that must be filed by Friday, you care more about efficiency. You should put the filing date on a calendar and plan your work accordingly based on clock time. But when you go to the grocery store, the order and timing of what you do matter less and you care more about effectiveness. You should make a list of items to buy and use event time to make sure you don't leave the grocery store until you have every ingredient necessary to make dinner.

—

Philip Zimbardo, an emeritus professor at Stanford, is best known for running a controversial experiment in which he locked two dozen student volunteers in the basement of a building at Stanford and randomly assigned half to be "guards" and half to be "prisoners." (Zimbardo had to end the experiment after six days because the students had so completely taken on their roles.) But his true legacy is his research about psychology and time.

Zimbardo and his coauthor John Boyd call human beings "living anachronisms." They say we are hardwired to live in the slow time of hunter gatherers and have become "hertz machines living in a megahertz world."[2] According to Zimbardo, one of our central struggles as human beings is to get our old physiology to keep pace with rapidly accelerating technology. He has designed tests to measure people's attitudes about time, with the hope that if we understand our unconscious views of time, we can consciously try to control how we react, learn, and make decisions.*

Zimbardo and Boyd argue that we can improve our lives by understanding how the modern economy has changed the human relationship to time. Clocks and calendars and timekeeping overall became much more precise during and after the industrial revolution, when people began wearing pocket watches, countries adopted standardized measures of time (particularly Britain and Greenwich Mean Time), and trains began to run according to these standard measures rather than different local clocks. According to Zimbardo and Boyd, "The transition from event time to clock time profoundly changed society, especially economic relations. We transitioned from an event-based and product-based economy to a time-based economy in which we are paid per unit sold, if hourly, or lump sum, if salaried."[3]

For many of us, clock time dictates what we do at work. The importance of clock time in the workplace can be traced back to Frederick Winslow Taylor. In 1909, Taylor, a former lathe operator, engineer, and management consultant, published *The Principles of Scientific Management,* a book advocating the use of time as a tool for improving workplace efficiency.[4] Taylor argued that companies should replace rules of thumb for accomplishing tasks with precise instructions based on scientific analysis of the timing of tasks. He told factory managers to break jobs into parts and use stopwatches to time their workers and determine how long each

---

* Zimbardo's survey tests are available at http://www.thetimeparadox.com/surveys. They are a useful way to understand how we think about the past, present, and future relative to other people, as well as compared to what Zimbardo calls the "ideal time perspective." (I found that the test accurately describes my own time perspective: I am a "present hedonist" who doesn't think much about the past. I had low scores on "past negative" and "present fatalism," which is good, but I also had low scores on "past positive." I need to think happier thoughts about the past. I probably could use some work on my "future" score as well, but I'll do that later.)

part should take. Then, according to Taylor, once they had found the "One Best Way" to do a job they should require that everyone follow that exact approach, every day, all the time.

So-called Taylorism briefly became a prominent part of American culture, and it continues to be influential in some industries and some planned economies. Although the original version of Taylorism proved too strict and inhuman for much of modern society, the basic idea hasn't gone away. There is still tension between employers who want employees to work harder, and employees who are selling their most precious commodity: time.

———

If you are like most people, you feel there aren't enough hours in the day. You perceive you are working longer and harder than in the past. You believe time is scarcer than ever before.[5] But there is one problem with these perceptions: they are wrong.

It is well documented and undeniable that people *feel* more time pressure today. Yet in fact the median number of hours that people *actually* work has remained relatively constant during the previous five decades and has declined in recent years.[6] With unemployment high and underemployment higher, many people are not working much or at all. If you actually work longer hours than your parents did, you are an outlier.

There are many culprits making us feel time-stressed about work. Technology is the most obvious. The modern workplace is a fast ride. When we flit among emails, phone calls, social media, meetings, and online searches, the hours seem longer than they really are. Ironically, the intense focus required by multitasking makes us slower and less efficient at our jobs, even as it stretches our perception of work time.[7] Work is becoming a slow-motion version of a 150-foot free fall (which, as we learned in Chapter 7, feels like it lasts four seconds even though it really takes just three).

Technology also has allowed more of our personal lives to merge into work time. We spend more time at leisure, social planning, and Internet surfing during the workday. A generation ago we spent forty hours a week working; today we spend fifty hours a week "working," but only thirty of those hours on our actual job.

Commuting also has lengthened the average workday. Long commutes are bad for all sorts of obvious reasons—traffic, fuel, stress, accidents, and distance from family. Studies show that our commute generally is the worst part of our day, and that a longer commute make us less happy, even if it helps us make more money.[8] Commuting also makes people feel locked into the workplace, so they stay at work longer even if they don't work more. One recent study found that, for every hour of commuting, people spend an extra thirty-five minutes at work.[9] Some of these changes are difficult to control: if your boss doesn't leave work until 8:00 PM, you might feel obligated to stay late as well, or you might take on a longer commute if that is the only way you can afford to buy a house.

In addition, the degree to which our perception of work time matches reality depends on what kind of work we are doing. For many of us, from plumbers and painters to accountants and lawyers, the most noxious influence on how we think about work is the billable hour, or fraction of an hour. It isn't as addictive as nicotine, but it's close, and it might be even less healthy, especially for highly paid workers.

———

Hourly billing—clock time, not event time—creates perverse incentives to focus on the amount of time spent doing a job instead of the job itself. It leads workers to equate time and money in harmful ways.

After World War II, labor economists predicted that the role of hourly pay in the US economy would decline.[10] They were correct for a couple of decades, but since the 1970s the number of American workers paid on an hourly basis has steadily increased.[11] Today more than 58 percent of all wage and salary workers in the United States are paid at hourly rates.[12] The average size of hourly pay is increasing, and hourly wages are increasingly common among the middle class and in upwardly mobile professions, including not only law, accounting, and consulting but increasingly medicine. Although one-fifth of hourly workers are under age twenty-five, fewer than 5 percent of hourly jobs are at or below the minimum wage.[13]

To many people, independent hourly work seems an ideal alternative to working for a large organization. In a 1998 article for *Wired* magazine and in a subsequent book, *Free Agent Nation,* author Dan Pink eloquently describes how tens of millions of workers have become frustrated with work politics, incompetent bosses, and unfair treatment and left the organized workplace to go it alone, make more money, and have more control over their time.[14] As Pink explains, free agent workers benefit from increased autonomy and control. The quintessential free agent is a midcareer professional who works alone or in a small group and charges by the hour.

During the late 1990s, three prescient researchers, James Evans, Gideon Kunda, and Stephen Barley, conducted a two-and-a-half-year ethnographic field study of free agent workers, including contractors, engineers, software developers, technical writers, and information technology specialists.[15] They found that, throughout the United States, one of the most significant differences in how people approach work is whether they are paid on an hourly basis.

Although hourly workers often benefit from their independence, they suffer some punishing costs from being on clock time. In a wide range of jobs and income levels, people who are paid hourly work longer and care less about nonwork activities. They suffer from higher stress during downtime, and they worry more about whether they will have enough work. When work is available, they are tempted to work as much as possible, every available hour of the day. Evans, Kunda, and Barley found that the hourly contractors they interviewed would "calculate precisely the cost of an hour of leisure or family time" and were "acutely aware that every hour they failed to work was lost compensation."[16] A vacation or even a day off meant a loss of money.

Free agent workers might imagine hourly pay as an ideal, flexible approach that will empower them and create free time and flexibility. They certainly benefit from greater increased autonomy and control. But people who are paid by the hour come to think about time and money differently than people who are paid a salary. Hourly workers are more likely to see hours not spent working as wasted. They tend to feel stress about the amount of work they do.[17] They do less volunteering and charitable work.[18] They come to realize, as Benjamin Franklin did, that time is money. Yet when time is money, hourly pay can become a trap.

The effect of hourly pay on the way work is perceived is a particularly important issue for both recent graduates and retooling midcareer workers who are reconsidering their paths. But even someone who is stuck with hourly pay forever can benefit from understanding that the way we are paid changes the way we view time. Many people want a balanced, happy, and fulfilling life plus a career. But to have both, we need to make a conscious effort to be sure that the method of payment at work does not have a negative impact on our nonwork life.

Counterintuitively, time pressure gets worse as we make more money. Studies show that higher income generates more time stress, even when the number of hours worked is held constant.[19] Just watch people graduate from school and move up the business ladder to become managing directors or partners or executive vice presidents. As they make more money, they feel like they have less time.

Why is this? The answer is simply supply and demand: we tend to believe that the more valuable an object is, the scarcer it is. When a Matisse painting sells for $100 million, we assume there aren't very many Matisse paintings. When Kobe beef sells for $10 per ounce, we assume it is less common than ground beef. If water becomes expensive, we assume there must be a drought.

As we make more money, we perceive, correctly, that our time has higher value. But as a result, we also feel like we have less time. In one recent experiment by Sanford DeVoe—the University of Toronto professor who made people read 20 percent faster by subliminally exposing them to fast-food logos—people performed a task and were told to keep track of their time in six-minute increments. Half of them believed their work was being billed out at $90 per hour; the other half believed their rate was $9 per hour. After the subjects finished their work, they answered questions about the degree of time pressure they felt. Those billing at the higher rate felt significantly more time pressure, even though everyone did exactly the same work under the same conditions for the same amount of time.[20]

In another study, DeVoe and Jeffrey Pfeffer, a Stanford business professor, asked 128 undergraduate students to check one of eleven boxes indicating how much money they had in their checking accounts. For half of the students, the boxes all had low numbers, so that even students with a relatively small amount of money would be at the top of the range and "feel rich." For the other half, the boxes had much higher numbers, so that even students with a fair amount of money would be at the bottom of the range and "feel poor."

Changing these labels didn't change how much money was in the students' checking accounts, but it significantly altered their emotional states. The students on the "feel rich" end of the spectrum experienced greater time pressure and generally felt more rushed. As with DeVoe's fast-food study, they also read more quickly, and for briefer periods. If you are worried about time stress, feeling rich is as bad as being subliminally flashed a McDonald's logo.

DeVoe also has found that even just thinking about our hourly wage impairs our ability to enjoy leisure time. In one experiment, he and his coauthor Julian House asked people to estimate the number of hours they expected to work in a year, as well as their expected annual salary. Half of the group also was asked to calculate their hourly wage. Everyone then spent ten minutes on a pleasurable leisure activity, playing a game or communicating with friends. The subjects who were asked to calculate their hourly wage reported feeling less happy. The mere act of dividing their salary by the number of hours to figure out their hourly wage made their leisure activities less fun.[21]

As with many other influences, the main way to combat the effects of the billable hour and increasing wealth is simply to think about it. If we are aware of how charging for our time can influence our personal lives, we can help separate the way we think about work from the way we think about the rest of life.

Another solution is even more basic: stop billing by the hour. Professionals could instead charge a fee based on the service provided: a fixed amount to file a legal brief or complete an audit or repair a leak. Lawyers, accountants, and other professionals increasingly are trying to find ways to charge flat fees instead of hourly rates. This is particularly true at large law firms, where the combination of economic pressure and low morale among associates is leading partners to search for alternative approaches to billing.

Economists and consultants say flat fees are more efficient than billable hours because they encourage workers to internalize the costs and capture the benefits of time spent on a project. But if you charge by the hour, there is another compelling argument in favor of switching to flat fees: it will reduce your stress and make you happier. It will get you off the clock.

———

In the not-too-distant past, people went to work for a company and planned to spend their career there. If they stayed, they were rewarded with an attractive retirement package, health insurance, and other benefits. If they left early, they lost much or all of this. While they were employed, their salary was relatively low—enough to live on, but nothing extravagant. A large share of their overall compensation was measured either in very long-term clock time (thirty or forty years) or in event time (retirement). This model created incentives for employees to care about the future of their employers and colleagues. It even applied to Wall Street, where investment banks were partnerships, and most of the partners' wealth was invested in the business. Partners did not sell their partnership shares until retirement; before that, they earned a relatively modest draw on the partnership's income. It seems impossible to believe given Wall Street's current mercenary character, but banks really were like families once.

Today, compensation at most companies is focused on shorter-term clock time. The highest-paid managers are paid most of their income on an annual basis, well before retirement. The average tenure of a CEO is just a few years, yet average annual pay for a CEO is in the range of $10 million, 250 times that of the average worker. Under pressure to make as much money as they can, as fast as they can, and then get out, CEOs' incentives have become skewed. Their pot of gold is bigger than ever, and it is at the end of a very short rainbow.

In contrast, the lowest-paid workers are paid based on even briefer increments of clock time: weeks and hours. For them, there is no pot of gold. There isn't even a rainbow.

These pay inequities have grown in part because of the massive shift in compensation policies from long-term event time to short-term clock time. Whereas pay used to be split more evenly among managers and employees over the course of decades, now a much larger share goes to the most senior executives each year in the form of annual bonuses and stock awards. Income inequality has grown as the most important unit of time for executive pay policies has become the year instead of the career.

As shorter-term clock time comes to dominate our work and the pay gap widens, there are two potentially serious consequences. First, for many people, work becomes less satisfying overall. Ideally, at the end of our lives we want to be able to look back on our accomplishments as events that followed a long arc; we derive satisfaction from seeing that some of the seeds planted early in our careers have grown and matured. If we are motivated to accomplish something important in our work, we will be willing to wait decades and understand that the jobs we start might not be finished until long after we are gone. Hourly pay and annual bonuses eat away at this philosophy and ultimately make work less fulfilling.

The second risk is that the accelerating pace of technology and the relentless ticking of the clock will make companies less profitable over the long term. As companies manage to the media cycle—not just for quarterly and annual disclosures of financial information but for more frequent product releases, daily blogs and website updates, and nearly continuous reactions to customers—employees inevitably think and act at a faster pace. As we saw with master professionals, quick responses are important and useful, but so is strategic perspective. Workers who are accustomed to instant gratification and continuous access to information expect major advances to come quickly. But what if that doesn't happen? What if the most important engines of economic growth run at a much slower pace than modern life?

There is a familiar story about innovation that you probably have heard in some version. It has been referenced in numerous business books and studies.* I even saw it recently in one of my daughter's sixth-grade textbooks. Yet although this story is told frequently, it is almost always inaccurate and incomplete, often so much so that we are led to precisely the wrong conclusions about innovation. This story is such a classic and has become such a part of business lore that we should get it right once and for all, with every colorful detail.

---

* Jonah Lehrer tells a brief version of this story in *Imagine*, his fascinating 2012 study of creativity, though he focuses on a shorter time period than I do in Chapter 13.

13 A LIFETIME OF INNOVATION

Art Fry and Spencer Silver were tinkerers. Fry spent his childhood in rural Iowa, where much of his learning came from taking apart and reassembling appliances and machines he and his dad picked up at the local dump. Fry built toboggans out of scrap lumber and was educated in a one-room schoolhouse.[1] He attended the University of Minnesota, where he majored in chemical engineering.

In 1953 Fry began working in the new product development group at the Minnesota Mining and Manufacturing Company. Fry fit right in with the other engineers and experimenters. He loved it when his bosses said, "If it's a dumb idea, you'll find out. You'll smack right into that brick wall, then you'll stagger back and see another opportunity that you wouldn't have seen otherwise."[2]

Spencer Silver was a decade younger than Arthur Fry, and by Minnesota standards at the time he was downright cosmopolitan: he was born in San Antonio, Texas, attended college in Arizona, and received a PhD in organic chemistry from the University of Colorado. He was a painter and liked to work with pastels and oils.

Silver joined Minnesota Mining's research team in 1966 and was immediately set loose to experiment. Like Fry, he loved the company's freethinking approach—it made him think of Thomas Edison's adage that the best inventions came from small groups of people with varied backgrounds.[3]

Minnesota Mining was a massive conglomerate, with thousands of employees, so at first these two men did not work together, or even meet. Silver's group was more like an academic faculty than a business: it was a hotbed of freethinkers, with dedicated scientists, and wasn't directly connected to Fry's more practical-minded group of product developers. Silver found that "I could talk to an analytical chemist, a physicist, people working in biology and organic chemistry—people in all the sciences. They were all within 50 yards."[4] Art Fry, and the firm's customers, were farther away.

Like a lot of chemists, Silver was interested in sticky stuff: glue, gum, cement, and other adhesives. After two years of experimenting, he discovered that he could make an adhesive out of tiny, indestructible acrylic spheres. He was excited about this new technology, but wasn't sure what to do about it other than tell everyone he saw. In addition to the normal water cooler talk, he began giving small seminars to show people these amazing little sticky spheres. He described his new discovery as "a solution waiting for a problem to solve."[5]

—

Art Fry was an avid golfer, and one of the perks of working at Minnesota Mining was the company's private golf club, Tartan Park, on a secluded 480-acre wildlife sanctuary at Lake Elmo, nine miles east of St. Paul. The course was open to all employees. Fry played in a golf league there, and he enjoyed the leisurely pace of his conversations with other employees he met through the club. He described golf as "a combination of things. You're walking, so the natural harmony of walking helps you to think. But it's also a social thing."[6] Fry thought golf's mix of outdoor exercise, social-izing, and natural harmony put him in the right state of mind to think cre-atively. (I've been playing golf for more than thirty years, and I make precisely this argument to my wife to explain why it is so important for me to spend five hours beating the cover off a little white ball.)

During one otherwise forgettable golf round in 1968, two years after Spencer Silver joined Minnesota Mining, Fry "was playing in one of the golf leagues there and on the second hole of the red nine I asked the fellow that I was playing with what was happening in his department. He said we've got a guy, Spence Silver, he's come up with these sticky micro-spheres, they're little bitty spheres and they're sticky but they don't know what to stick to. They're real interesting. You can't dissolve them. You can't melt them. It's like sticking to a bunch of marbles."[7]

Fry thought the new adhesive sounded intriguing. The next day he went to a Minnesota Mining "technical forum," one of many roundtable dis-cussions the company held to promote the diffusion of new research among employees in different groups. Silver was there, describing how he could vary the strength of his new, nimble adhesive just by putting the lit-tle spheres farther apart or closer together. Unlike most glues, his adhesive was reusable—it kept sticking, because the little spheres remained intact. Silver suggested some possible uses: maybe a sticky spray, or an adhesive bulletin board where notices could be easily posted and removed. Fry was fascinated, but he didn't think those applications made sense, and at that moment he couldn't come up with any others.[8]

We like eureka stories. Popular lore is filled with this kind of thing. One warm evening, Isaac Newton is sitting under an apple tree in his garden when an apple falls and bonks him on the head; he instantly discovers gravity.[9] Thomas Edison is staying up all night at Menlo Park, frantically experimenting, when suddenly he creates a new lightbulb that glows continuously for thirteen-and-a-half hours.[10] Tim Berners-Lee is helping some scientists share data when out of the blue an idea hits him and he invents the World Wide Web.[11]

But these stories are rarely accurate. Newton had been working on the problem of gravity for years, and neither he nor his biographer said an apple hit him on the head. The first incandescent bulb was invented seventy-five years before Edison's innovation, which was not the bulb itself, but a filament made of bamboo. Tim Berners-Lee mocks the notion that he suddenly discovered the Internet, as if he "just had to take the hypertext idea and connect it to the Transmission Control Protocol and domain name system ideas and—ta-da!—the World Wide Web."[12]

The most important innovations of modern times—the automobile, camera, computer, cotton gin, lightbulb, penicillin, sewing machine, steam engine, telephone, television—were not overnight epiphanies. They took decades or longer to invent and develop. And although the cycles are getting faster, the most dramatic innovations of the modern era—from

Apple, Google, and Facebook—have taken years. In most cases these innovations began not when the inventors and entrepreneurs first began seeing and pushing their big ideas, but when they were children, building the creative base for their later insights.

In his brilliant book *Where Good Ideas Come From,* Steven Johnson shows that important discoveries typically do not come from calculated judgments. They cannot be forced out by rigorous analysis. Instead, intuition plays a central role in these discoveries. But the form of intuition is slow, not snap. As Johnson concludes, "The snap judgments of intuition—as powerful as they can be—are rarities in the history of world-changing ideas."[13]

Johnson describes innovative ideas the same way Art Fry and Spence Silver talk about the big ideas at Minnesota Mining: "They start with a vague, hard-to-describe sense that there's an interesting solution to a problem that hasn't yet been proposed, and they linger in the shadows of the mind, sometimes for decades, assembling new connections and gaining strength."[14] Innovation is not deductive. Scientific innovators at work are similar in kind to fireground commanders at a burning house, or chess masters "chunking" the location of game pieces—except that they are several million times slower. New technological insights emerge almost magically from our unconscious processing or even while we are asleep, but they do so at a glacial pace.[15] Steven Johnson has the perfect term for this kind of gradual intuition. He calls it the "slow hunch."

———

For five years after Art Fry's post-golf introduction to Spence Silver, the sticky acrylic spheres were just another idea percolating within Minnesota Mining. Fry and his colleagues were good at coming up with new products—the company already made thousands of them—and they kept trying to figure out what to do with Silver's new adhesive. But they kept drawing blanks. Then, one Sunday in 1973, Fry had a thought:

"I was singing in the Sunday church choir. I had just gotten up to sing and the little paper marker I had put in to mark a spot from rehearsal on Wednesday night had fallen out and everybody else was singing and I was trying to figure out what page we were on and I thought I wish I could have a bookmark that would stick to the paper but wouldn't pull it apart. How could I do that? So I thought about the microspheres. I remembered if they are spread apart they will be less sticky. There should be some magic spacing that would be just right for this paper. So I went back to Spence Silver the next day, got samples of his microspheres and we started experimenting. That's how it got started."[16]

After a series of new experiments, Fry and Silver created an adhesive that was just barely strong enough to hold two pieces of paper together. If you wanted to pull the pages apart, you could do it without tearing them. They coated part of a strip of paper with the adhesive, so the sticky part could stick to a page inside a book but the protruding part wouldn't be sticky. Finally, after five years, there was a product: a bookmark that would stay put.

When innovation comes this slowly, it is vulnerable. Steven Johnson calls slow hunches "fragile creatures, easily lost to the more pressing needs of day-to-day issues."[17] These kinds of discoveries need nurturing.

When Fry finally thought they had perfected the sticky bookmark, he pitched the idea to his bosses. They were underwhelmed and skeptical. Bookmarks generally worked fine already. Bookmarks were a small market. Besides, Fry and Silver couldn't keep the adhesive from spreading, so the prototypes left behind a sticky residue. Customers wouldn't want the pages of their books to get stuck together after a bookmark touched them. Fry and Silver worked on these manufacturing problems for more than a year, but their bosses still didn't think they could sell more than $750,000 of the bookmarks annually. That wasn't enough to get anyone excited about some little sticky pieces of paper. Fry's choir epiphany fell short.

At many companies, Fry's bosses would have shut the project down. It had been a failure, a mistake. But Minnesota Mining had a supportive culture. Employees were encouraged to spend 15 percent of their time on whatever they wanted.[18] The firm's managers understood the importance of nurturing new products, even if they weren't succeeding.

The man responsible for this family-like culture was William McKnight, the firm's longtime visionary leader. McKnight had become Minnesota Mining's president three months before the stock market crash of 1929, the worst possible time for anyone to begin running a company. Yet McKnight saw the Great Depression as an opportunity to encourage creativity and growth. He made it clear that "Mother Mining" would take care of its flock, and over two decades he developed the McKnight Principles, which are more than half a century old but seem drawn from an inspirational speech by a start-up technology chief executive today.

> As our business grows, it becomes increasingly necessary to delegate responsibility and to encourage men and women to exercise their initiative. This requires considerable tolerance. Those men and women, to whom we delegate authority and responsibility, if they are good people, are going to want to do their jobs in their own way. Mistakes will be made. But if a person is essentially right, the mistakes he or she makes are not as serious in the long run as the mistakes management will make if it undertakes to tell those in authority exactly how they must do their

jobs. Management that is destructively critical when mistakes are made kills initiative. And it's essential that we have many people with initiative if we are to continue to grow.[19]

The McKnight Principles were a truly radical policy to implement just after World War II, when most companies had a rigid nine-to-five work culture and managers were mostly men wearing blue suits and crisp white shirts.

McKnight stepped aside as chairman of the company's board in 1966, the same year Spence Silver joined the firm. But the culture he created lived on, shaping the firm.[20] Fry and Silver were good people, with initiative. Their bosses had faith in them and gave them lots of responsibility. They were permitted to make mistakes, even if that meant spending years on a sticky bookmark. Minnesota Mining employees appreciated this faith, and they gave it right back with long hours and dedication.[21]

———

The word *Einstellung* means "attitude" in German. The Einstellung effect refers to our tendency to become stuck in our ways, to act or think in the same manner we've always acted or thought, even when we are presented with alternatives that are obviously better. The best innovators—people like Art Fry and Spence Silver, or Newton and Edison, or Steve Jobs—are skilled at overcoming the Einstellung effect. They follow the old Apple Computer slogan and "think different." They do not develop an attitude.

To see how the Einstellung effect matters to innovation, and to help finish the story of the sticky bookmark, we are going to revisit Peter McLeod, the neuroscientist from Oxford who showed us how the best cricket batsmen delay hitting the ball until the last split-second. McLeod (who, incidentally, is a terrible procrastinator) and two other scientists, Merim

Bilalíc and Fernand Gobet, have been quantifying how the Einstellung effect arises when we make decisions, even when we are experts.[22] Their conclusions are important for virtually every area of new discovery, from science to politics to business. But they start with chess.

McLeod and his colleagues set up a chessboard with a three-move solution to checkmate that is counterintuitive and requires innovative thinking. Most of us would never see these moves on our own.

The solution involves moving your queen three times: first, to force your opponent's king into the corner; then to a spot where a pawn has been positioned to take your queen but cannot do so with the king in the corner because doing so would expose the cornered king to check from your bishop near the opposite corner; and then finally, to take a pawn and put the king in check.

Three-move Checkmate Only

The three-move checkmate begins with the white queen moving up to e6 to put the black king in check. When the black king moves to the corner to escape check (it can't move to f8, because then the white knight would take the pawn at h7: checkmate), the white queen moves to h6. Black can't take the white queen with its pawn, because that would open the black king to white's bishop. At this point, black is done: no matter what it does, the white queen will be able to take one of its pawns on the next move, leaving the black king in checkmate (1. Qe6+ Kh8 2. Qh6! Rd7 3. Qxh7 mate, or 2. . . . Kg8 3. Qxg7 mate).

They recruited chess players of varying skills and showed them the board. Although many average players did not see the innovative three-move solution, expert players did. Of the strongest players, ranging from candidate master to international master, 100 percent spotted the moves. And it took them just thirty-seven seconds on average.

Then McLeod changed the board setup slightly, moving just one piece, the circled bishop, so that the three-move solution to checkmate was still there, but now there was *also* a five-move solution.

Both Three-move and Five-move Checkmates

In the five-move checkmate, the white queen again moves to e6, forcing the black king into the corner. Then the white knight moves to f7, putting the king in check. The black king has no choice but to move back to g8, its original position. Now the white knight moves to h6, again exposing the black king to check from the white queen. When the black king retreats back to the corner, the white queen attacks the black king by moving right next to it. The black rook is forced to take the queen, leaving the king trapped, or "smothered," by its own piece. Finally, the white knight moves back to f7 for checkmate (1. Qe6+ Kh8 2. Nf7+ Kg8 3. Nh6++ Kh8 4. Qg8+ Rxg8 5. Nf7 mate).

Both the three-move and five-move checkmates are available in the second diagram, immediately above. But the five-move checkmate doesn't work in the first diagram, because the black bishop is covering f7, preventing the white knight from moving there.

Most of us wouldn't see this five-move solution either (it's a version of "smothered mate," where the king becomes trapped by its own pieces). But for master-level players, the five-move solution is a familiar tried-and-true strategy. They know those five moves cold.

When the researchers asked a new group of players to find the shortest route to checkmate, something strange happened. The experts recognized the five-move solution right away. But they couldn't see the three-move solution. Not a single candidate master player found it. Only 18 percent of master-level players saw it. And even among the most highly skilled players, at the level of international master, only half figured out the three-move solution.

There's something stranger still: even after McLeod moved the pieces back to the original setup, the experts who hadn't seen the three-move solution continued to have trouble seeing it—even though the five-move solution was no longer available. The distorting effects of seeing the familiar solution lived on, like a ghost haunting their ability to find anything new. These experts eventually found the three-move solution, but it took them more than twice as long as the experts who had never seen the five-move solution. The players who had seen it became stuck in their ways.

We normally think of chess as rewarding creative genius. It requires tremendous brainpower and innovative thinking. Yet even chess masters are vulnerable to the Einstellung effect when they are exposed to familiar situations. The five-move checkmate was a well-worn path, like a predictable task at work. When chess experts saw that solution, they instinctively knew what they were looking at—they had seen this game before. And that effect, that *attitude,* persevered, even when they were put in a new situation. McLeod concluded that the Einstellung effect exerts a constant influence: it "continues to distract experts even when it is removed."[23]

The challenge for innovation is that the Einstellung effect persists even when we believe we are doing everything in our power to avoid it. The experts told McLeod they were looking all around the board. They insisted they were examining every possible piece and move, trying to spot a new, creative solution. They truly believed they were looking for an innovative checkmate.

But McLeod is a skeptic, like Stephen Porges, the psychiatrist who studies how heart rate variability is related to emotional well-being. These scientists are more interested in what people do than what they say.

So McLeod precisely tracked the players' eye movements to determine which squares they were focusing on. He found that where they looked depended on whether they had been exposed to the five-move solution. When they had not been exposed to it, their eyes darted all around the board until they settled on the squares that mattered for the innovative three-move checkmate. But the experts who had seen the five-move solution dwelled on the squares and pieces relevant to that strategy. They didn't look at the squares involved in the three-move solution, even though they claimed that they did.

McLeod and his colleagues concluded that the "eye movement data demonstrate how a pattern of thought, once activated, can prevent other patterns of thought becoming active."[24] These brilliant chess masters believed they were looking everywhere, not just at the tried-and-true squares on the chessboard. They insisted they were doing their best to be creative and open-minded. But their eyes weren't moving.

―――

There are two ways to defend against the Einstellung effect in order to protect our fragile creatures of innovation. One is to avoid known, comfortable situations, or at least to be acutely aware of their potential drawbacks. This is why many organizations, including successful technology firms and the most innovative parts of government, require that employees switch jobs every couple of years. It is why they fund pure research and development, why they insulate some groups of employees from the short-term pressure of quarterly profits, and why they encourage workers to spend 15 percent of their time on something new. The goal is to push employees out of their comfort zones. As John Maynard Keynes wrote, "The difficulty lies, not in the new ideas, but in escaping from the old ones, which ramify, for those brought up as most of us have been, . . . into every corner of our minds."[25]

The second way is to expose work projects to people who are likely to have a different frame of reference. This is why firms ask employees to "cross-fertilize" by sharing with other groups so that people in unrelated areas will react to each other's ideas from new perspectives. It is why diversity has become so popular, not just as social policy, but for business innovation. It is why so many new businesses have open-architecture offices—so employees will be frequently exposed to others with a different perspective. It is why Minnesota Mining had research teams, technical forums, and golf leagues.

A chess player might try to minimize the Einstellung effect by consciously looking for alternatives when a scenario is familiar or by practicing with people who have different styles. Some of this approach requires fast behavior during games. But some of it can be slower, as a player analyzes games over a period of years.

Today, many smart business leaders protect against the dangers of the Einstellung effect, even if they haven't heard of it, by using a similarly fast-and-slow approach. Some technology companies host "hackathons," periodic one- or two-day breaks from normal work life where employees gather to develop new ideas or products. A hackathon combines focus on the short term and the long term: the event itself is brief, but it can be preceded by several months of anticipation and followed by several months of reaction. Hackathons help a company's engineers and programmers see better alternatives and possibly major new innovations. The idea for Twitter, for example, came from a hackathon.

Likewise, some online retailers harness the power of the Internet to avoid what Keynes called the ramification of old ideas. Shop It To Me, the popular free online personal shopper, takes suggestions from customers and runs experiments in real time, tweaking its website and emails continuously to see which features customers prefer. Would you use a new filter that sends you information about a particular Diane von Furstenberg dress immediately when it goes on sale? Would you like to set a maximum price or minimum discount? When do you want to receive notifications?

The company runs quick experiments, some lasting just a few minutes, so they can precisely test the effects of one change in isolation. It also tests the exact opposite of what customers say they want. If you request more search filters, the company might let you try more filters, but also test what you do with fewer filters. Shop It To Me's employees have discovered that when we say we want X, we really might want Y. By assessing the data from these quick experiments over much longer periods of months or even years, they get a much more complete understanding of how their customers behave, not just what they say. The genius is to let innovative answers bubble up from the company's own diverse group of customers and then respond at a strategically slower speed, observing and orienting, to make better decisions about serving customers over the long term. This fast-and-slow approach is like the military's OODA Loop, and it works: as of early 2012, Shop It To Me had more than four and a half million subscribers.[26]

As Art Fry continued to try to come up with other products using Spencer Silver's tiny adhesive spheres, others at Minnesota Mining began using the sticky paper in their daily work lives. Some used them as bookmarks, the way Fry had envisioned. But others saw the sticky paper in a new light. They hadn't already assumed the sticky notes were bookmarks, so they used them for all kinds of other purposes. They wrote on them. They scribbled messages to their bosses, and their bosses scribbled back. They passed along samples to other employees, who also wrote notes to themselves and others. Given Minnesota Mining's open culture and environment, word spread.

Fry started to see these little pieces of paper all over different offices around the firm, stuck on desks and calendars. Employees who had nothing to do with the development of the sticky notes saw the checkmate Fry hadn't spotted before. For years he and Silver had seen only the sticky bookmark. Finally, with the help of his colleagues and their own humility, a new product emerged. As Fry explains, "It wasn't a bookmark at all, but a note. This was the insight. It was a whole new concept in pressure-sensitive adhesives. It was like moving from the outer ring of the target to the bull's eye."[27]

It took several more years, but by 1977 Fry had persuaded his bosses that the sticky notes had enough potential to support some market research. They called them "Press 'n' Peel" and tested them with potential customers in four major cities. The results were lukewarm, however, and the idea sputtered again. The managers still saw them as bookmarks. Yet Fry persisted.

Meanwhile, the staff at Minnesota Mining had become addicted to the sticky notes. They couldn't get enough of Fry's samples. At first, he gave out just one pad at a time, so he could keep track of how many notes people used. His data showed that within the company people were using between seven and twenty pads per year. Soon they were demanding even more. There were entire pallets of the sticky notes stacked up in the hallways. By comparison, the company's customers used only about one roll per year of Magic Tape, a popular and hugely profitable product. Fry saw the potential of the sticky notes and refused to give up.[28]

After yet another year, Fry persuaded his bosses to try one last market research effort. They decided to distribute samples widely in one town, to see if they would catch on in the same way they had caught on within the firm. They selected Boise, Idaho, and doled out the sticky notes throughout the city in what they called the "Boise blitz." By now Fry and his colleagues had refined them. The sticky notes were small and yellow. They had just the right size and feel. The adhesive reliably stayed on the note.

Within days, the notes were a hit. More than 90 percent of the people in Boise who tried them said they would buy them. Looking back, everyone at Minnesota Mining saw the innovation as obvious.

On April 6, 1980, twelve years after Spence Silver invented the sticky spheres and a fortuitous golf round led Art Fry to hear about them, seven years after Fry was at church and thought about adhesive bookmarks, and several years after Minnesota Mining's employees became obsessed with sticky notes in their daily lives, the company's new product finally debuted in the United States. More than three decades later, they are everywhere and over a trillion have been sold.

———

The "invention" of the Post-it® is often told as a eureka story, as if the Post-it was an instant and brilliant idea, an epiphany like Newton's apple or Edison's lightbulb.

The facts are different. The innovation that led to the Post-it was not like flipping a switch. It was a long-term, multistage process that took more than a decade. It was a slow hunch.

The Post-it depended on several people, not just Fry and Silver. Fry's golf partners and coworkers played important roles. So did the employees at Minnesota Mining who didn't know the sticky note was intended to be used as a bookmark. These people weren't experts in adhesive spheres, and they weren't burdened by prior understanding. They had fresh eyes. They helped Fry overcome the Einstellung effect.

Experts like Steven Johnson worry that companies today are giving up long-term innovation to get short-term efficiency. Even companies with innovative cultures are restricting the freedom they once gave employees. Google had one-upped Minnesota Mining's 15 percent free time policy with its own 20 percent "innovation time off" program, which was the source of as many as half of its newly launched products in a given year, including Gmail, Google News, and Google Earth.[29] But in late 2011 Google abandoned that program (though it continues to fund new ideas through a cutting-edge research arm). Other companies, such as Hewlett-Packard, have imposed limits on their free time policies.

Johnson says, "Part of the secret to having great ideas lies in creating a working environment where those fragments are nurtured and sustained over time. This obviously poses some difficulty in modern work environments, with deadlines and quarterly reports and annual job reviews."[30] Not many CEOs appreciate learning that an employee has a hunch about a product that will not generate profits, if at all, for more than a decade. Yet Minnesota Mining once had just that kind of visionary leadership.

In 2001, in the aftermath of the collapse of Enron, Minnesota Mining hired as its new leader James McNerney, an executive at General Electric who had lost the competition to replace Jack Welch as GE's CEO.

McNerney was by all accounts an accomplished professional manager, but he was not a scientist. He was not a tinkerer. McNerney implemented the "six sigma" system of cutting costs and improving efficiency. During his first two years, Minnesota Mining cut nearly 10,000 jobs and closed a dozen plants. It changed its name to 3M. After two more years focused on efficiency, McNerney left to become CEO of Boeing. So much for Mother Mining.

During his four years at the helm, the company's culture became less patient. McNerney's replacement, Sir George William Buckley, slashed another 6,000 jobs. Today 3M's future leaders confront an even more difficult economic climate as well as increased competition. It is unclear whether the company will be able to balance its focus on quarterly and annual profits with its hope for future growth. Given the firm's cost-cutting, how many employees will feel free to pursue their dreams? Will they have the time and support to find the next Post-it? Or will they get stuck in the muck?

There are still plenty of creative people at 3M, and the company spends over $1 billion a year on research and development, about 5 percent of its net sales. But how many 3M employees feel the kind of loyalty Fry and Silver felt? How many have a similar sense that their jobs have an important long-term purpose? Looking back, Fry thinks of the products he worked on as part of his family: "It's like having your children grow up and turn out to be happy and successful. When Post-its are still used after I am gone, it will be as if a part of me will live on forever."[31]

It is no coincidence that Fry, Silver, and others remember Minnesota Mining as a kind of family, or that they use the word *children* so frequently when talking about their work. They began innovating when they were kids, and they never lost that childlike spark. Fry never forgot about building toboggans out of scrap wood; Silver never stopped painting. Thinking like a kid is a big part of innovation.

Behind every innovator is a playful, experimental childhood. When Steve Jobs was five or six years old, his adoptive father gave him a piece of his workbench and some tools and, according to Jobs, "spent a lot of time with me . . . teaching me how to build things, how to take things apart, put things back together."[32] Larry Page, cofounder of Google, has a similar story of growing up in a house full of computers and gadgets and having an older brother who showed him how stuff worked.[33] Apple was established in 1976, and Google in 1996, but really they began long before.

One of the most debated topics in the history of innovation is Joseph Priestley's "discovery" of oxygen. Some historians point to Priestley's special moment of insight on Monday, August 1, 1774, when, at the age of forty-one, he heated a sample of mercuric oxide with a burning lens to obtain a curious form of "pure" air.[34] Others credit Carl Wilhelm Scheele or Antoine Lavoisier with the discovery and say Priestley merely followed in their footsteps. Some point to Priestley's collaboration with Benjamin Franklin, who sparked his ideas about plants, and others cite the new developments, particularly air pumps, that permitted Priestley to move air in and out of a jar.

But what most people miss about the story is that Priestley's insight arose from his childhood fixation on sealing spiders, mice, and frogs into glass jars to see how long they would live. The boy from rural Yorkshire who watched those creatures die knew deep down that something strange was happening.[35] He was a genius child, to be sure.[36] Yet it was not merely his genius but also his necrological glass-jar obsession that paid off three decades later.

When the older Priestley began working on the relationship between plants and air, he naturally wanted to see whether a mouse would survive longer inside a jar if it had a plant as company. When he found that a plant did something to help mice stay alive longer, it was only a matter of time before he figured out the puzzle of oxygen.

Priestley's key experiments as an adult weren't prompted by a sudden insight. They were built on an almost compulsive idea that had been in the back of his mind since he was eleven years old. As Steven Johnson concludes, "Most great ideas grow the way Priestley's did, starting with some childhood obsession, struggling through an extended adolescence of random collisions and false starts, and finally blooming decades after they first took root."[37] Innovation seems like it should be fast, but it almost never is.

———

Somewhere out there is a kid thinking about an idea that might ultimately lead to a discovery as important as gravity or oxygen, or something as routinely ubiquitous as the Post-it. Right now, the idea behind that discovery is unformed, a dim thought in the back of this child's mind as she plays with a video game, observes her family's dog, or rebuilds a broken toy. If the discovery comes, it will not be a lightbulb suddenly going on. It will be the culmination of a decades-long process.

Whether she comes through will depend on much more than her own genius. It will matter whether she, like Art Fry and Spencer Silver, has nurturing teachers and family, people who encourage her to think creatively. Her success will require an open workplace environment, a company or research institution that allows her to develop outside-the-box thinking and encourages her to share ideas with her colleagues. She will need mentors and bosses who think about the long run, who are willing to overlook quarterly and annual earnings targets and look beyond short-term performance reviews and bonuses to support new thinking, even if it is not immediately apparent how an idea might generate profits. She will need to live for a long time in a culture of innovation, where she spends not merely hours and days, but months and years, just tinkering.

14 GO LONG

Most of life's big questions need to be answered over the long term. How, then, should we approach decisions about our happiness, health, safety, and well-being? What investment should we make to sustain the quality of our planet for future generations? What value should we place on human life? These questions might seem unrelated to fencing or pigeons or the discovery of oxygen, but in fact, understanding shorter-term decision-making can help us handle the epic questions more completely and thoughtfully. An appreciation of the minuscule gives us a better chance at tackling the massive.

These big topics are also a good test of our patience. It is hard to think about them for very long. The questions are abstract and complicated, and the answers tend to be vague and unsatisfying. Instead of finding the definitive answer, we often can answer these questions only by asking yet more questions. Given the fast pace of modern life we don't practice this kind of thinking for sustained periods of time; instead, we favor quick, finite responses. We are like athletes who exercise our fast-twitch muscle fibers but not our slow ones and then try to run a marathon. Many of us aren't in long-term thinking shape.

***

In February 2008, seven months before the collapse of the investment bank Lehman Brothers, the flamboyant conservative French president, Nicolas Sarkozy, asked economists Joseph Stiglitz, Amartya Sen, and Jean Paul Fitoussi to create a commission to study the drawbacks of using gross domestic product (GDP) to assess a country's economic performance. As Sarkozy put it, "I felt the urgent need to do away with the set of ideas and dogmas that had locked in all our thinking and action, that were making us lie to ourselves."[1]

GDP is a standard measure of the value of what is produced within a country during a particular year. When we say, "China is growing," or, "The United States is in a recession," what we really mean is, "China's GDP increased," or, "US GDP declined." President Sarkozy said he wanted help replace GDP with something that better measured social progress. Some critics accused Sarkozy of grandstanding, opportunistically claiming the world needed a new measure of well-being so he could move the goalposts and make France's economy look better. In any event, the new commission was a controversial move. Sarkozy asked Stiglitz to chair the effort.

Stiglitz had come a long way since waiting for his friend George Akerlof to send him a box of clothes from India. In 1979 he won the John Bates

Clark Medal, awarded every other year to the top American economist younger than forty. He had held posts at Columbia, Duke, Oxford, Princeton, Stanford, and Yale. He had been the chief economist of the World Bank and chaired the Council of Economic Advisers under President Clinton. He had won the Nobel Prize in Economics.

Stiglitz also had been working for decades on what he calls "the measurement issue." The assignment from President Sarkozy fit right in with his own long-term thinking, and that of his colleagues. He told me, "We began in the early 1990s, trying to get the US government to talk about 'Green GDP.' We knew it wouldn't happen overnight. And we knew measurement by itself wouldn't change behavior, but the process would start to change behavior, because it was changing cognition, what people see. An idea thrown out fifteen or twenty years ago is finally moving into the collective consciousness."

GDP numbers neglect many important factors that, at least until recently, we have not measured at all. They omit leisure and quality of life. They do not account for "externalities," an economist's term for the costs that some people's activities, like polluting, impose on the rest of us. Nor do they address inequality. GDP might suggest a country's prosperity is increasing, yet poverty and income disparity might be increasing too.

The commission made some recommendations to fix these problems. Its report concluded that, in addition to economic production, we should measure health, education, political voice, and social relationships. We should focus on inequality and the environment. We should use subjective quality-of-life surveys as well as objective measures of economic growth. We should measure happiness instead of merely production. Such reforms would take many years, probably decades, to implement.[2]

When it appeared, the report generated a flurry of popular support. There was favorable coverage from leading newspapers and magazines, on television and online, and in speeches by politicians. Sarkozy reiterated that the changes were fundamental and required a sustained commitment: "The kind of civilization we build depends on the way we do our accounts quite simply because it changes the value we put on things. It is not the fruit of the instantaneous confrontation of supply and demand."[3] His soaring rhetoric inspired people around the world to think about their long-term futures. For a little while.

But then the European financial crisis hit. By 2012, the numerical measures that Sarkozy was urging people to move beyond had become the object of daily obsessive observation as markets crashed. The media and the public focused relentlessly on these plummeting numbers, as happens when there is a spike in the murder rate or a sudden decline in math test scores. GDP growth was down; unemployment was up. Even France's AAA credit rating was downgraded. Suddenly, Sarkozy faced a more immediate crisis than the long-term search for the right ways to measure well-being: the numbers were hurting his chances in an already tough reelection campaign. Measuring well-being moved to the back burner. Meanwhile, in the United States, the issue of GDP measurement never even made it into the kitchen.

Today virtually no politician, including Sarkozy, talks about replacing GDP in the long term; instead, everyone has zeroed in on how to increase GDP in the short term. We are accepting a quick answer when instead we should be asking a slow question.

———

Sustainability is an even longer-term concept. The word *sustainability* sounds like a label that should be applied to 1960s hippies who wear tie-dye shirts and hug trees. But sustainability isn't really left-leaning or partisan—

even when we are talking about the environment. The question is simply whether a short-term level of income and wealth can be sustained over the longer term.

If we care only about the consequences over a one-year time horizon, we might raze an entire forest right away. But if we think about future decades, we should instead harvest only a portion of the forest now, and we should periodically replant where we have cut. We should do this not because we love trees necessarily but because we care about the next generation's needs. Sustainability is a hard-nosed approach to thinking about the future, like the difference between a steady investment and a get-rich-quick scheme. Warren Buffett is sustainable; Bernie Madoff is not.

Sustainability is also related to GDP measurement. GDP tells us how well we did last year and may give us a limited sense of the short-term future. But it doesn't say anything about the long term. It doesn't tell us whether a country's citizens are consuming too much of their current wealth, or whether there are enough natural resources and human capital for future decades. It doesn't predict how long a country's transportation and technology infrastructure will last, or whether its next generation of workers will be sufficiently educated and trained. Focusing narrowly on GDP is like driving a car and only looking at how fast you are going. Sustainability means you should also ask how much gas is left in the tank or whether you need to adjust your position on a winding road.[4]

Sustainability is a long-term global version of the challenges we confront as individuals when we are tempted to overconsume alcohol, smoke, gamble, or overeat, when we focus too much on the short term and give lower priority to future well-being. Today seems worth a lot more than tomorrow, so we overindulge today. As we have seen, the key variable in these kinds of questions, for both humans and animals (even pigeons), is the discount rate.

Like all of us, policymakers tend to have high discount rates, especially in the short term.[5] Recall that a discount rate is the interest rate we use to compare future benefits and costs to current benefits and costs. The rate that governments use to assess future benefits and costs is sometimes called the "social discount rate." It can dramatically affect whether government decisions look good or bad. If the social discount rate is high, it means the decision-maker values the future less. Given the influence of the media and election cycles, it shouldn't be surprising that politicians value the short term a lot more than the long term.

For two decades, the US Office of Management and Budget (OMB) has set a "base rate" of 7 percent for investments and regulatory programs designed for the general public.[6] Meanwhile, other parts of the federal government, such as the General Accounting Office and Congressional Budget Office, use a discount rate closer to 1 percent.[7] For many government decisions, the difference between 7 percent and 1 percent is night and day.

For example, the Federal Emergency Management Agency requires that project applications for flood mitigation programs, such as dams, levees, and retrofitting of homes, include an analysis of future benefits based on the OMB's 7 percent rate. Because the benefits of these programs are expected over a very long period of time—decades or even centuries—those benefits will appear to be worth a lot less today if they are discounted at a higher rate. At a 1 percent rate, a $100 benefit in one hundred years is worth $37 in today's terms. But at a 7 percent rate, that same benefit is worth just twelve cents today. Hurricanes Andrew and Katrina illustrated the importance of flood mitigation and long-term planning. Yet proposals for FEMA projects have little chance when they use a 7 percent discount rate. Consequently, we are underprotected against future floods.

The starkest example of how discount rates matter in answering questions about sustainability is climate change. Although politicians and the media focus on allegations about falsified evidence and questions about whether the climate really is changing, the most crucial question about climate change is about discount rates. The world's top economists assume climate change will destroy the planet, but ask what is the cost of that future destruction in today's terms. These experts are locked in a heavyweight battle over discount rates.

One group, led by Nicholas Stern, the chair of the Grantham Research Institute on Climate Change and the Environment at the London School of Economics, says we should use a low discount rate, just a fraction of a percent.[8] Using a low rate, Stern concludes that governments must immediately enact far-reaching reforms in order to prevent long-term disaster. The other group, led by William Nordhaus, the Sterling Professor of Economics at Yale University, says we should use a higher discount rate.[9] Nordhaus assumes climate change will be every bit as harmful as Stern assumes it will be, but using a higher rate, he concludes that the threat of climate change is not sufficiently great to justify major expenditures today.

Which group should we believe? Is climate change a major crisis or an inconvenience we can punt down the road for our children and grandchildren to manage? If we use a low discount rate—say half a percent—a $100 trillion loss that will occur in five hundred years is comparable to a cost of several trillion dollars today. That means we should be willing to spend a fortune to prevent such a future catastrophe. But if we use a high discount rate—say the 7 percent OMB rate—the same future loss is comparable to a cost of just *twenty cents* today. That means, if we have the choice between twenty-five cents today and saving the entire world's economy in five hundred years, we should take the quarter.

We might be tempted to make judgments about climate change right away, perhaps as fast as we tend to react in our personal lives. But just as we are better off personally when we take time to think about how much we should drink, smoke, gamble, or eat, we also will be better off as a society if we take time to think about sustainability.

Choosing the right discount rate requires more than just number crunching.[10] It requires a fundamental decision about how much we care about future generations. Can we ethically justify favoring the well-being of a person today over the well-being of a person born in the future? If so, how much less should we assume future generations are worth? Do we have an obligation, consistent with the philosopher John Rawls's argument that we should protect the least-well-off member of society, to maximize the well-being of the poorest generation, whenever that generation might live?

There are no easy answers, at least not for now. The thing we need to do is stay focused on these questions, not short-term distractions. And subsumed within these difficult questions is an even bigger one, our last: how much is a human life worth?

When our legislators and regulators enact new rules, they are supposed to weigh benefits versus costs. Should all lighters be childproof? Should food labeling be more detailed? Should airlines carry survival equipment for inadvertent water landings? Should cars and factories reduce carbon emissions? Government officials are supposed to put numbers on the pros and cons of these questions.

Doing so inevitably requires making decisions about the value of a human life. How much money should we be willing to spend to save a person from dying? And how much does it matter that the life will be saved?

Every day regulators answer such seemingly unanswerable philosophical questions, and they do it in ways that the Office of Management and

Budget understands: they come up with a number. Today, they put the value of a human life in the range of $7 million to $9 million.

Why these numbers and not, say, "42"? Some clever economists estimate the value of a human life based on the choices we make about risky behavior: smoking cigarettes, driving a car, eating undercooked meat, or working a risky job.[11] As Adam Smith noted, people's wages reflect a trade-off regarding "the ease or hardship, the cleanliness or dirtiness, the honourableness or dishonourableness of the employment."[12] There have been more than one hundred studies that attempt to determine the value of a human life based on the value we place on our lives in private decisions.[13]

One way to calculate the value of a human life is to look at how much more money a worker earns for doing a risky job. Suppose working in a coal mine pays $10,000 a year more than working a safer desk job, and that coal miners have a 1 percent greater chance of dying on the job; some economists would say that this trade-off suggests people value a human life at $1 million. They assume the increased cost of working as a coal miner (which, on average, is $1 million multiplied by 1 percent, or $10,000) is reflected in increased pay.

Another method is based on our behavior. How much will we pay for safety features such as bicycle helmets or antilock brakes? When we have the choice to drive faster, even at increased risk of death, how much faster do we go? In 1987, when the US government permitted states to raise the speed limit from 55 to 65 miles per hour, many states did so, and drivers saved time by driving about two miles per hour faster on average. But fatality rates rose by about one-third. Overall, people saved about 125,000 hours of driving per lost life. At average wages, the trade-off between the time savings and the increased risk of fatalities suggested that state decision-makers were putting the value of a human life at about $1.5 million.[14] Today, the United Kingdom is considering increasing the maximum speed on its motorways from 70 to 80 miles per hour; that change would lead to more deaths and by doing so would illuminate the question of how much regulators there think human life is now worth.

These studies all have various problems and biases. And it is highly controversial to use them to calculate the specific value of an individual life: they are generalizations. Should we assume the lives of terminally ill elderly people have the same value as the lives of healthy toddlers? Should we ask medical experts to adjust our assessment of a life's value based on its quality or the probability of death?[15] There is no perfect methodology, but over the years researchers have reached a consensus that $1.5 million is much too low. Kip Viscusi, a professor at Vanderbilt University, and other prominent economists have persuaded regulators to increase their assumed values, and they have done so. As of 2011, the Environmental Protection Agency assumed the value of a human life was $9.1 million, the Food and Drug Administration put it at $7.9 million, and the Department of Transportation figure was around $6 million.[16] Are any of these the right answer?

The question gets tougher. Even if we assume a human life today is worth $7 million to $9 million, what should a future life be worth? If a policy choice puts future generations at risk, what discount rate should we use for valuing those lives? Should it be in the range of 3 to 5 percent, as some economists suggest? The 7 percent GAO rate? A fraction of a percent?

As we have seen from the debate about discount rates and climate change, these rates can seem arbitrary and produce widely divergent outcomes. If a human life is worth $8 million, then how much should we pay today to prevent an event that would result in the loss of 10 billion human lives in five hundred years? If we use a 7 percent discount rate, that number is shockingly small: $162.63. If we use a low discount rate, the number would be so big that it would have too many zeros to fit on this page.

Our most important policy decisions—about the economy, jobs, health care, defense, the environment, and foreign relations—require that smart people spend long periods of time thinking strategically. It will take years to construct measures of happiness, health, safety, and well-being other than GDP, and perhaps even longer to understand what we should do to sustain our planet. We might never figure out how much a future human life is worth in numerical terms. But if we ask life's biggest questions for long enough, eventually we will get better answers.

We should approach the longest-term questions with the same two-step framework that, as we already have seen, works well for short-term decisions. First, estimate the relevant time period for a particular decision. For the big questions, these time periods might be ten or twenty years. We might have a public debate focused exclusively on what that time period should be and how we should try to answer the questions, perhaps as part of a major election cycle.

Then, second, we should recruit and incentivize a group of experts to study the question throughout this period of time, but tell them we don't want an answer until the very end. Governments could implement a series of long-term research programs designed to address the most important policy questions using this framework.[17] We might embed a series of shorter questions in the programs to avoid inertia.[18] But in each case, we should not expect a decision until the last possible moment.

Author Douglas Adams famously wrote: "The Answer to the Ultimate Question of Life, the Universe, and Everything is . . . 42." We'd like to specify that kind of clear-cut answer for our decisions: the exact number of milliseconds before we react to a tennis serve or high-frequency trade, the precise duration of a first date, or the perfect interval between a sin and an apology.

But wisdom doesn't come from definitive answers. It is more important to ask the right question. The trouble in *The Hitchhiker's Guide to the Galaxy* is that no one can remember the question.

Here is the right question: "For how long should we delay?"

When we ask this question repeatedly about different kinds of decisions, we begin to see that similar patterns of good decision-making recur for decisions that take different amounts of time—the elements of a good decision within milliseconds (a baseball hitter following see-prepare-hit) resemble the elements of a good decision within seconds (a fighter pilot following observe-orient-decide-act), and so forth for minutes or months or years. The central element of good decision-making during any of these time periods is a person's ability to manage delay.

This sameness across time suggests that some aspects of decision-making are universal and even fundamental to the human condition. We are hardwired to react quickly. Modern society taps into that hardwiring, tempting us to respond instantly to all kinds of information and demands. Yet we are often better off resisting both biology and technology. As Robert J. Sternberg, a Yale psychologist, says, "The essence of intelligence would seem to be in knowing when to think and act quickly, and knowing when to think and act slowly."[19]

The most insightful writing about decision-making has addressed delay indirectly by focusing on how human beings deal with uncertainty about the future. In the preface to Roberta Wohlstetter's classic book on the Japanese surprise attack at Pearl Harbor, Thomas Schelling wrote that "there is a tendency in our planning to confuse the unfamiliar with the improbable. The contingency we have not considered seriously looks strange; what looks strange is thought impossible; what is improbable need not be considered seriously."[20] These unconsidered contingencies are what Donald Rumsfeld, the former secretary of defense, referred to as "unknown unknowns." They are what the economist Frank Knight labeled unquantifiable "uncertainty" (as opposed to risk, which can be measured). Or what Nassim Taleb called "black swans." Or what the German military theorist Carl von Clausewitz wrote was the inevitability of surprise. Or what Charles Perrow labeled unanticipated "normal accidents." They are what Socrates meant when he said, "I neither know nor think that I know."[21]

For centuries, these leading thinkers and other people we have met in this book have told us not to jump to firm conclusions about the unknown. Yet today we jump faster and more frequently to firm conclusions. We like to believe there is wisdom in our snap decisions, and sometimes there is. But true wisdom and judgment come from understanding our limitations when it comes to thinking about the future. (Not even Maggie, the dog on the cover, can sit with a biscuit on her nose forever.) That is why it is so important for us to think about the relevant time period of our decisions and then ask what is the maximum amount of time we can take within that period to observe and process information about possible outcomes. Asking questions about timing is crucial, even if we cannot arrive at an answer as specific as "42."

The examination undertaken in this book is about more than improving personal and professional decisions. Thinking about the role of delay is a profound and fundamental part of being human. Questions about delay are existential: the amount of time we take to reflect on decisions will define who we are. Is our mission simply to be another animal, responding to whatever stimulations we encounter? Or are we here for something more?

Our ability to think about delay is a central part of the human condition. It is a gift, a tool we can use to examine our lives. Life might be a race against time, but it is enriched when we rise above our instincts and stop the clock to process and understand what we are doing and why. A wise decision requires reflection, and reflection requires a pause. The converse of Socrates's famous admonition is that the examined life just might be worth living.

Like any author, I hope future generations of leaders will read and digest the specific research and recommendations in this book to help them understand the complexities of human decision-making. But if that doesn't happen, if their attention spans have been shrunk by fast-food stimuli or the reptile workings of their vagal nerves, I can advise them in a simpler way. If I am limited to just one word of wisdom about decision-making for children born a hundred years from now, people who will have all of our advantages and limitations as human beings but will need to navigate an unimaginably faster-paced world than the one we confront now, there is no doubt what that word should be.

Wait.

ACKNOWLEDGMENTS

You would not be holding a book by me about the role of delay in decision-making if it weren't for the wisdom and advocacy skills of my super-agent, Theresa Park, who has stood by me over the years as I tackle increasingly obscure books that I am increasingly unqualified to write. Thank you, Theresa, for your judgment and honesty. I am grateful to Theresa's colleagues at the Park Literary Group: I have appreciated Abby Koons's sound judgment and advice, and I am delighted to be working with Emily Sweet and Peter Knapp as well. Thank you all.

You would not be holding an even moderately tolerable book by me about the role of delay in decision-making if it weren't for the creative genius of my editor, Clive Priddle. Clive turned my drafts upside down and inside out, ripped them to shreds, mixed in his own insight, and then let me put my name on what is in large part his work. Thank you, Clive, for your endurance and for telling me straight up when I've written a "truly horrible sentence."

I also benefited from several early conversations with Niki Papadopoulos, an editor and rising star of the publishing industry now at Penguin

Group, who left PublicAffairs during the summer of 2010, just as I was getting ready to start procrastinating my work on this book. I am grateful to everyone at PublicAffairs, particularly Melissa Veronesi, who was a tremendously efficient production editor, and Tessa Shanks, virtuoso publicist. Thanks to Peter Osnos and Susan Weinberg for believing in this project.

Andrew Franklin of Profile Books was dazzling, as always, helping me stay on track and then swooping in at the last minute with colorful editorial suggestions. Andrew's loyalty since 1997 is rivaled only by that of my wife and dog; this is the fourth book the four of us have done together. Thank you, once again, to everyone at Profile Books.

Numerous people talked to me about the various topics in this book. I am especially grateful for conversations with Bill Ackman, Julian Alexander, Michael Ashner, Lanny Breuer, Yaron Brook, Jeff Campbell, Dana Carney, Kathy Casey, Walker Clark, Simon Copleston, Jeff Critchfield, Patrick Daniels, Hernando de Soto, Sanford DeVoe, Gurpreet Dhaliwal, Andrew Dittmer, Jesse Eisinger, Anne Erni, Allen Farrell, Jerome Fons, Mary Fricker, Koji Fukumura, Maria Gavrilovic, Gordon Gerson, Jonathan Glater, Francesco Guerrera, Scott Harrison, Margaret Heffernan, Sheena Iyengar, James Jacoby, Rob Jafek, Roy Katzovicz, Adam Kolber, Eric Kolchinsky, Unni Krishnan, Steve Kroft, Stephen Labaton, Irene LaCota, Vice Chancellor Travis Laster, Angel Lau, Donald Lawrence, Joe Lonsdale, Angel Lopez, John Lovi, Jeff Madrick, Peter McLeod, Ralph Nader, Chuck O'Kelley, André Perold, Stephen Porges, Ernesto Reuben, Christine Richard, Darren Robbins, John Rogers, Jennifer Schenker, Todd Simkin, Robert P. Smith, Yves Smith, Mark Snell, Michael Solender, Judge Stanley Sporkin, Joseph Stiglitz, Richard Thaler, David Westbrook, and David Viniar.

I was able to test-drive some of the ideas in this book in two speeches during October 2011, at the Seattle University School of Law's Berle Center Corporate Governance Colloquium and the French-American Foundation's Young Leaders program. I am grateful to both organizations, and I benefited tremendously from the active questioning and feedback from both groups.

Several people gave me helpful comments on drafts, as well as in numerous conversations and correspondence. I especially appreciated advice from Jennifer Curran, Charlie Graham, Justin Graham, Peter H. Huang, Paul Kedrosky, Alex Krongard, Shaun Martin, Trace McCreary, Joel Mick, Lisa Partnoy, and JB Tropp. I owe special thanks to my law professor/author cabal of Kent Greenfield and Adam Winkler, who read an early manuscript and offered helpful comments, sober and not.

I am grateful to the University of San Diego and want to thank previous dean Kevin Cole, current dean Stephen Ferruolo, provost Julie Sullivan, and president Mary Lyons.

And finally, thanks to my family: my wife, Laura Adams, for trying to keep me in line; our kids, Natasha and Zachary, for inspiring me, helping me explain some difficult passages, and repeatedly asking how many pages I had written; and Fletch, for lying patiently at my feet throughout the writing of this book.

NOTES

Introduction

1. Rebecca J. Leonardi, Sarah-Jane Vick, and Valérie Dufour, "Waiting for More: The Performance of Domestic Dogs (*Canis familiaris*) on Exchange Tasks," *Animal Cognition* 15(1, 2012): 107–120. If you are interested in a literature survey of experiments on delayed gratification in animals, Leonardi, Vick, and Dufour's article is a go-to source.

2. Some other animals, especially primates, are also very good at delaying gratification. Chimpanzees will wait up to eighteen minutes for their favorite food. Theodore A. Evans and Michael J. Beran, "Chimpanzees Use Self-Distraction to Cope with Impulsivity," *Biology Letters* 3(2007): 599–602.

3. The recent popular books I have in mind when I refer to what many psychologists call systems 1 (automatic/intuitive) and 2 (deliberative/analytical) and to behavioral economists' claims that our biases are predictable are Daniel Kahneman, *Thinking, Fast and Slow* (Farrar, Straus and Giroux, 2011), and Dan Ariely, *Predictably Irrational: The Hidden Forces That Shape Our Decisions* (Harper Perennial, 2010). See also Venkatesh Guru Rao, *Tempo: Timing, Tactics and Strategy in Narrative-Driven Decision-Making* (Ribbonfarm Inc., 2011).

4. The Harvard psychologist Daniel Gilbert concludes that "*the human being is the only animal that thinks about the future*" (emphasis Gilbert's). Daniel Gilbert, *Stumbling on Happiness* (Knopf, 2006), p. 3.

5. For example, research on the importance of willpower does not draw from studies that show how heart rate variability matters to our ability to regulate our emotions (a topic we will explore in Chapter 1). In 2010, Walter Mischel and his coauthors suggested that the Bing Nursery experiments and studies of willpower (including brain imaging) are converging on an explanation of self-control that focuses on cognitive and neural mechanisms; they do not mention heart rate variability. See Walter Mischel et al., "'Willpower' over the Life Span: Decomposing Self-Regulation," *Social Cognitive and Affective Neuroscience Advance Access* (September 19, 2010): 1–5. Likewise, Roy Baumeister's pathbreaking research on "willpower" tends to focus more on cognition and brain function than on heart rate variability. See Roy F. Baumeister and John Tierney, *Willpower: Rediscovering the Greatest Human Strength* (Penguin Press, 2011).

Chapter 1

1. Porges's full title illustrates the wide-ranging scope of his expertise and research: Professor of Psychiatry (and Bioengineering) and Director of the Brain-Body Center in the Department of Psychiatry, College of Medicine, University of Illinois at Chicago. He is also an adjunct professor in the psychology department, but told me he labels himself a "behavioral neuroscientist" because his orientation and perspective differ from those of modern psychology.

2. The tenth cranial nerve is termed "vagal" or "vagus," derived from the Latin term for "wandering," because its path is so diverse and connected to so many organs. The "wandering" label, however, is a bit misleading. The vagal nerve carries signals down several paths that run through our bodies, but it doesn't do so slowly. It does it fast. Really fast. Porges's research background and several of his most important articles are described in his book *Polyvagal Theory* (W. W. Norton & Co., 2011), which excerpts and summarizes much of his previously published research. Porges also has explained his theories in several public interviews and lectures. See Ravi Dykema, "How Your Nervous System Sabotages Your Ability to Relate: An Interview with Stephen Porges About His Polyvagal Theory," *Nexus* (March–April 2006), http://www.nexuspub.com/articles_2006/interview_porges_06_ma.php.

3. Charles Darwin (1872), quoted in *The Expression of the Emotions in Man and Animals* (University of Chicago Press, 1965), p. 69.

4. For Porges's early work on heart rate variability, see Stephen W. Porges, "Heart Rate Variability and Deceleration as Indexes of Reaction Time," *Journal of Experimental Psychology* 92(1, 1972): 103–110. Porges's early work was prescient; he even noted in his early studies of attention that there is a distinction among the time frames in which people react, beginning with a short-term (less than one second) deceleration, followed by a slightly longer-term (two- to six-second) variable response, followed finally by a sustained response. See Stephen W. Porges, "Peripheral and Neurochemical Parallels of Psychopathology: A Psychophysiological Model Relating Autonomic Imbalance to Hyperactivity, Psychopathy, and Autism," *Advances in Child Development and Behavior* 11(1976): 35–65, at 47–53; see also Gary F. Walter and Stephen W. Porges, "Heart Rate and Respiratory Responses as a Function of Task Difficulty: The Use of Discriminant Analysis in the Selection of Psychologically Sensitive Physiological Responses," *Psychophysiology* 13(6, 1976): 563–571; Stephen W. Porges and David C. Raskin, "Respiratory and Heart Rate Components of Attention," *Journal of Experimental Psychology* 81(3, 1969): 497–503.

5. Porges, *Polyvagal Theory*.

6. Ibid., p. 111.

7. Ibid., p. 112.

8. Changes in the timing of the heart rate, known as cardiac vagal regulation, is measured by a variable known as respiratory sinus arrhythmia (RSA). Since Porges's early work, numerous studies have confirmed that differences in RSA are related to both children's and adult's emotional experiences and regulation. For recent examples, see Bradley M. Appelhans and Linda J. Luecken, "Heart Rate Variability as an Index of Regulated Emotional Responding," *Review of General Psychology* 10(2006): 229–240; Paul D. Hastings et al., "Applying the Polyvagal Theory to Children's Emotional Regulation: Social Context, Socialization, and Adjustment," *Biological Psychology* 79(2008): 299–306; and Lisa M. Diamond, Angela M. Hicks, and Kimberly D. Otter-Henderson, "Individual Differences in Vagal Regulation Moderate Associations Between Daily Affect and Daily Couple Interactions," *Personality and Social Psychology Bulletin* 37(6, 2011): 731–744.

9. Porges, *Polyvagal Theory*, p. 145.

10. Diamond, Hicks, and Otter-Henderson, p. 732.

11. John Mordecai Gottman and Lynn Fainsilber Katz, "Children's Emotional Reactions to Stressful Parent-Child Interactions: The Link Between Emotional Regulation and Vagal Tone," in Richard A. Fabes, ed., *Emotions and the Family*, pp. 265–283 (Haworth Press, 2002). Interestingly, Gottman and Katz further found that a kid's ideal response varies depending on which parent is doing the criticizing. A variable heart rate is important in responding to both Mom and Dad, but in opposite directions. When a father mocks a

child, the response that best predicts later emotional health in the child is a quick drop in heart rate. Apparently, the central nervous system of a child has become hardwired to react in the way stereotypes about male parents might suggest children should react. The ideal response to criticism from a father seems to be a calm and levelheaded one. But when a mother is the source of negative criticism, the child's best response is to increase the heart rate. The infant central nervous system responds to criticism from a female parent by inducing a more emotionally charged reaction, with a fast-pounding heart. This opposite response is also what hardwiring and stereotypes might suggest: emoting is the best way to respond to Mom. We will revisit Gottman's pioneering work on emotional reactions in Chapter 6, when we explore "thin slicing."

12. Diamond et al., "Individual Differences in Vagal Regulation."

13. Stephen W. Porges, "Orienting in a Defensive World: Mammalian Modifications of Our Evolutionary Heritage: A Polyvagal Theory," *Psychophysiology* 32(1995): 301–318. Porges called his theory "polyvagal theory" because there are multiple strands of the vagal nerve and they have different effects. To simplify his theory, we focus here on the distinction between the reptilian and mammalian strands of the vagal nerve. Since the speech, Porges has given several interviews, some published, on polyvagal theory. See "The Polyvagal Theory for Treating Trauma: A Teleseminar Session with Stephen W. Porges, PhD, and Ruth Buczynski, PhD," National Institute for the Clinical Application of Behavioral Medicine (NICABM), http://www.childhood.org.au/Assets/Files/618688a6-c955-4a1d-9608-ce33e945cc1e.pdf, 1–28; "The GAINS Anniversary Interviews: Stephen Porges: Interviewed by Lauren Culp," *Connections and Reflections: The Global Association for Interpersonal Neurobiology Studies Quarterly* (Autumn–Winter 2010): 57–64.

14. Formally, what I am calling the old reptilian vagus is referred to in the literature as the dorsal motor nucleus (DMNX); the new mammalian vagus is referred to as the nucleus ambiguous (NA).

15. Porges expands the comparison of the old vagus and new vagus to the story about the race between the tortoise and the hare: "Reptiles locomote with a reliable but underpowered engine and mammals locomote with a supercharged engine that can function for only short periods of time without refueling." Porges, *Polyvagal Theory*, p. 31.

16. Ibid., p. 46.

17. Ibid., ch. 14.

18. Ibid., pp. 222–223.

19. Ibid., p. 227.

20. Ibid., p. 241.

21. Porges has coined the term "neuroception" to describe how neural circuits distinguish whether a situation or person is safe or dangerous. See Stephen W. Porges, "Neuroception: A Subconscious System for Detecting Threats and Safety," *Zero to Three* (May 2004): 19.

22. Programs such as Stop Now And Plan (SNAP) have been effective in helping young children who might be predisposed to criminal behavior learn to delay trigger reactions that can cause trouble in stressful situations; these programs might incorporate findings about heart rate variability. See the SNAP website at http://www.stopnowandplan.com.

23. The original study is Walter Mischel, Ebbe B. Ebbesen, and Antonette Raskoff Zeiss, "Cognitive and Attentional Mechanisms in Delay of Gratification," *Journal of Personality and Social Psychology* 21(1972): 204–218. Subsequent studies include: Harriet Nerlove Mischel and Walter Mischel, "The Development of Children's Knowledge of Self-Control Strategies," *Child Development* 54(1983): 603–619; Walter Mischel, Yuichi Shoda, and Philip K. Peake, "The Nature of Adolescent Competencies Predicted by Preschool Delay of Gratification," *Journal of Personality and Social Psychology* 54(1988): 687–699; Walter Mischel, Yuichi Shoda, and Monica L. Rodriguez, "Delay of Gratification in Children," *Science* 244(1989): 933–938; and Walter Mischel and Ozlem Ayduk, "Willpower in a Cognitive-Affective Processing System: The Dynamics of Delay of Gratification," in Roy F. Baumeister and Kathleen D. Vohs, eds., *Handbook of Self-Regulation: Research, Theory, and Applications*, pp. 99–129 (Guilford, 2004).

24. Yuichi Shoda, Walter Mischel, and Philip K. Peake, "Predicting Adolescent Cognitive and Self-Regulatory Competencies from Preschool Delay of Gratification: Identifying Diagnostic Conditions," *Developmental Psychology* 26(6, 1990): 978–986; John Mordecai Gottman and Lynn Fainsilber Katz, "Children's Emotional Reactions to Stressful Parent-Child Interactions: The Link Between Emotional

Regulation and Vagal Tone," in Richard A. Fabes, ed., *Emotions and the Family,* pp. 265–283 (Haworth Press, 2002).

25. See Walter Mischel et al., "'Willpower' over the Life Span: Decomposing Self-Regulation," *Social Cognitive and Affective Neuroscience Advance Access* (September 19, 2010): 1–5, at 2.

26. Jonah Lehrer, "Don't!," *The New Yorker,* May 18, 2009.

27. One experiment found that in order to distinguish between two different time intervals, ADHD children needed for the difference to be 50 milliseconds longer than the difference in time that a control group needed. In this experiment, the children were shown two circles on a computer screen and asked which circle appeared for a longer period of time. The control group could distinguish intervals that differed by less than 190 milliseconds, whereas for the ADHD children the intervals needed to be 240 milliseconds apart to be distinguishable. This difference is statistically significant, but would be imperceptible to an observer trying to determine whether a child has ADHD. See Anna Smith et al., "Evidence for a Pure Time Perception Deficit in Children with ADHD," *Journal of Child Psychology and Psychiatry* 43(4, 2002): 529–542.

28. For example, fMRI studies have found significant differences in the brain patterns of children with ADHD and conduct disorders when the children are presented with tasks that require them to exercise inhibition. See Katya Rubia et al., "Dissociated Functional Brain Abnormalities of Inhibition in Boys with Pure Conduct Disorder and in Boys with Pure Attention Deficit Hyperactivity Disorder," *American Journal of Psychiatry* 165(2008): 889–897.

29. Robert Sanders, "Advance Makes MRI Scans More Than Seven Times Faster," UC Berkeley News Center, January 5, 2011, http://newscenter.berkeley.edu/2011/01/05/functionalmri.

Chapter 2

1. David Foster Wallace, "Federer as Religious Experience," *New York Times,* August 20, 2006. Wallace committed suicide on September 12, 2008, three days before the Lehman Brothers bankruptcy. Given his expertise in mathematics (see David Foster Wallace, *Everything and More: A Compact History of ∞* [W. W. Norton, 2003]), he surely would have written wisely about the connections between the financial crisis and snap decision-making, and perhaps the relationship to tennis as well.

2. When I say most people can react in about two hundred milliseconds, I base that conclusion on hundreds of studies done during the previous century. Two hundred milliseconds might seem fast, but it's slow for our neurons, which can send signals in one millisecond, the time it takes a mosquito to beat its wings. And visual reaction time is about as slow as our brains get. For example, we see about 20 percent more slowly than we hear, because it takes longer for the 100 million rods and cones in our retinas to process visual information than it takes the 20,000 cochlear hair cells in our ears to process sound. If you are curious about how you compare to others in reaction speed, here are some findings: men are a few milliseconds faster than women; young and old people are slower than people in their forties and fifties; caffeine, exercise, and exhaling speed us up; alcohol and illness slow us down. If you want to know how fast you are, take a break now, do an Internet search for "visual reaction time tests," and check your speed. I'm betting that, unless you are a healthy, sober, fifty-year-old man who has just drunk a pot of coffee, you can't consistently beat two hundred milliseconds—not by much anyway. Robert J. Kosinski, a biology professor at Clemson University, has posted an excellent review of the literature on reaction time (September 2010) at http://biology.clemson.edu/bpc/bp/Lab/110/reaction.htm. In Kosinski's experiments at Clemson, the average reaction time to a simple visual stimulus is 268 milliseconds. Interestingly, an early study by Francis Galton reported a mean reaction time for teenagers of 187 milliseconds, so perhaps we are getting slower. Francis Galton, "On Instruments for (1) Testing Perceptions of Differences of Tint and for (2) Determining Reaction Time," *Journal of the Anthropological Institute* 19(1899): 27–29. Another good source is Stefan Klein's excellent book, *The Secret Pulse of Time: Making Sense of Life's Scarcest Commodity* (Da Capo Press, 2007), which has a particularly insightful discussion about the very short term in Chapter 5 and also cites various reaction time studies.

Notes to Chapter 2

3. "WTF: Andy Roddick Monday Press Conference," Tennis Connected, November 23, 2010, http://tennisconnected.com/home/2010/11/23/wtf-andy-roddick-monday-press-conference.

4. Robert Levine, *A Geography of Time: On Tempo, Culture, and the Pace of Life* (Basic Books, 1997), p. 33. This book has several interesting anecdotes and quotes from professional athletes in the zone.

5. Noriyuki Kida, Shingo Oda, and Michikazu Matsumura, "Intensive Baseball Practice Improves the Go/Nogo Reaction Time, but Not the Simple Reaction Time," *Cognitive Brain Research* 22(2005): 257–264. Numerous studies have reached similar conclusions about superfast sports, ranging from baseball and tennis to skeet shooting. See Bruce Abernethy and Robert J. Neal, "Visual Characteristics of Clay Target Shooters," *Journal of Science and Medicine in Sports* 2(1999): 1–19; Antti Mero, Laura Jaakola, and Paavo V. Komi, "Neuromuscular, Metabolic, and Hormonal Profiles of Young Tennis Players and Untrained Boys," *Journal of Sports Sciences* 7(1989): 95–100; Darhl Nielsen and Carl McGown, "Information Processing as a Predictor of Offensive Ability in Baseball," *Perceptual and Motor Skills* 60(1985): 775–781. The Kyoto study also was consistent with prior research showing that even long-term practice does not improve visual reaction ability. Interestingly, when the researchers asked subjects to respond to a "Go/Nogo" stimulus—they were told *not* to respond to visual cues outside a defined "strike zone"—the professional baseball players still were just as fast, but the others were significantly slower, as much as 100 milliseconds slower.

6. These findings are reported in Peter McLeod, "Visual Reaction Time and High-Speed Ball Games," *Perception* 16(1987): 49–59. Given that cricket is the world's second most popular sport (after soccer), it is perhaps not surprising that there is an extensive literature on the reaction times of cricket batsmen. The studies are not as voluminous as baseball statistics, but they are close. There even is a "classic work" on the subject, H. T. A. Whiting, *Acquiring Ball Skill: A Psychological Interpretation* (Bell and Hyman, 1969). As with baseball, cricket studies generate disputes over certain hot-button issues, such as whether cricket batsmen can accurately predict the speed and location of the ball based on early cues from the bowler. Some studies have found that expert batsmen glean information from a one-second video of the bowler's windup. See Jonah Lehrer, *How We Decide* (Houghton Mifflin, 2009), p. 25. Other researchers have concluded that skilled batsmen can predict ball flight parameters better than chance. Bruce Abernethy and David G. Russell, "Advance Cue Utilisation by Skilled Cricket Batsmen," *Australian Journal of Science and Medicine in Sport* 16(1984): 2–10. However, it is possible that the viewer subjects in an experimental setting focus more than they normally would on the visual cues available before the ball is thrown. See McLeod, "Visual Reaction Time," p. 57, n. 3. What is not disputed in these studies is the consistency of our visual reaction time: sports scholars agree that professionals are no faster than amateurs.

7. See British Fencing, "Foundation Programme for Beginners—Epee," http://www.britishfencing.com/academy/academy-resources/foundation-programme-for-beginners-epee.

8. Lehrer, *How We Decide,* ch. 1.

9. For example, in *How We Decide,* Lehrer says: "So how does a quarterback do it? How does he make a decision? It's like asking a baseball player why he decided to swing the bat at a particular pitch: the velocity of the game makes thought impossible. Brady can afford to give each receiver only a split second of attention before he has to move on to the next" (p. 8). Yet, as Lehrer notes, there is a difference between having three seconds to think about four receivers and having half a second to react to one pitch.

10. One of the most vexing questions in superfast sports is whether there is an advantage to going first. In tennis and baseball, the answer generally is yes. The server typically wins more tennis games. Pitchers give up hits less than half the time. Yet in other one-on-one battles, such as fencing or a pistol duel, the answer is less clear. In legend and film, it is often the gunslinger who draws first who gets shot. Scientists have long speculated that human beings are faster when reacting than when acting. Niels Bohr, a physicist, suggested decades ago that it takes people longer to initiate a movement than to react to the same movement, and recent experiments have found that people playing a gunslinging game in fact moved about 10 percent faster when reacting to their opponent than when they went first. Apparently, we use a faster neural circuit when we react. Of course, that doesn't mean we should prefer to go second. On the street—as opposed to the movies—the first shooter usually wins. Fencers often are better off attacking than defending. Nevertheless, win or lose, we seem to be faster when we react than when we act. See Andrew E. Weichman

et al., "The Quick and the Dead: When Reaction Beats Intention," *Proceedings of the Royal Society: Biological Sciences* 277(2010): 1667–1674; Ed Yong, "Why Does the Gunslinger Who Draws First Always Get Shot?" Not Exactly Rocket Science, February 2, 2010, http://scienceblogs.com/notrocketscience/2010/02/why_does_the_gunslinger_who_draws_first_always_get_shot.php.

11. Libet's central finding also is the kind of discovery that deserves a Nobel Prize, except that Alfred Nobel did not include psychology among the eligible disciplines. A group at the University of Klagenfurt in Austria has attempted to remedy this oversight by establishing a "Virtual Nobel Prize in Psychology." Instead of a "call from Stockholm" and a seven-figure monetary award, the recipient receives just a "letter from Klagenfurt"—and no money. Still, it is something of an honor, and the inaugural award in 2003 went to Libet "for his pioneering achievements in the experimental investigation of consciousness, initiation of action, and free will."

12. Libet was born in Chicago, where he received his doctorate at the University of Chicago, and he spent most of his life in or near large cities in the United States. When he received the Virtual Nobel Prize in Psychology, he declined an invitation to present a Nobel Lecture in Europe, saying, "I do not have any present plans for a trip." See his letter of July 8, 2003, accepting the award, at: http://cognition.uni-klu.ac.at/nobel/libetanswer.jpg. Instead, he posted a brief acceptance speech on YouTube. And apparently he was not much of a cricket fan.

13. Benjamin Libet, *Mind Time: The Temporal Factor in Consciousness* (Harvard University Press, 2005), pp. 109–110.

14. Libet, *Mind Time*, pp. 110–111.

15. Ibid., p. 110.

16. Artificial intelligence research is focused on many of the same questions as decision-making research overall, including problem solving, knowledge, reasoning, uncertainty, communicating, perceiving, and acting. The question of whether computers have "learned" the art and science of delay is a big and interesting one we can only begin considering in the next chapter. See generally Stuart Russell and Peter Norvig, *Artificial Intelligence: A Modern Approach*, 3rd ed. (Prentice-Hall, 2010).

Chapter 3

1. I described this trip in *F.I.A.S.C.O.: Blood in the Water on Wall Street* (W. W. Norton, 1997), p. 168. The locker-room antics at the NYSE and on Wall Street generally—which I describe in that book—have subsided with the move to more impersonal, computer-driven business. As a result, investment banking has become less colorful, but perhaps more tolerable.

2. Quoted from the Security and Exchange Commission's lengthy publication on high-frequency trading and other complex issues related to advances in trading technology, "Concept Release on Equity Market Structure," release 34-61358, file S7-01-10 (2010), p. 45.

3. It isn't just travel. Interfacing with networks, processing and buffering information or decoding speech, putting data into packets—all of this takes time. Brooktrout Technology, a leading hardware and software supplier in the electronic messaging market, recommends making a latency budget, just like a personal budget, except with milliseconds instead of dollars. Here is an example, not for you to use, but to illustrate that the optimal amount of latency depends on costs and objectives. A high-frequency trader would scoff at this latency budget, whereas a telecommunications company might say it is fine.

ITEM	MILLISECONDS
Network interface	1
Framing	30
Processing time	10
Packetization	30
Media access delay	10
Routing	50
Jitter buffering	30
Total latency	161

Alan Percy, "Understanding Latency in IP Telephony," TelephonyWorld.com (2011), http://www .telephonyworld.com/training/brooktrout/iptel_latency_wp.html.

4. See Spread Networks, "Vision & Background," http://www.spreadnetworks.com/about-us/vision -and-background; Christopher Steiner, "Wall Street's Speed War," *Forbes*, September 27, 2010.

5. This section is taken from Frank Partnoy, "Don't Blink: Snap Decisions and Securities Regulation," *Brooklyn Law Review* 77 (2011): 151–179, which I wrote as part of my Abraham L. Pomerantz Lecture on securities regulation, delivered March 15, 2011, at Brooklyn Law School.

6. The details of the "flash crash" were reported in "Findings Regarding the Market Events of May 6, 2010," report of the staffs of the Commodities Futures Trading Commission (CFTC) and the Securities and Exchange Commission (SEC) to the Joint CFTC-SEC Advisory Committee on Emerging Regulatory Issues, September 30, 2010.

7. Joel Hasbrouck and Gideon Saar, "Low-Latency Trading," Johnson School Research Paper Series 35-2010, September 1, 2011, available at: http://papers.ssrn.com/sol3/papers.cfm?abstract_id=1695460; see also Jonathan A. Brogaard, "High-Frequency Trading and Market Quality," Working Paper Series, July 17, 2010, available at: http://papers.ssrn.com/sol3/papers.cfm?abstract_id=1970072; Andrei Kirilenko, Albert S. Kyle, Mehrdad Samadi, and Tugkan Tuzun, "The Flash Crash: The Impact of High-Frequency Trading on an Electronic Market," Working Paper Series, May 26, 2011, available at: http://papers.ssrn .com/sol3/papers.cfm?abstract_id=1686004.

8. Frank Zhang, "The Effect of High-Frequency Trading on Stock Volatility and Price Discovery," Working Paper Series, December 2010, available at: http://papers.ssrn.com/sol3/papers.cfm?abstract _id=1691679.

9. Charles Perrow, *Normal Accidents: Living with High-Risk Technologies* (Princeton University Press, 1999).

10. CFTC and SEC staffs, "Findings Regarding the Market Events of May 6, 2010," p. 6. In a later pro-nouncement, the joint CFTC-SEC committee recommended additional safeguards related to the five-second trading limit and the limit-up/limit-down process, as well as expansion of the scope of existing circuit breakers. See "Recommendations Regarding Regulatory Responses to the Market Events of May 6, 2010," summary report of the Joint CFTC-SEC Advisory Committee on Regulatory Issues, February 18, 2011, http://www.cftc.gov/ucm/groups/public/@aboutcftc/documents/file/jacreport_021811.pdf, pp. 4–5. In-terestingly, the number of circuit breaker halts appears to have increased recently. See Nick Baker, "Clear-wire Is Latest Stock Halted by Circuit Breakers," Bloomberg News, February 4, 2011, http://www .bloomberg.com/news/2011-02-04/clearwire-is-latest-stock-halted-by-circuit-breakers-table-.html.

11. Other post-crash solutions include a "limit-up/limit-down" mechanism that prevents trading out-side of a set price band, the elimination of stub quotes, and the use of an audit trail to detect disturbances in the market. See "Plan to Address Extraordinary Market Volatility Submitted to the Securities and Ex-change Commission," http://www.sec.gov/news/press/2011/2011-84-plan.pdf; see also Michael Mackenzie and Telis Demos, "Fears Linger of New 'Flash Crash,'" *Financial Times*, May 5, 2011.

12. Takako Iwatani and Kana Nishizawa, "Tokyo Bourse Will Start Shorter Lunch Break on May 9," Bloomberg News, February 6, 2011, http://www.bloomberg.com/news/2011-02-07/tokyo-bourse-will -start-shorter-lunch-break-on-may-9-tse-says.html; "Most Investors Oppose Ending TSE Lunch Break," Japan Times Online, September 25, 2010, http://www.japantimes.co.jp/text/nb20100925a4.html.

Chapter 4

1. One of the most insightful discussions of subliminal messaging in *Fight Club* is "11 Hidden Secrets in Fight Club," 11 Points, September 14, 2009, http://www.11points.com/Movies/11_Hidden_Secrets _in_Fight_Club_spv. An Internet search for "fight club subliminal penis" in early 2012 generated more than 98,000 results.

2. Now formats can be faster and more varied, but even in the slower 24p format one frame runs by at preconscious speed.

3. The University of Connecticut maintains an archive of James Vicary's correspondence, publications, surveys, and business records in its Thomas J. Dodd Research Center in Storrs; see James A. Vicary Papers, Archives and Special Collections, http://doddcenter.uconn.edu/asc/findaids/Vicary/MSS19980320.html.

4. The game title, which used macrons above the *u*'s, should not be confused with the 1980s Minneapolis punk band Hüsker Dü, which replaced the macrons with umlauts.

5. Although I have focused on subliminal video messages, there are numerous examples of subliminal audio messages, both real and imagined, particularly from rock songs played backward. Although the Beatles are credited with making such "backmasking" popular, it became more widely known when religious groups claimed that rock bands were using backmasking to help them recruit Satan worshipers or persuade listeners to kill themselves. One subliminal phrase allegedly hidden in the Judas Priest heavy metal song "Better by You, Better Than Me" was the subject of a year-long trial after the parents of a boy who attempted suicide in 1985 claimed that he was influenced by a hidden "do it" in that song. The protests against satanic backmasking led some bands to respond with backmask jokes or caricatures of religiously inspired messages. In his 1984 song "Nature Trail to Hell," Weird Al Yankovic declares in reverse that "Satan eats Cheese Whiz." And in "Darling Nikki," a song from the same year by the artist formerly known as Prince, the lyrics when the song is played forward are graphic descriptions of a sex fiend, but in reverse Prince is saying, "The Lord is coming soon."

6. If you want to see the topless Disney woman, try Snopes.com, "The Rescuers," http://www.snopes.com/disney/films/rescuers.asp. She is lurking there in the window, just behind the rodent heroes Bianca and Bernard, who are tucked into a sardine box strapped to Orville the albatross. The two frames are exhibits A and B for anyone who might question whether traditional animation was a tedious job crying out for comic relief, particularly at Disney during the 1970s.

7. For a trace memory study for pictures, see Andreas T. Breuer, Michael E. J. Masson, A. Cohen, and D. Stephen Lindsay, "Long-Term Repetition Priming of Briefly Identified Objects," *Journal of Experimental Psychology: Learning, Memory, and Cognition* 35(2009): 487–498. For a trace memory study for words, see Thorsten Albrecht and Dick Vorberg, "Long-Lasting Effects of Briefly Flashed Words and Pseudowords in Ultrarapid Serial Visual Presentation," *Journal of Experimental Psychology* 36(2010): 1339–1345.

8. Gráinne M. Fitzsimons, Tanya L. Chartrand, and Gavan Fitzsimons, "Automatic Effects of Brand Exposure on Motivated Behavior: How Apple Makes You 'Think Different,'" *Journal of Consumer Research* 35(2008): 21–35.

9. Henk Aarts and Ap Dijksterhuis, "The Silence of the Library: Environment, Situational Norm, and Social Behavior," *Journal of Personality and Social Psychology* 84(2003): 18–28.

10. John A. Bargh, Mark Chen, and Lara Burrows, "Automaticity of Social Behavior: Direct Effects of Trait Construct and Stereotype Activation on Action," *Journal of Personality and Social Psychology* 71(2, 1996): 230–244. Other recent research shows we are capable of making aesthetic judgments at astonishingly fast speeds as well: for example, when we see fifty-millisecond flashes of websites on their own, not preceded or followed by other images, we reach conclusions about their appeal that are highly correlated with our longer-term judgments after longer views. See Gitte Lindgaard, Gary Fernandes, Cathy Dudek, and J. Brown, "Attention Web Designers: You Have 50 Milliseconds to Make a Good Impression," *Behaviour and Information Technology* 25(March–April 2006): 115–126.

11. Chen-Bo Zhong and Sanford E. DeVoe, "You Are How You Eat: Fast Food and Impatience," *Psychological Science* 21(2010): 619–622.

12. National Endowment for the Arts, "To Read or Not to Read: A Question of National Consequence," research report 47, November 2007, http://www.nea.gov/research/ToRead_ExecSum.pdf.

13. The unpublished working paper, which was under invited revision for publication at the *Journal of Consumer Research* as of early 2012, is "No Time to Smell the Roses: Happiness in the Era of Impatience."

14. Bahador Bahrami, Nilli Lavie, and Geraint Rees, "Attentional Load Modulates Responses of Human Primary Visual Cortex to Invisible Stimuli," *Current Biology* 17(6, 2007): 509–513.

15. The reports were posted at Google's help forum, http://www.google.com/support/forum/p/Web%20Search/thread?tid=42196a7ddc220675&hl=en.

Chapter 5

1. Kahneman, *Thinking, Fast and Slow*, p. 415.

2. A box score for the game is available at Pro-Football-Reference.com, http://www.pro-football -reference.com/boxscores/197811190nyg.htm.

3. The details about Ron Jaworski are available at Pro-Football-Reference.com, http://www.pro -football-reference.com/play-index/comeback.cgi?player=JawoRo00.

4. Antonio Damasio, *Descartes' Error: Emotion, Reason, and the Human Brain* (Penguin, 2005), ch. 6.

5. Ibid., p. 119.

6. Ibid.

7. Stefan Klein, *The Secret Pulse of Time*, pp. 199–200.

8. Gary Klein, *Sources of Power: How People Make Decisions* (MIT Press, 1998), pp. 7–8.

9. Ibid., p. 11.

10. Ibid., p. 17.

11. Ibid., pp. 75–76.

12. Ibid., p. 150.

13. There are numerous studies showing that expert chess players instinctively pick the best moves, even in high-speed blitz games. See Roberta Calderwood, Gary A. Klein, and Beth W. Crandall, "Time Pressure, Skill, and Move Quality in Chess," *American Journal of Psychology* 101(1988): 481–493.

14. Chess grand masters can look at a board for five seconds and burn the placement of pieces into memory with 90 percent accuracy. They do this by "chunking," using their experience to put together large blocks of information. Instead of memorizing the board piece by piece, they tap into a memorable game from the past, or a particular strategy. If pieces are placed randomly on the board, so that experts can't "chunk," they do no better than novices. For an incredible journey through these memory concepts through the eyes of a participant in the US Memory Championship, see Joshua Foer, *Moonwalking with Einstein: The Art and Science of Remembering Everything* (Penguin Press, 2011).

15. The leading study is Michael Bar-Eli, Ofer H. Azar, Ilana Ritov, Yael Keidar-Levin, and Galit Schein, "Action Bias Among Elite Soccer Goalkeepers: The Case of Penalty Kicks," *Journal of Economic Psychology* 28(5, 2007): 606–621. Some researchers have questioned this study, however, and soccer goalkeepers continue to ignore its findings, jumping left and right. See Roger Berger, "Should I Stay or Should I Go? Optimal Decision Making in Penalty Kicks," Arbeitspapier des Lehrstuhls IV No. 1, January 2009, available at: http://papers.ssrn.com/sol3/papers.cfm?abstract_id=1628776; Paul Kedrosky, "Soccer Goalkeepers: Action Bias or Not?" September 3, 2010, available at: http://paul.kedrosky.com/archives/2010/09/soccer _goalkeep.html.

16. Gary Klein, *Sources of Power*, Chapter 6.

17. Ibid., pp. 21–22.

18. Ray Didinger, "Didinger's Game I'll Never Forget," CSNPhilly.com, September 4, 2009, http:// www.csnphilly.com/09/04/09/Didingers-Game-Ill-Never-Forget-The-Mira/landing_insider_didinger .html?blockID=73181&feedID=2227.

19. Several versions of the video of the "Miracle at the Meadowlands" are available through YouTube.

20. Steve Serby, "True Blue Fans Set for Final Game at Stadium," *New York Post*, December 26, 2009.

21. Hank Gola, "30 Years Later, Giant Disappointment of 'The Fumble' Still Lingers," *New York Daily News*, November 18, 2008.

22. Greg Garber, "Pisarcik Eager to Set Record Straight; Others Aren't," ESPN, December 2, 2008, http://sports.espn.go.com/nfl/columns/story?columnist=garber_greg&id=3694635. The word "we" was omitted from the original quote.

23. For one of the leading papers, see David Romer, "It's Fourth Down and What Does the Bellman Equation Say? A Dynamic-Programming Analysis of Football Strategy," February 2003, http://emlab .berkeley.edu/users/dromer/papers/nber9024.pdf. Belichick discussed this paper with *New York Times*

reporter David Leonhardt and said he had read and understood it. See David Leonhardt, "Incremental Analysis, with Two Yards to Go," *New York Times,* February 1, 2004.

Chapter 6

1. For example, see Alexander R. Green, Dana R. Carney, Daniel J. Pallin, Long H. Ngo, Kristal L. Raymond, Lisa I. Iezzoni, and Mahzarin R. Banaji, "Implicit Bias Among Physicians and Its Prediction of Thrombolysis Decisions for Black and White Patients," *Journal of General Internal Medicine* 22(9, September 2007): 1231–1238.

2. In addition, when the researchers asked how likely it was that Mr. Thompson's chest pain was due to heart disease, the doctors answered that heart disease was the cause (as opposed to a heart attack) more frequently for blacks than for whites.

3. Statistically, the racial disparity arose because doctors more frequently diagnosed coronary artery disease among black patients, but recommended thrombolysis roughly equally for black and white patients. The researchers' judgment was stark: "Equal treatment in the face of unequal diagnosis between the two groups constitutes a disparity." Green et al., "Implicit Bias Among Physicians," p. 7.

4. Dana R. Carney and Greg Willard, "Racial Prejudice Is Contagious," working paper, available at: http://www.columbia.edu/~dc2534/Contagion.pdf.

5. Nalini Ambady and Robert Rosenthal, "Thin Slices of Expressive Behavior as Predictors of Interpersonal Consequences: A Meta-Analysis," *Psychological Bulletin* 111(1992): 256–274.

6. Nalini Ambady and Robert Rosenthal, "Predicting Teacher Evaluations from Thin Slices of Nonverbal Behavior and Physical Attractiveness," *Journal of Personality and Social Psychology* 64(3, 1993): 431–441.

7. Gordon W. Allport, *Personality: A Psychological Interpretation* (Holt, 1937).

8. Malcolm Gladwell, *Blink: The Power of Thinking Without Thinking* (Little, Brown, 2005), p. 8.

9. Garner Resources Consulting, "Thin Slicing Your Way to Better Hiring Decisions," http://www.grgc.com/pages/117_thin_slicing_your_way_to_better_hiring_decisions.cfm.

10. Virtulink LLC, "Consulting Services," http://www.virtulinksystems.com/rfp-procurement-it-emr-ehr-consulting.php.

11. Derek Thompson, review of *Blink* by Malcolm Gladwell, http://www.wnur.org/lit/reviews/blink.php.

12. Gladwell, *Blink,* p. 8; Gladwell.com, "What Is *Blink* About?" http://www.gladwell.com/blink/index.html.

13. Nalini Ambady, Mary Anne Krabbenhoft, and Daniel Hogan, "The 30-Sec Sale: Using Thin-Slice Judgments to Evaluate Sales Effectiveness," *Journal of Consumer Psychology* 16(1, 2006): 4–13, at 5.

14. The Gottman Relationship Institute, http://www.gottman.com.

15. Gladwell, *Blink,* p, 34.

16. Nicholas Rule and Nalini Ambady, "Brief Exposures: Male Sexual Orientation Is Accurately Perceived at 50ms," *Journal of Experimental Social Psychology* 44(4, 2008): 1100–1105.

17. Dana R. Carney, C. Randall Colvin, and Judith A. Hall, "A Thin Slice Perspective on the Accuracy of First Impressions," *Journal of Research in Personality* 41(2007): 1054–1072, at 1058.

18. Ibid.

19. For example, Ekman and his colleagues have shown, controversially, that although most of us cannot tell when people are lying, some highly trained officials can pick out a liar about 80 percent of the time based on small movements in face muscles. See Paul Ekman, Maureen O'Sullivan, and Mark G. Frank, "A Few Can Catch a Liar," *Psychological Science* 10(3, 1999): 263–266.

20. Nicholas O. Rule and Nalini Ambady, "Judgments of Power from College Yearbook Photos and Later Career Success," *Social Psychology and Personality Science* 2(2, 2011):154–158.

21. Nicholas O. Rule and Nalini Ambady, "She's Got the Look: Inferences from Female Chief Executive Officers' Faces Predict Their Success," *Sex Roles* 61(2009): 644–652, at 651; see also Nicholas O. Rule and Nalini Ambady, "The Face of Success: Inferences from Chief Executive Officers' Appearance Predict Company Profits," *Psychological Science* 19(2008): 109–111.

22. Many of these studies are summarized in Alan Feingold, "Good-Looking People Are Not What We Think," *Psychological Bulletin* 111(2, 1992): 304–341. An excellent and more recent survey of the literature, with a particular focus on employment, is included in Bradley J. Ruffle and Ze'ev Shtudiner, "Are Good-Looking People More Employable?" Working Paper Series, October 2011, available at: http://papers.ssrn.com/sol3/papers.cfm?abstract_id=1705244.

23. Niclas Berggren, Henrik Jordahl, and Panu Poutvaara, "The Looks of a Winner: Beauty and Electoral Success," *Journal of Public Economics* 94(2010): 8–15.

24. Daniel S. Hamermesh and Jeff E. Biddle, "Beauty and the Labor Market," *American Economic Review* 84(5, 1994): 1174–1194.

25. Jeff E. Biddle and Daniel S. Hamermesh, "Beauty, Productivity, and Discrimination: Lawyers' Looks and Lucre," *Journal of Labor Economics* 16(1, 1998): 172–201.

26. Matthew Parrett, "Beauty and the Labor Market: Evidence from Restaurant Servers," 2007, unpublished paper.

27. There are hundreds of interesting books on the topic, ranging from Dr. Timothy Perper's *Sex Signals: The Biology of Love,* a serious and heavily footnoted 1985 classic (red cupid on the cover), to Leil Lowndes's more instructive and prurient 2001 book, *Undercover Sex Signals* (blond bombshell's dangling cleavage on the cover). If you want to understand biosocial functionality, Perper is a good guide. If you want to "learn how to become a sexual polygraph machine," Lowndes is a better choice.

28. Rule and Ambady, "She's Got the Look," p. 651; see also Rule and Ambady, "The Face of Success."

29. Ruffle and Shtudiner, "Are Good-Looking People More Employable?"

30. Ibid., p. 24.

31. Others have made similar points to Ruffle and Shtudiner. See Ramit Mizrahi, "'Hostility to the Presence of Women': Why Women Undermine Each Other in the Workplace and the Consequences for Title VII," *Yale Law Review* 113(2004): 1579–1621; Joan Marques, "Sisterhood in Short Supply in the Workplace: It's Often the Women Who Hold Back Their Female Colleagues," *Human Resource Management International Digest* 17(5, 2009): 28–31.

32. Similar conclusions hold for brain scans as for the BioPac Systems physio-measurement. Although scientists don't understand precisely why our brains react so strongly to stereotypes, some answers are emerging from brain imaging studies about the likely home of our unconscious biases. Nalini Ambady and three other researchers put sixteen volunteers in a Siemens 3T Tim Trio scanner and asked them to make a series of three-second judgments about people based on photographs. See Jonathan B. Freeman, Daniela Schiller, Nicholas O. Rule, and Nalini Ambady, "The Neural Origins of Superficial and Individuated Judgments About Ingroup and Outgroup Members," *Human Brain Mapping* 31(2010): 150–159. Half of the judgments were "superficial" and half were "individuated." A superficial judgment involves putting a person into a social category based exclusively on their appearance ("Evan is male; is he aggressive?"). An individuated judgment involves putting a person into a social category based on their idiosyncratic attributes and qualities ("Evan likes fighting; is he aggressive?").

Unlike Ambady's other work, the point of these questions was not to test whether the subjects were biased or would answer correctly (the questions were intentionally ambiguous). The point was to see which parts of their brains were triggered by superficial questions versus individuated ones. The brain scans of the subjects showed that they made superficial judgments primarily in the amygdalae, the neural regions that specialize in automatic processing, while individuated judgments were spread around a neural network of several other brain regions. It appears from this research that the amygdalae, though important and useful in numerous ways, also play a major role when we form implicit biases.

33. Dana R. Carney, Amy J. C. Cuddy, and Andy Yap, "Power Posing: Brief Nonverbal Displays Affect Neuroendocrine Levels and Risk Tolerance," *Psychological Science* 21(10, 2010): 1363–1368.

34. Ibid., p. 9. Testosterone has been shown to blunt social emotions such as guilt, embarrassment, and anxiety; it makes both men and women feel less empathy. See Erno Jan Hermans, Peter Putman, and Jack van Honk, "Testosterone Administration Reduces Empathetic Behavior: A Facial Mimicry Study," *Psychoneuroendocrinology* 31(2006): 859–866; Erno Jan Hermans, Peter Putman, Johanna M. Baas, Nynke

M. Gecks, J. Leo Kenemans, and Jack van Honk, "Exogenous Testosterone Attenuates the Integrated Central Stress Response in Healthy Young Women," *Psychoneuroendocrinology* 32(2007): 1052–1061. For example, people with high testosterone are more likely to have demonstrated greater success on Wall Street. In a separate study, Carney and Malia Mason, a professor at Columbia, found that men and women are more likely to be utilitarian in their choices—tallying up costs and benefits instead of referring to a moral code of right and wrong—if they have higher levels of testosterone. See Dana R. Carney and Malia F. Mason, "Moral Decisions and Testosterone: When the Ends Justify the Means," *Journal of Experimental and Social Psychology* 46(4, 2010): 668–671.

35. John Gottman, Julie Gottman, and Joan DeClaire, *Ten Lessons to Transform Your Marriage: America's Love Lab Experts Share Their Strategies for Strengthening Your Relationship* (Crown, 2006). Although John Gottman claims that his models for predicting which newlywed couples will remain married is 80 to 95 percent accurate, some commentators have disputed Gottman's predictive power. According to journalist Laurie Abraham, "What Gottman did wasn't really a prediction of the future but a formula built after the couples' outcomes were already known. This isn't to say that developing such formulas isn't a valuable—indeed, a critical—first step in being able to make a prediction. The next step, however—one absolutely required by the scientific method—is to apply your equation to a fresh sample to see whether it actually works. That is especially necessary with small data slices (such as 57 couples), because patterns that appear important are more likely to be mere flukes. But Gottman never did that." Laurie Abraham, "Can You Really Predict the Success of a Marriage in 15 Minutes?" *Slate*, March 8, 2010. The Gottmans dispute this claim and say that their model is predictive. In any event, couples continue to flock to the Gottmans, and the Gottmans continue to use two days, not two minutes, as the benchmark length of their program.

36. Carney and Willard, "Racial Prejudice Is Contagious," p. 13.

37. Ibid., p. 12.

Chapter 7

1. George Zebrowski, interview with Arthur C. Clarke, *Sci Fi Weekly*, June 30, 2008, http://web.archive.org/web/20080723051103/, http://www.scifi.com/sfw/interviews/sfw19051.html.

2. Stefan Klein, *The Secret Pulse of Time*, p. 54.

3. Even migraine headaches can cause time to slow down or rush forward. See Joseph Dooley, Kevin Gordon, and Peter Camfield, "The Rushes: A Migraine Variant with Hallucinations of Time," *Clinical Pediatrics* (Philadelphia) 29(9, 1990): 536–538.

4. See Chess Stetson, Matthew P. Fiesta, and David M. Eagleman, "Does Time Really Slow Down During a Frightening Event?" *PLoS One* 2(12, 2007): e1295. Eagleman describes several related experiments, as well as his more general theories about identity and the brain, in his fascinating book *Incognito: The Secret Lives of the Brain* (Canongate/Pantheon Books, 2011).

5. Eagleman's interpretation of this event is controversial, but we don't need to enter this fray to get the central point: duration dilation is a real, real-time experience. For a critique of the free-fall study, see Marshal Barnes, "Duration Dilation and the Flawed Frightening Experiment," 2007, http://aet-radal.blogdrive.com. The main critique is that subjects overestimate the time because landing in the net is so smooth. (And of course, no one wants to test falling sixteen stories to land on a hard surface.)

6. David M. Eagleman, "Brain Time," Eagleman Laboratory for Perception and Action, June 24, 2009, http://www.eaglemanlab.net/time/essay-brain-time.

7. Levine, *A Geography of Time*, p. 34, n. 21.

8. Clark is a huge fan of "flow" theory, from the 1990 national best-seller *Flow: The Psychology of Optimal Experience*, by Mihaly Csikszentmihalyi, which describes various ways in which human beings can obtain joy, creativity, and a process of total involvement with life. Clark uses the word "flow" a lot, so I will too.

9. Institute for Social Research (ISR), "Persuasive Speech: The Way We, Um, Talk Sways Our Listeners," ISR Sampler, May 16, 2011, http://www.sampler.isr.umich.edu/2011/research/persuasive-speech-the-way -we-um-talk-sways-our-listeners/.

Chapter 8

1. Dr. Iannis's line about love appears in both Louis de Bernières's book *Corelli's Mandolin: A Novel* (Vintage, 1995) and in the 2001 film *Captain Corelli's Mandolin*. See "Memorable Quotes for *Captain Corelli's Mandolin*," http://www.imdb.com/title/tt0238112/quotes.

2. For an excellent article on the various online dating sites, see Nick Paumgarten, "Looking for Someone," *The New Yorker*, July 4, 2011.

3. Tamar Caspi Shnall, "More Picture Perfect," JDate.com, http://www.jdate.com/blog/2010-07/more -picture-perfect.

4. Paumgarten, "Looking for Someone."

5. Thomas Suddendorf and Michael C. Corbalis, "The Evolution of Foresight: What Is Mental Time Travel, and Is It Unique to Humans?" *Behavioral and Brain Sciences* 30(2007): 299–351.

6. Elizabeth H. M. Sterck and Valérie Dufour, "First Test, Then Judge Future-Oriented Behavior in Animals," *Behavior and Brain Sciences* 30(3, 2007): 333–334.

7. See Thomas R. Zentall, "Mental Time Travel in Animals: A Challenging Question," *Behavioral Process* 72(2, 2006): 173–183.

8. Sterck and Dufour, "First Test," p. 334.

9. In 2011 scientists published a study of bonobos that replicated experiments with young children from the 1950s: both groups learned to delay gratification for similar periods of time when the source of the reward was more reliable. Jeffrey R. Stevens, Alexandra G. Rosati, Sarah R. Heilbronner, and Nelly Mühlhoff, "Waiting for Grapes: Expectancy and Delayed Gratification in Bonobos," *International Journal of Comparative Psychology* 24(2011): 99–111. The bonobos that delayed longer probably wouldn't later score well on the Scholastic Aptitude Test, though.

10. Daniel Gilbert, *Stumbling on Happiness* (Knopf, 2006), p. 16.

11. Robert Browning, "A Grammarian's Funeral" (1896), available at: http://www.online-literature .com/robert-browning/2768.

12. Helen Fisher, *Why We Love: The Nature and Chemistry of Romantic Love* (Holt Paperbacks, 2004).

13. See C. Sue Carter and Lowell L. Getz, "Monogamy and the Prairie Vole," *Scientific American* 268(1993): 100–106; and Lowell L. Getz and C. Sue Carter, "Prairie-Vole Partnerships," *American Scientist* 84(1, 1996): 56–62. Sue Carter is married to Stephen Porges, the behavioral neuroscientist who studies heart rate variation, making them perhaps the only human couple to form a strong monogamous bond while researching strong monogamous bonds.

14. See Robert Coram, *Boyd: The Fighter Pilot Who Changed the Art of War* (Back Bay Books/Little, Brown, 2002), ch. 24. The primary difference between my "observe-process-act" approach and Boyd's is that I collapse "orient-decide" into "process" to avoid complexities that arise from interpreting the overlap between "orientation" and "decision," as well as between "decision" and "action." The other crucial aspect of the OODA Loop is that it is a loop, repeatedly cycling from "act" back to "observe." This dynamic is particularly important during battle, when action and interaction quickly create a new environment and what a person sees unfolding will guide his future orientation and decisions. Military strategists who are wedded to OODA and resist my friendly amendment might still use the OODA Loop for battle, but adopt "observe-process-act" for other daily decisions.

15. One major relationship question is how long to wait before responding to a marriage proposal. The ideal amount of delay depends on several factors, including how much time you have spent together, your previous relationships, your age, any previous conversations about marriage, and whether the person proposing is sober. If someone proposes during a first date, you probably should politely say you need

some time to get to know each other better first. But if the proposal is expected and your reaction is positive, delay will only leave your future spouse with an uncomfortable memory and maybe even a few suspicions—you should just say yes right away.

Chapter 9

1. Susan Schmidt, "Teamsters Contribution to Clinton Effort Probed," *Washington Post*, October 9, 1997, p. A01; Thomas Galvin, "GOP's Prez Bombshell Is a Dud," *New York Daily News*, October 9, 1997, p. 34; Michael Kranish, "Thompson Apologizes to Clinton," *Boston Globe*, October 9, 1997, p. A1.

2. In January 2002, I was called as an expert to testify during the first Senate hearings on the collapse of Enron. When I raised questions about footnote 16 of Enron's 2000 annual report, which contained cryptic disclosures of some of that company's most opaque and horrific deals, Senator Thompson interrupted me to remark that he was familiar with footnote 16. But when I became excited about our apparent parallel understanding of the Enron fiasco, he interrupted me again and said he was only joking. Since this was such a dramatic moment for me, and since most people don't believe this story when I tell them, here is the full, unedited, official transcript of our brief back-and-forth (see Partnoy, *F.I.A.S.C.O.*, p. 258):

MR. PARTNOY: I would draw your attention to footnote 16 of Enron's 2000 Annual Report.
SEN. THOMPSON: I'm very familiar with it.
MR. PARTNOY: If you can tell me what's going on—
SEN. THOMPSON: Just kidding.

3. Stephen F. Hayes, "From the Courthouse to the White House," *The Weekly Standard*, April 23, 2007, cover; Matea Gold and Scott Collins, "Reality Role for a Television DA," *Chicago Tribune*, July 27, 2005, p. 3; Eleanor Clift, Evan Thomas, and Michael Isikoff, "The Role of a Lifetime," *Newsweek*, February 3, 1997, p. 30.

4. Schmidt, "Teamsters Contribution to Clinton Effort Probed," p. A01; Galvin, "GOP's Prez Bombshell Is a Dud," p. 34; Kranish, "Thompson Apologizes to Clinton," p. A1.

5. Aaron Lazare, *On Apology* (Oxford University Press, 2004), p. 171.

6. Ibid.

7. Cynthia McPherson Frantz and Courtney Bennigson, "Better Late Than Early: The Influence of Timing on Apology Effectiveness," *Journal of Experimental Social Psychology* 41(2005): 201–207. Previous studies had demonstrated the general effectiveness of apologies, but mentioned the importance of timing and delay only in passing. See, for example, Jeffrey Z. Rubin, Dean G. Pruitt, and Sung Hee Kim, *Social Conflict: Escalation, Stalemate, and Settlement*, 2nd ed. (McGraw-Hill, 1994), p. 165 ("if improperly timed or meant insincerely, an apology can arouse suspicion on the part of the Other"); Christina E. Mitchell, "Effects of Apology on Marital and Family Relationships," *Family Therapy* (1989): 282–287, at 285 ("If an abbreviated apology is given immediately following a transgression, it may be perceived as superficial and insincere").

8. Frantz and Bennigson, "Better Late Than Early," p. 204.

9. Ibid., p. 205.

10. Some unpublished research appears to support these studies. See Erinn Squires and Michael J. A. Wohl, "Timing Is Everything: When an Apology Is Given Affects Empathy, Perceived Responsibility, Relationship Closeness, and Willingness to Forgive," poster presented at the eleventh annual meeting of the Society for Personality and Social Psychology (SPSP), Las Vegas (January 2010); Erinn C. Squires, "Timing Is Everything: The Time at Which an Apology Is Given Affects Willingness to Forgive," master's thesis, Carleton University (2009); Sarah J. Zilzer and Cynthia McPherson Frantz, "The Influence of Timing on Apology Effectiveness: Exploring the Phenomenon of a 'Too Late' Apology," poster presented at the annual meeting of the American Psychological Society, New Orleans (June 2002).

11. Lazare, *On Apology*, p. 171.

12. Aaron Lazare, "Apology in Medical Practice: An Emerging Clinical Skill," *Journal of the American Medical Association* 296(11, 2006): 1401–1404, at 1402.

13. TMZ.com, the online celebrity gossip site, which reported on Tracy Morgan's slurs, also covered Morgan's attempts to repair the damage. See "Tracy Morgan: I'm Going Back to Nashville to Apologize,"

TMZ.com, June 13, 2011, http://www.tmz.com/2011/06/13/tracy-morgan-glaad-anti-gay-comedy-routine-homophobic-stab-son-homeless-ali-forney-center-new-york-tennessee.

14. Dave Itzkoff, "Comedian, Chastened, Gets Back to Laughs," *New York Times,* June 27, 2011, p. 1.

Chapter 10

1. Akerlof and Stiglitz shared the 2001 Nobel Memorial Prize in Economic Sciences with Michael Spence for their work on information asymmetry, the idea that markets do not efficiently allocate resources when there is a large gap between the information available to sellers and buyers. Akerlof's most famous paper—one of the most frequently cited papers in the history of economics—is George A. Akerlof, "The Market for Lemons: Quality Uncertainty and the Market Mechanism," *Quarterly Journal of Economics* 84(3, 1970): 488–500. In this paper, Akerlof uses the market for used cars as an example of the "lemon effect": where the quality of cars is low, the owners of good cars will not put their cars up for sale because buyers, who lack information, will assume those good cars are merely average. As a result, the overall quality of used cars being sold is low, and it is difficult for sellers and buyers of higher-quality used cars to find each other. Five years after Akerlof's article was published, the federal government passed a national "lemon law" to protect buyers and try to improve this "lemons" problem.

2. Piers Steel, "The Nature of Procrastination: A Meta-Analytic and Theoretical Review of Quintessential Self-Regulatory Failure," *Psychological Bulletin* 133(1, 2007): 65–94, at 66.

3. Peter F. Drucker, *The Effective Executive: The Definitive Guide to Getting the Right Things Done* (HarperCollins, 1967).

4. Jane B. Burka and Lenora M. Yuen, *Procrastination: Why You Do It, What to Do About It* (Da Capo Press, 1983).

5. Stephen R. Covey, *The Seven Habits of Highly Effective People* (Simon & Schuster, 1989); Stephen R. Covey, A. Roger Merrill, and Rebecca R. Merrill, *First Things First* (Simon & Schuster, 1994).

6. David Allen, *Getting Things Done: The Art of Stress-Free Productivity* (Penguin Putnam, 2001).

7. Piers Steel, *The Procrastination Equation: How to Stop Putting Things Off and Start Getting Things Done* (HarperCollins, 2011).

8. Timothy A. Pychyl, Jonathan M. Lee, Rachelle Thibodeau, and Allan Blunt, "Five Days of Emotion: An Experience Sampling Study of Undergraduate Student Procrastination," *Journal of Social Behavior and Psychology* 15(2000): 239–254.

9. Jesse S. Harriott and Joseph R. Ferrari, "Prevalence of Procrastination Among Samples of Adults," *Psychological Reports* 78(1996): 611–616.

10. On May 15, 2008, Slate used the title "Procrasti-Nation" in publishing a list of comments giving a "glimpse at the panoply of American procrastination," from cowboys, astronauts, forest rangers, imams, and even federal judge and author Richard Posner, at http://www.slate.com/articles/life/procrastination/2008/05/procrastination.html. Judge Posner is adamantly anti-procrastination: "It causes problems for the people who are counting on you to complete things in a timely fashion and it makes your own life more difficult."

11. Although there were negative references to procrastination before the eighteenth century, many scholars argue that the industrial revolution was a turning point for procrastination because of the time deadlines that arose from technology. Some of the early critiques of procrastination, including a speech by Cicero denouncing Antonius, some musings by Thucydides, an admonition by the poet Hesiod that "a sluggish worker does not fill his barn," and a passage by Krishna, are collected in Steel, *The Nature of Procrastination.* Steel recognizes the increased focus on procrastination beginning around 1750, but argues that the concept nevertheless has been important throughout human history. He also notes that at least one of the alleged historical works on procrastination, cited in the scholarly literature, was actually an elaborate joke: a book about procrastination that was never completed (Steel, *The Nature of Procrastination,* p. 66). So much for peer review and cite checkers.

12. Angela Hsin Chun Chu and Jin Nam Choi, "Rethinking Procrastination: Positive Effects of 'Active' Procrastination Behavior on Attitudes and Performance," *Journal of Social Psychology* 145(2005): 245–264.

13. "Fans of Procrastination Say It Boosts Control, Preserves Self-Esteem," *Wall Street Journal,* February 9, 2005, p. B1.

14. Steel, *The Procrastination Equation,* p. 3.

15. Sidney J. Blatt and Paul Quinlan, "Punctual and Procrastinating Students: A Study of Temporal Parameters," *Journal of Counseling Psychology* 31(1967): 169–174; W. Hugh Missildine, *Your Inner Child of the Past* (Simon & Schuster, 1964); Laura J. Solomon and Esther D. Rothblum, "Academic Procrastination: Frequency and Cognitive-Behavioral Correlates," *Journal of Counseling Psychology* 31(4, 1984): 503–509; William McCown, Thomas Petzel, and Patricia Rupert, "An Experimental Study of Some Hypothesized Behaviors and Personality Variables of College Student Procrastinators," *Personality and Individual Differences* 8(6, 1987): 781–786.

16. Chun Chu and Nam Choi, "Rethinking Procrastination"; Jin Nam Choi and Sarah V. Moran, "Why Not Procrastinate? Development and Validation of a New Active Procrastination Scale," *Journal of Social Psychology* 149(2, 2009): 195–211.

17. Carolyn Fischer, "Read This Paper Later: Procrastination with Time-Consistent Preferences," Discussion Paper 99-19 (Resources for the Future, April 1999), p. 28.

18. George A. Akerlof, "Procrastination and Obedience," *American Economic Review* 81(2, 1991): 1–19.

19. See Steel, *The Procrastination Equation,* p. 66.

20. See George Loewenstein, Scott Rick, and Jonathan D. Cohen, "Neuroeconomics," *Annual Review of Psychology* 59(2008): 647–672.

21. One excellent recent compilation of some of this wisdom, with a philosophical bent, is Chrisoula Andreou and Mark D. White, eds., *The Thief of Time: Philosophical Essays on Procrastination* (Oxford University Press, 2010).

22. Piers Steel's book *The Procrastination Equation* is the most thorough and recent attempt to frame a global theory; it is closely related to Akerlof's work and incorporates similar concepts.

23. Akerlof's lecture opened up research on procrastination with one simple sentence near the beginning that became a road map for a generation: "Procrastination occurs when present costs are unduly salient in comparison with future costs, leading individuals to postpone tasks until tomorrow without foreseeing that when tomorrow comes, the required action will be delayed yet again." Akerlof, "Procrastination and Obedience."

24. Sometimes the opposite is true, and we prefer to receive payment later. For example, On Amir and Dan Ariely have found that although we prefer to receive certain products and services right away, sometimes we like delay. If we are told we can kiss our favorite movie star, we generally prefer for the kiss to come later, not right away, so we can savor it. Likewise, Amir and Ariely found that the subjects of an experiment preferred to receive a piece of electronic equipment right away, but preferred receiving a ticket to a concert that would take place in the future later so they could savor the opportunity. On Amir and Dan Ariely, "Decisions by Rules: The Case of Unwillingness to Pay for Beneficial Delays," *Journal of Marketing Research* 44(2007): 142–152; see also George Loewenstein, "Anticipation and the Valuation of Delayed Consumption," *Economic Journal* 97(387, September 1987): 666–684. It wasn't likely that Stiglitz preferred receiving his box later.

25. Some economists fought back against Akerlof's views, labeling them "a radical rejection of the neoclassical economic model of man as a rational, self-interested utility maximizer." Gary M. Anderson and Walter Block, "Procrastination, Obedience, and Public Policy: The Irrelevance of Salience," *American Journal of Economics and Sociology* 54(2, 1995): 201–215, at 203. Anderson and Block concluded that, "if Akerlof is correct in asserting that this kind of behavior is common, this fact had radical, and troubling implications for economics" (204).

26. Akerlof didn't send the box until he could send it along with a friend's shipment to the United States. James Surowiecki, who writes "The Financial Page" at *The New Yorker,* has suggested that, "given the vagaries of intercontinental mail, it is possible that Akerlof made it back to the States before Stiglitz's shirts did." James Surowiecki, "Later: What Does Procrastination Tell Us About Ourselves?" *The New Yorker,* October 11, 2010.

27. Paying the same amount in the future, without any interest, is like getting a zero-interest loan. We should love zero-interest loans; they are like free money. While I was in law school, I got zero-interest-rate cash advances on several credit cards and simply put the money in the bank. After a few months, I withdrew the money, repaid the card balances, and kept the remaining amount. When I began working on Wall Street, a friend from the United Kingdom one-upped me: he told our employer he needed a line of credit to convert his pay from U.S. dollars, and then he used the zero-interest loan to make a quarter of a million dollars trading foreign currency derivatives.

28. Paul A. Samuelson, "A Note on Measurement of Utility," *Review of Economic Studies* 4(2, 1937): 155–161.

29. More specifically, the assumption was that humans discount *exponentially* in a *time-consistent* manner, meaning that for a given discount rate (r) over a specified time period (T), the value in today's terms of a future payment ($) equals $ divided by $(1 + r)^T$. For example, the "present value," or value in today's terms, of $110 in one year at a rate of 10 percent is $110/(1 + 0.1)^1 = \$100$.

30. Richard A. Thaler, "Some Empirical Evidence of Dynamic Inconsistency," *Economics Letters* 8(3, 1981): 201–207.

31. George Loewenstein and Richard H. Thaler, "Anomalies: Intertemporal Choice," *Journal of Economic Perspectives* 3(1989): 181–193.

32. George Ainslie, *Picoeconomics* (Cambridge University Press, 1992).

33. George A. Akerlof, "Behavioral Microeconomics and Macroeconomic Behavior," Nobel Prize Lecture, December 8, 2001.

34. James E. Mazur, "Tests of an Equivalence Rule for Fixed and Variable Reinforcer Delays," *Journal of Experimental Psychology: Animal Behavior Process* 10(1984): 426–436; James E. Mazur, "Theories of Probabilistic Reinforcement," *Journal of the Experimental Analysis of Behavior* 51(1989): 87–99.

35. Hyperbolic discounting follows a different equation than exponential discounting, one that Mazur showed better fits the actual behavior of pigeons (and, he suggested, sometimes human behavior as well). In the hyperbolic equation Mazur proposed, instead of dividing by $(1 + r)^T$, we divide by $(1 + K \times T)$, where K is a decay parameter that determines how quickly the rate declines. James E. Mazur, "Procrastination by Pigeons: Preference for Larger, More Delayed Work Requirements," *Journal of the Experimental Analysis of Behavior* 65(1996): 159–171; James E. Mazur, "Procrastination by Pigeons with Fixed-Interval Response," *Journal of the Experimental Analysis of Behavior* 69(1998): 185–197; see also Marvin Z. Deluty, "Self-Control and Impulsiveness Involving Aversive Events," *Journal of Experimental Psychology: Animal Behavior Processes* 4(1978): 250–266.

36. Sandi Kahn Shelton, "SCSU Prof James Mazur Finds We're a Lot Like Pigeons When It Comes to Procrastination," *New Haven Register*, September 11, 2011, http://www.nhregister.com/articles/2011/09/11/life/doc4e6d7ad9169a1961387742.txt?viewmode=fullstory.

37. David I. Laibson, "Golden Eggs and Hyperbolic Discounting," *Quarterly Journal of Economics* 62(1997): 443–478; David I. Laibson, "Hyperbolic Discount Functions, Undersaving, and Savings Policy," Working Paper 5635 (National Bureau of Economic Research, 1996).

38. The newer models include two components meant to describe the trade-offs between our immediate and future preferences. The idea is that one part of our brain (the "beta" part, in the corticolimbic regions) responds automatically in the short term and another part (the "delta" part, in the lateral prefrontal regions) responds more deliberatively in the long term. The beta system is impatient and emotional; the delta system thinks about the future using reason. For example, if you put people in an fMRI machine and ask them if they want an Amazon gift certificate today, the beta region will light up. If you ask them if they want the same gift certificate in a few weeks, the delta region will light up. See George Ainslie and John Monterosso, "A Marketplace in the Brain," *Science* 306(2004): 421–423; Samuel M. McClure, David I. Laibson, George Loewenstein, and Jonathan D. Cohen, "Separate Neural Systems Value Immediacy and Delayed Monetary Rewards," *Science* 306(2004): 503–507.

It is worth noting that when economists attempt to describe human behavior using high-level math, it often doesn't go particularly well. Because the math is complex, people are prone to rely on it without question. And the equations often are vulnerable to unrealistic assumptions. Most recently, the financial crisis was caused in part by overreliance on statistical models that didn't take into account the chances of declines in housing prices. But that was just the most recent iteration: the collapse of Enron, the implosion of the hedge fund Long-Term Capital Management, the billions of dollars lost by rogue traders Kweku Adoboli, Jerome Kerviel, Nick Leeson, and others—all of these fiascos have, at their heart, a mistaken reliance on complex math. Nassim N. Taleb has written widely and wisely about the deception in financial models, most notably in his book *The Black Swan: The Impact of the Highly Improbable* (Random House, 2007). In retrospect, many economic models look absurd. For my college honors thesis, I wrote computer code, using something called "simplicial algorithms," that was supposed to accurately depict Mexico's economy. Though not particularly useful, the model looked cool and I received credit for the thesis. But it didn't account for the chances of the Mexican government radically devaluing the peso, as it did in December 1994.

39. The mathematical language that economists use to describe human "utility functions" is complicated, and there is an ongoing debate about the role of "normal" exponential discounting and "abnormal" hyperbolic discounting in human decision-making. We cannot possibly resolve that debate here, and I don't want to try, but I do want to acknowledge its existence to any economists who might read this book (and who make it back to this endnote). I am using the term "present biased" to describe how modern economic theory reflects our preference for immediate returns and our aversion to immediate costs. Ted O'Donoghue and Matthew Rabin have developed more nuanced models of present bias that depend on our degree of sophistication. See Ted O'Donoghue and Matthew Rabin, "Choice and Procrastination," *Quarterly Journal of Economics* 66(2001): 121–160; and Ted O'Donoghue and Matthew Rabin, "Doing It Now or Later," *American Economic Review* 89(1999): 103–124.

40. Some studies have found that time preferences don't fit hyperbolic discounting. In fact, some studies show that we sometimes have negative discounting, where essentially we would rather just get something out of the way, even though it would be less costly to incur the cost in the future. In one experiment, subjects were told that they would have to listen to an annoying noise for twenty minutes. They listened to a three-minute sample and then expressed their preferences. A majority of the subjects said they preferred listening to the noise that day over two or four weeks later. Marco Casari and Davide Dragone, "Impatience, Anticipatory Feelings, and Uncertainty: A Dynamic Experiment on Time Preferences," Jena Economic Research Papers 2010-087 (Friedrich Schiller University and Max Planck Institute of Economics, 2010). So-called quasi-hyperbolic discounting is rarely used by psychologists, but is used more extensively by economists. John R. Doyle, "Survey of Time Preference, Delay Discounting Models," http://papers.ssrn .com/sol3/papers.cfm?abstract_id=1685861, p. 11.

41. Piers Steel has suggested that there is a "procrastination equation," which is similar to hyperbolic discounting. The procrastination equation, in its simple form, says that we can calculate our level of motivation by dividing "expectancy times value" by "impulsiveness times delay." The numerator captures the concept of "expected value," the weighted-average payoff we will get from some activity. The more likely we are to get something, or the more valuable it is, the higher this payoff will be. Conversely, the denominator captures the reduction in value that comes from our impulsiveness and delay. The more impulsive we are, or the longer we have to wait, the lower this payoff will be. The challenge is to reduce our impulsiveness, so we can more accurately gauge future payoffs. The procrastination equation predicts that our work pace will start off slow and then spike at the end, like a hyperbola. See Steel, *The Procrastination Equation*, ch. 2.

42. Shelton, "SCSU Prof James Mazur Finds We're a Lot Like Pigeons When It Comes to Procrastination."

43. Christopher F. Chabris et al., "Individual Laboratory-Measured Discount Rates Predict Field Behavior," *Journal of Risk and Uncertainty* 37(2008): 237–269. Alcohol and drug abusers, smokers, and pathological gamblers all have higher discount rates than average. James MacKillop et al., "Alcohol Demand, Delayed Reward Discounting, and Craving in Relation to Drinking and Alcohol Use Disorders," *Journal of Abnormal Psychology* 119(1, 2010): 106–114. Heroin users have discount rates that are twice as high as those of non-addicts. Kris N. Kirby, Nancy M. Petry, and Warren K. Bickel, "Heroin Addicts Have Higher Discount Rates for Delayed Rewards Than Non-Drug-Using Controls," *Journal of Experimental Psychology: General* 128(1999): 78–87. Impatience and impulsivity, the hallmarks of a high-discount-rate

person, are correlated with sexual motivation as well. Men appear to have higher discount rates after they view photographs of attractive women, but not after viewing photos of unattractive women. (Women's discount rates apparently don't change when they view photographs of men, attractive or not.) Margo Wilson and Martin Daly, "Do Pretty Women Inspire Men to Discount the Future?" *Biology Letters* 271(2004): S177–S179.

44. Stephan Meier and Charles Sprenger, "Present-Biased Preferences and Credit Card Borrowing," *American Economic Journal: Applied Economics* 2(1, 2010): 193–210. People who ask for and receive credit counseling have lower discount rates than those who do not. Stephan Meier and Charles Sprenger, "Discounting Financial Literacy: Time Preferences and Participation in Financial Education Programs," IZA Discussion Paper 3507 (Institute for the Study of Labor, 2008).

45. Daniel Kahneman and Dan Lovallo, "Timid Choices and Bold Forecasts: A Cognitive Perspective on Risk and Risk Taking," *Management Science* 39(1, 1993): 17–31.

46. Marianne Bertrand and Adair Morse, "Information Disclosure, Cognitive Biases, and Payday Borrowing," Chicago Booth Research Paper 10-01 (University of Chicago, Booth School of Business, October 2009), http://papers.ssrn.com/sol3/papers.cfm?abstract_id=1532213.

47. Mattias Sutter, Martin G. Kocher, Daniela Rützler, and Stefan T. Trautmann, "Impatience and Uncertainty: Experimental Decisions Predict Adolescents' Field Behavior," IZA Discussion Paper 5404 (Institute for the Study of Labor, 2010).

48. Marco Castillo, Paul Ferraro, Jeff Jordan, and Ragan Petrie, "The Today and Tomorrow of Kids: Time Preferences and Educational Outcomes of Children," *Journal of Public Economics* 95(11–12, 2011): 1377–1385.

49. Angela L. Duckworth and Martin E. P. Seligman, "Self-Discipline Outdoes IQ in Predicting Academic Performance of Adolescents," *Psychological Science* 16(12, 2005): 939–944.

50. Researchers have found that impatience and procrastination are related to the same underlying "present bias" phenomenon. See O'Donoghue and Rabin, "Doing It Now or Later"; see also George Loewenstein, Daniel Read, and Roy F. Baumeister, eds., *Time and Decision: Economic and Psychological Perspectives on Intertemporal Choice* (Russell Sage Foundation, 2003).

51. Ernesto Reuben, Paola Sapienza, and Luigi Zingales, "Procrastination and Impatience," Working Paper Series, May 1, 2010, http://papers.ssrn.com/sol3/papers.cfm?abstract_id=1915467.

52. For a comprehensive discussion of legal issues related to procrastination, see Manuel Utset, "Procrastination and the Law," in Andreou and White, *The Thief of Time*, pt. III(15).

53. The psychologist Piers Steel says this kind of planning can be helpful: "Impulsive people find it difficult to plan work ahead of time and even after they start, they are easily distracted. Procrastination inevitably follows." Steel, *The Procrastination Equation*, p. 14.

54. Bertrand and Morse, *Information Disclosure, Cognitive Biases, and Payday Borrowing*.

55. Richard H. Thaler and Cass R. Sunstein, *Nudge: Improving Decisions About Health, Wealth, and Happiness* (Yale University Press, 2008).

56. See Henri C. Schouwenburg, Clarry H. Lay, and Timothy A. Pychyl, *Counseling the Procrastinator in Academic Settings* (American Psychological Association, 2004); Henri C. Schouwenburg and JanTjeerd Groenewoud, "Study Motivation Under Social Temptation: Effects of Trait Procrastination," *Personality and Individual Differences* 30(2, 2001): 299–340. In one experiment, Dan Ariely and Klaus Wertenbroch recruited students to proofread three ten-page texts during a three-week period. Payment would depend on how many grammar and spelling errors they caught (there were 100 total). They divided the proofreaders into three groups: a "last minute" group was told simply to submit all three texts at the end of three weeks; a "weekly deadlines" group was told to submit one text at the end of each week; and a "you decide" group was told to set their own deadlines. The "last minute" group spent the least amount of time on the task, just fifty-one minutes, and they found the fewest errors. The "weekly deadlines" group spent the most time on the task, eighty-four minutes, and found the most errors. The "you decide" group was in between. The implication is that for this kind of straightforward task, if we want students to do well we should give them deadlines. Just as the "you decide" group didn't do as well as the "weekly deadlines" group, students left to their own devices won't perform as well as they will when we give them specific deadlines.

In a related (and more famous) experiment that was reported along with the proofreading study, Ariely and Wertenbroch told students to set deadlines for themselves for three papers required for a course. They could pick any date they wanted in the fourteen-week course, including the last day of class. On average, the dates were thirty-three, twenty, and ten days before the end of the term, for each paper. When Ariely and Wertenbroch repeated the experiment with just one paper, students chose an even earlier deadline— forty-two days before the end of the term. Giving the students flexibility instead of just telling them the papers were due at three fixed times during the semester resulted in lower grades. Dan Ariely and Klaus Wertenbroch, "Procrastination, Deadlines, and Performance," *Psychological Science* 13(3, 2002): 219–224. One puzzle in this study was that, even though they were paid less, the "last minute" participants reported enjoying the task far more than the others. Getting things done might not be fun.

57. David M. Garner and Susan C. Wooley, "Confronting the Failure of Behavioral and Dietary Treatments of Obesity," *Clinical Psychology Review* 11(1991): 767.

58. Tara Parker-Pope, "The Fat Trap," *New York Times Magazine,* December 28, 2011.

59. George Ainslie, "Procrastination: The Basic Impulse," paper presented at the CUNY Workshop, New York (July 9, 2008), p. 9.

60. Paul Graham, "Good and Bad Procrastination," December 2005, http://www.paulgraham.com/procrastination.html.

61. John Perry, "How to Procrastinate and Still Get Things Done," *Chronicle of Higher Education,* February 23, 1996.

62. Many writers follow something close to Perry's model. We do other tasks first and delay writing until the last possible moment. In September 2011, PublicAffairs, the publisher of this book, had already created the book's cover, fixed a publication date of June 26, 2012, and posted the book for pre-order on Amazon.com. Yet at that time I had only just sent Clive Priddle, my editor, the first three chapters, and had not even started writing what is now the second half of this book. You might rebuke me for procrastinating (I am typing this endnote on January 31, 2012), but I am in good company. For example, the brilliant writer Michael Lewis says this about how he approaches a day of writing: "Well, I get up, take my child to school, then come back to my office and usually procrastinate until I panic, and then I write. I procrastinate to a point where I'm filled with self-loathing and then I start writing. It's usually a state of self-loathing that gets me going." Lewis follows a similar approach over the longer term: he puts off the actual writing of a book as long as he can, and then he writes really fast. For *The Big Short,* he says, "I did a year of wandering around and learning, but the first words were laid down on paper on August 15 and I finished the book the beginning of January. But I wasn't through the first thirty or forty pages until early October." Alicia Whitaker, "Magic and Self-Loathing in Berkeley," Huffington Post Books, March 22, 2010, available at: http://www.huffingtonpost.com/alicia-whitaker/magic-and-self-loathing-i_b_507965.html.

Chapter 11

1. The authors of this study analyzed Cramer's recommendations from June 2005 and February 2009. Joseph Engelberg, Caroline Sasseville, and Jared Williams, "Market Madness? The Case of *Mad Money*," *Management Science* 58(2, 2012): 351–364.

2. See Robert J. Shiller, *Irrational Exuberance* (Crown Business, 2006); George A. Akerlof and Robert J. Shiller, *Animal Spirits: How Human Psychology Drives the Economy, and Why It Matters for Global Capitalism* (Princeton University Press, 2010); Jason Zweig, *Your Money and Your Brain: How the New Science of Neuroeconomics Can Make You Rich* (Simon & Schuster, 2007); Hersh Shefrin, *Beyond Greed and Fear: Finance and the Psychology of Investing* (Oxford University Press, 2000); Edward Chancellor, *Devil Take the Hindmost: A History of Financial Speculation* (Plume, 2000); Gur Huberman and Tomer Regev, "Speculating on a Cure for Cancer: A Non-Event That Made Stock Prices Soar," *Journal of Finance* 56(2001): 387–396. Professor Peter H. Huang has written widely about the role of emotions in investing and market regulation. See Peter H. Huang, "How Do Securities Laws Influence Affect, Happiness, and Trust?" *Journal of Business and Technology Law* 3(2, 2008): 1301–1351; Peter H. Huang, "Regulation, Irrational Exuberance, and Anxiety in Securities Markets," in Francesco Parisi and Vernon L. Smith, eds., *The Law and Economics*

of Irrational Behavior (Stanford University Press, 2005). There is a wave of recent empirical research, most prominently in a series of studies by Eldar Shafir, a professor of psychology and public affairs at Princeton, that goes well beyond the thought experiments of the previous generation of research to test the errors people make in real life. For example, Shafir was recently part of a group that analyzed a direct-mail field experiment in South Africa to understand how different advertising approaches (including a photo of an attractive woman or describing how the loan proceeds might be used) affected people's demand for loans. Marianne Bertrand, Dean Karlan, Sendhil Mullainathan, Eldar Shafir, and Jonathan Zinman, "What's Advertising Content Worth? Evidence from a Consumer Credit Marketing Experiment," *Quarterly Journal of Economics* 125(1, 2010): 263–306. Shafir also has studied, with economist Richard Thaler, some of the puzzles of how and why we delay gratification. Eldar Shafir and Richard Thaler, "Invest Now, Drink Later, Spend Never: On the Mental Accounting of Delayed Consumption," *Journal of Economic Psychology* 27(5, 2006): 694–712.

3. Nassim Taleb in particular has demonstrated that human beings make all sorts of cognitive mistakes in assessing risk. See Nassim Nicholas Taleb, *Fooled by Randomness: The Hidden Role of Chance in Life and Markets* (Random House, 2008), and Taleb, *The Black Swan*.

4. Men appear to be more overconfident than women about their trading: one study shows that men trade 45 percent more than women, which costs them almost a full percentage point in terms of their net annual returns. See Brad M. Barber and Terrance Odean, "Boys Will Be Boys: Gender, Overconfidence, and Common Stock Investment," *Quarterly Journal of Economics* (February 2010): 261–292.

5. Interestingly, even among high-frequency trading firms, the best traders and managers also have a long-term perspective. Firms such D. E. Shaw and Susquehanna might have computer algorithms that trade within milliseconds, but their investment strategies are focused on multiple-year returns.

6. These remarks of Buffett's, from a 1974 interview published in *Forbes,* have been widely cited. He and his partner Charlie Munger have made similar comments over the years. Roger Lowenstein describes Buffett's patience and includes the fat-pitch quotation in his excellent biography, *Buffett: The Making of an American Capitalist* (Random House, 1995), p. 161.

7. 1998 Berkshire Hathaway annual meeting, Omaha, Nebraska.

8. Warren Buffet, letter to Berkshire Hathaway shareholders, March 1, 1991.

9. For the MBIA story, see Christine S. Richard, *Confidence Game: How Hedge Fund Manager Bill Ackman Called Wall Street's Bluff* (Bloomberg Press, 2010).

10. Ibid., p. 46.

11. Jerome Kassirer, John Wong, and Richard Kopelman, *Learning Clinical Reasoning,* 2nd ed. (Lippincott Williams & Wilkins, 2010), p. xvii–xviii.

12. Atul Gawande, *The Checklist Manifesto: How to Get Things Right* (Picador, 2009).

13. Ibid., p. 154.

14. The concept of a diagnostic time-out is raised in John W. Ely, Mark L. Graber, and Pat Croskerry, "Checklists to Reduce Diagnostic Errors," *Academic Medicine* 86(3, 2011): 1–7, an excellent recent article exploring the use of checklists in diagnostic decision-making, particularly under uncertainty and time pressure.

15. Dhaliwal also sounds almost exactly like Michael Ashner, the successful chairman and CEO of Winthrop Realty Trust, who told me this about business decisions: "What you are relying on is your experience. The difference between smart and not smart is how you utilize experience. Everyone has intuition. But it's what you do to mine your experience and apply it analytically and dispassionately."

16. Yen Chen Liu, Amisha Desai, Bryan Lee, and Malathi Srinivasan, "It's Not Behçet's," *Journal of General Internal Medicine* 26(5, 2010): 559–560.

17. Ibid.

18. Al Tompkins, "Steve Kroft Explains Why He Broke Interviewing Rules When Questioning Obama About Bin Laden Death for *60 Minutes,*" Poynter.org, May 9, 2011, http://www.poynter.org/latest -news/als-morning-meeting/131544/dissecting-the-kroftobama-60-minutes-interview.

19. For the entire interview, see "Obama on Bin Laden: The Full Interview," 60 Minutes Overtime, CBSNews.com, May 8, 2011, http://www.cbsnews.com/video/watch/?id=7365426n&tag=mncol;lst;8.

20. When I told Kroft about observe-orient-decide-act, he immediately saw the parallels to television journalism: "You have to manage the person you are interviewing. You might say you want short answers. You can't get outsmarted. After doing this for a while, you learn that this is the way I've got to approach this person. Sometimes you ask the hardest question, the most off-the-wall question, at the very beginning to get control. I did that with Bill and Hillary. They had no idea the first question was going to be about Gennifer Flowers. So I started with: 'Who is Gennifer Flowers?' I tried to put them off guard so they didn't go into their preassigned bullet points."

21. "Verbal fencing" is my spin on the phrase "verbal judo." See George Thompson, *Verbal Judo: The Gentle Art of Persuasion* (William Morrow, 2004). There is even a Verbal Judo Institute, which "teaches a philosophy of how to look creatively at conflict and use specific strategies and tactics to find peaceful resolutions." See http://verbaljudo.org.

22. Tompkins, "Steve Kroft Explains Why He Broke Interviewing Rules."

23. See "*Wall Street Journal* Names Francesco Guerrera Editor of Money & Investing," Globe Newswire release via BioPortfolio, April 28, 2011.

24. There are counterexamples to journalism's predominantly fast pace. ProPublica has a newsroom of thirty-four working journalists, including about twenty reporters as well as editors, researchers, and others. Each year they publish several hundred stories of various lengths, but their crowning achievement is the roughly twenty annual "deep dives," stories that require significant investigations and long lead times. See http://www.propublica.org/about/. Jesse Eisinger, a ProPublica reporter who was a coreicipient of the 2011 Pulitzer Prize for National Reporting for just such a "deep dive," told me ProPublica's approach has several important advantages: "We can put more time into our stories. We can think in a wider, top-down, bigger way. We can reflect on the past." Eisinger also writes a biweekly column for the *New York Times,* but even two weeks is much longer than the typical journalist's deadline.

25. Tompkins, "Steve Kroft Explains Why He Broke Interviewing Rules."

26. One of the stories Kroft interviewed me for was about the lack of criminal prosecutions of Wall Street. His team had worked for months with whistleblowers who had incriminating information about what the senior executives of several financial institutions knew and when they knew it. Kroft said they could have done the story faster, especially if they thought they were in danger of being scooped. However, he said, the quick story "wouldn't have the power that I think this will have when it's right." You can judge its power for yourself (and see me subjected to Kroft's questioning) by watching the two-segment "Prosecuting Wall Street" story, which aired on December 4, 2011. See http://www.cbsnews.com/8301-18560_162-57336042/prosecuting-wall-street/.

27. Jeffrey K. Riley, "Examining Potential Demographic Trends in the Opinions of Undergraduate Journalism Professors Concerning the Topic of Technological and Traditional Journalism Skills and Theories," master's thesis, Scripps College of Communication, Ohio University, August 2011, p. 14.

Chapter 12

1. Tamar Avnet and Anne-Laure Sellier, "Clock Time Versus Event Time: Temporal Culture or Self-Regulation?" Working Paper Series, December 20, 2010, http:/ssrn.com/abstract=1665936.

2. Philip Zimbardo and John Boyd, *The Time Paradox: The New Psychology of Time That Will Change Your Life* (Free Press, 2008), p. 30.

3. Zimbardo and Boyd, *The Time Paradox,* pp. 38, 40.

4. Frederick Winslow Taylor, *The Principles of Scientific Management* (1909).

5. See, for example, Heather Menzies, *No Time: Stress and the Crisis of Modern Life* (Douglas & McIntyre, 2005).

6. Mark Aguiar and Erik Hurst, "Measuring Trends in Leisure: The Allocation of Time over Five Decades," *Quarterly Journal of Economics* 112(2007): 969–1006. According to the HarrisInteractive annual poll of work and leisure time, from 1980 until recently the median weekly work hours for Americans has held in the range of forty-seven to fifty-one. The peak period of fifty to fifty-one hours was from 1993 to 2001. By 2008, median work hours had declined to forty-six. HarrisInteractive asks the following question: "How many hours would

you estimate you spend at work, housekeeping or studies, including any travel time to and from the job or school?" See http://www.harrisinteractive.com/Insights/HarrisVault.aspx?PID=980.

7. Multitaskers also are less creative and efficient; for example, they take up to 30 percent longer to complete parallel tasks and they commit twice as many errors. Eyal Ophir, Clifford Nass, and Anthony D. Wagner, "Cognitive Control in Media Multitaskers," *Proceedings of the National Academy of Sciences of the United States of America* 106(37, 2009): 15583–15587.

8. Daniel Kahneman, Alan B. Krueger, David A. Schkade, Norbert Schwarz, and Arthur A. Stone, "A Survey Method for Characterizing Daily Life Experience: The Day Reconstruction Method," *Science* (December 3, 2004): 1776–1780; Alois Stutzer and Bruno S. Frey, "Stress That Doesn't Pay: The Commuting Paradox," *Scandinavian Journal of Economics* 110(2, 2008): 339–366. For an excellent recent summary of research on the negative effects of commuting, as well as related policy recommendations, see Peter H. Huang, "Experiences Versus Memories: Should Law and Policy Care More About Your First Love or Your Memories of It?" Temple University Legal Studies Research Paper 2011-03 (November 3, 2011), available at http:// http://papers.ssrn.com/sol3/papers.cfm?abstract_id=1743025.

9. J. Ignacio Gimenez-Nadal and José Alberto Molina, "Commuting Time and Labor Supply: A Causal Effect?" IZA Discussion Paper 5529 (Institute for the Study of Labor, February 2011).

10. Paul John William Pigors and Charles A. Myers, *Personnel Administration: A Point of View and a Method* (McGraw-Hill, 1973).

11. Sanford E. DeVoe, Byron Y. Lee, and Jeffrey Pfeffer, "Hourly Versus Salaried Payment and Decisions About Trading Off Time and Money over Time," *Industrial and Labor Relations Review* 63(4, 2010): 627–640, at 638.

12. US Department of Labor, Bureau of Labor Statistics, "Labor Force Statistics from the Current Population Survey: Characteristics of Minimum Wage Workers: 2009," http://www.bls.gov/cps/minwage2009.htm#1 (updated March 1, 2010).

13. Ibid.

14. Daniel H. Pink, "Free Agent Nation," *Fast Company* (December–January 1998): 131–147; Daniel H. Pink, *Free Agent Nation: How America's New Independent Workers Are Transforming the Way We Live* (Warner Business Books, 2011).

15. James A. Evans, Gideon Kunda, and Stephen R. Barley, "Beach Time, Bridge Time, and Billable Hours: The Temporal Structure of Technical Contracting," *Administrative Science Quarterly* 49(2004): 1–38, at 21.

16. Ibid., p. 30.

17. DeVoe, Lee, and Pfeffer, "Hourly Versus Salaried Payment," p. 640.

18. Sanford E. DeVoe and Jeffrey Pfeffer, "The Stingy Hour: How Accounting for Time Affects Volunteering," *Personality and Social Psychology Bulletin* 36(4, 2010): 470–483.

19. Sanford E. DeVoe and Jeffrey Pfeffer, "Time Is Tight: How Higher Economic Value of Time Increases Feeling of Time Pressure," *Journal of Applied Psychology* 96(2011): 655–676; Sanford E. DeVoe and Jeffrey Pfeffer, "When Time Is Money: The Effect of Hourly Payment on the Evaluation of Time," *Organizational Behavior and Human Decision Processes* 104(2007): 1–13.

20. DeVoe and Pfeffer, "Time Is Tight."

21. Sanford E. DeVoe and Julian House, "Time, Money, and Happiness: How Does Putting a Price on Time Affect Our Ability to Smell the Roses?" *Journal of Experimental Psychology* 48(2, 2012): 466–467.

Chapter 13

1. Lemelson-MIT, "Inventor of the Week Archive: Art Fry and Spencer Silver: Post-it® Notes," http://web.mit.edu/invent/iow/frysilver.html.

2. 3M, *A Century of Innovation: The 3M Story* (3M, 2003), p. 68.

3. Ibid., p. 19.

4. Ibid.

5. Ibid., p. 38.

6. "Podcast: Art Fry's Invention Has a Way of Sticking Around," Smithsonian Lemelson Center, May 20, 2008, http://invention.smithsonian.org/video/vid-popup.aspx?clip=1&id=518.

7. Ibid.

8. Ibid.

9. The story originates from a passage in a biography of Newton, *Memoirs of Sir Isaac Newton's Life*, written by one of his contemporaries, William Stukeley, and published more than two decades after Newton's death. The relevant passages from the book are available online at The Royal Society, "Newton's Apple," http://royalsociety.org/library/moments/newton-apple/.

10. Thomas Edison Center at Menlo Park, "Young Edison," http://www.menloparkmuseum.org/thomas-edison-and-menlo-park (excerpted from Westfield Architects and Preservation Consultants, *Preservation Master Plan, Edison Memorial Tower, Museum, and Site* (2007).

11. "Answers for Young People," http://www.w3.org/People/Berners-Lee/Kids.html; Tim Berners-Lee, *Weaving the Web: The Original Design and Ultimate Destiny of the World Wide Web* (HarperOne, 1999).

12. "Answers for Young People." Newton and Edison also rejected the notion that their discoveries were eureka stories. Remember these quotes? From Newton: "If I have seen a little further it is by standing on the shoulders of Giants." And from Edison, "Genius is 1 percent inspiration and 99 percent perspiration." Even the original eureka story—that Archimedes discovered the laws of buoyancy in the bath and then ran outside naked shouting, "Eureka! Eureka!"—is probably not true. See David Biello, "Fact or Fiction? Archimedes Coined the Term 'Eureka!' in the Bath," *Scientific American*, December 8, 2006.

13. Steven Johnson, *Where Good Ideas Come From* (Riverhead, 2010), p. 77.

14. Ibid.

15. See Scott Berkun, *The Myths of Innovation* (O'Reilly Media, 2007); Mihaly Csikszentmihalyi, *Creativity: Flow and the Psychology of Discovery and Invention* (Harper Perennial, 1997).

16. "Podcast: Art Fry's Invention Has a Way of Sticking Around."

17. Johnson, *Where Good Ideas Come From*, p. 77.

18. "Podcast: Art Fry's Invention Has a Way of Sticking Around."

19. 3M, "McKnight Principles," http://solutions.3m.com/wps/portal/3M/en_WW/History/3M/Company/McKnight-principles.

20. See Kaomi Goetz, "How 3M Gave Everyone Days Off and Created an Innovation Dynamo," Co Design, February 1, 2011, http://www.fastcodesign.com/1663137/how-3m-gave-everyone-days-off-and-created-an-innovation-dynamo.

21. 3M, *A Century of Innovation*, p. 33.

22. Merim Bilalić, Peter McLeod, and Fernand Gobet, "The Mechanism of the Einstellung (Set) Effect: A Pervasive Source of Cognitive Bias," *Current Directions in Psychological Science* 19(2, 2010): 111–115.

23. Ibid., p. 115.

24. Ibid., p. 113.

25. John Maynard Keynes, *The General Theory of Employment, Interest, and Money* (Macmillan, 1973), p. xxiii.

26. Full disclosure: Charlie Graham, the founder and CEO of Shop It To Me, is my brother-in-law.

27. 3M, *A Century of Innovation*, pp. 38–39.

28. "Podcast: Art Fry's Invention Has a Way of Sticking Around."

29. See Marissa Mayer's talk at Stanford University, June 30, 2006, http://www.youtube.com/watch?v=soYKFWqVVzg.

30. Johnson, *Where Good Ideas Come From*, p. 82.

31. "Sticking Around—The Post-it Note Is 20," BBC News, April 6, 2000, http://news.bbc.co.uk/2/hi/uk_news/701661.stm.

32. Daniel Morrow, "Learning to Use Tools," interview with Steve Jobs, Smithsonian Oral and Video Histories, April 20, 1995, http://americanhistory.si.edu/collections/comphist/sj1.html#tools; see also Walter Isaacson, *Steve Jobs* (Simon & Schuster, 2011).

33. Sergey Brin, Google's other cofounder, had a childhood similarly devoted to exploring whatever he was curious about, as well as family members who were supportive and equally curious. See Virginia Scott, *Google* (Greenwood Publishing Group, 2008), pp. 1–4.

34. See also Steven Johnson, *The Invention of Air* (Riverhead, 2008); Robert E. Schofield, *The Enlightened Joseph Priestley: A Study of His Life and Work from 1773 to 1804* (Pennsylvania State University Press, 2004), p. 105. In marking the bicentenary of Joseph Priestley's death, the Bath Royal Literary and Scientific Institution noted that Priestly had "discovered Oxygen gas on 1 August 1774 in the laboratory at Bowood House, Wiltshire, England." See Bath Royal Literary and Scientific Institution, "The Man Who Discovered Oxygen," February 6, 2004, http://www.brlsi.org/notable/Priestley.htm.

35. Johnson, *The Invention of Air*, pp. 65–67.

36. For example, Priestley memorized all 107 questions and answers of the Westminster Shorter Catechism at the age of four; he learned French, Italian, German, Latin, and Greek and then took on Hebrew, Arabic, Syrian, and Chaldean. Johnson, *The Invention of Air*, pp. 7, 40.

37. Ibid., p. 79.

Chapter 14

1. Sarkozy expressed his views in a foreword to the report. Joseph E. Stiglitz, Amartya Sen, and Jean-Paul Fitoussi, *Mis-Measuring Our Lives: Why GDP Doesn't Add Up* (The New Press, 2010), p. x.

2. The British government in particular has recently focused on measuring happiness. It remains unclear how a government might capture well-being, except through subjective questioning or surveys. Some researchers have proposed that instead of using GDP we should simply multiply the time people spend doing activities by the satisfaction generated by each activity. See Daniel Kahneman, Alan B. Krueger, David Schkade, Norbert Schwarz, and Arthur Stone, "Toward National Well-being Accounts," *AEA Papers and Proceedings* 94(2, 2004): 429–434.

3. Stiglitz, Sen, and Fitoussi, *Mis-Measuring Our Lives*, pp. xiv–xv.

4. I am grateful to Joseph Stiglitz for the speedometer–gas tank metaphor.

5. Evidence suggests that policymakers' discount rates are too high in the short term and then decline over time, like a roller-coaster drop. For example, one study found that for policy questions that involve saving human lives, we use a much higher discount rate in the relatively short term: about 17 percent for five years compared to 4 percent for one hundred years. See Richard T. Carson and Brigitte Roth Tran, "Discount Behavior and Environmental Decisions," *Journal of Neuroscience, Psychology, and Economics* 2(2, 2009): 123.

6. In 1992, OMB issued a pronouncement about discount rates stating that federal government decisions should include comprehensive estimates of the expected benefits and costs to society and setting forth several categories of decisions, along with a schedule of discount rates to be used in assessing each category's future benefits and costs. It set the "base rate" at 7 percent. (This is a "real" return, meaning a return after including inflation.) The rationale for this number was that 7 percent "approximates the marginal pretax return on an average investment in the private sector in recent years." See "Guidelines and Discount Rates for Benefit-Cost Analysis of Federal Programs," OMB circular A-94, October 29, 1992, http://www.whitehouse.gov/omb/circulars_a094, p. 9. The idea was that because public investments and regulation displace private investment, the government should only take on a project if it is expected to generate net future benefits when those benefits are discounted at the private-sector rate. Otherwise, the government should stay out of it and leave the program to the private sector. The OMB circular also noted that the discount rate for purely internal government programs, such as leasing a building for government use, would be based on the US Treasury's borrowing rate. OMB said discount rates for internal projects would be updated once a year, and it has done so. In contrast, the 7 percent rate has remained fixed, even though OMB said in 1992 that "significant changes in this rate will be reflected in future updates of this Circular" (p. 9). OMB also suggested that sensitivity analysis should be conducted using a range of discount rates; this kind of analysis can help to illustrate the inappropriateness of the 7 percent base rate in some contexts.

7. The GAO and CBO follow US Treasury borrowing rates, which, as of early 2012, were in the range of 1 percent.

8. In a 700-plus-page report for the British government in 2006, Stern warned that climate change would cause disastrous long-term harm. He framed this warning in terms of GDP: "If we don't act, the overall costs and risks of climate change will be equivalent to losing at least 5% of global GDP each year, now and

forever. If a wider range of risks and impacts is taken into account, the estimates of damage could rise to 20% of GDP or more." Nicholas Stern, *The Economics of Climate Change* (Cambridge University Press, 2007), p. xv. The Stern report is available at: http://www.hm-treasury.gov.uk/sternreview_index.htm.

9. William Nordhaus attacked the Stern report as a hastily prepared document that was not subject to peer review: "We could only wish that the Review's authors had taken a few more months and written a more concise and consistent treatise." William Nordhaus, "The *Stern Review* on the Economics of Climate Change," May 3, 2007, http://nordhaus.econ.yale.edu/stern_050307.pdf, p. 8. Although Nordhaus assumed that the report's assumptions about climate change were correct and that, on average, the world would lose GDP in the future (specifically, that the losses would be 0.4 percent of GDP in 2060, 2.9 percent in 2011, and 13.8 percent in 2200) without immediate action, he concluded that an appropriate discount rate was much higher than Stern's, in the range of 5.5 percent. Nordhaus criticized the Stern report by citing examples of the implications of using Stern's low discount rates, including that we should spend $7 trillion today to prevent damages of just 0.01 percent of GDP that would start in 2200 and then continue thereafter. He also noted that more than half of Stern's estimated damages would occur after the year 2800; those costs would be virtually impossible to measure today.

10. Decades ago, the economist Tjalling Koopmans warned policymakers to be careful not to make judgments about discount rates before they understand the implications of alternative choices. Tjalling C. Koopmans, "On the Concept of Optimal Economic Growth," *Academiae Scientiarum Scripta Varia* 28(1, 1965): 1–75.

11. For an overview of these studies, see W. Kip Viscusi and Joseph E. Aldy, "The Value of a Statistical Life: A Critical Review of Market Estimates Throughout the World," *Journal of Risk and Uncertainty* 27(1, 2003): 5–76.

12. Adam Smith, *The Wealth of Nations* (1776; University of Chicago Press, 1976), p. 112.

13. An excellent summary of the categories of methods is Ike Brannon, "What Is a Life Worth?" *Regulation* (Winter 2004–2005): 60–63.

14. Orley Ashenfelter and Michael Greenstone, "Using Mandated Speed Limits to Measure the Value of a Statistical Life," *Journal of Political Economy* 112(S1, February 2004): S226–S267.

15. For example, medical professionals now use both the quality-adjusted-life-year, or QALY, which values a future year of perfect health more highly than a future year with some affliction, and the micromort, a unit measuring a one-in-one-million risk of death.

16. Binyamin Appelbaum, "As US Agencies Put More Value on a Life, Businesses Fret," *New York Times*, February 16, 2011.

17. The definitive account of the recent financial crisis will require several more years, or perhaps decades, as was the case following the stock market crash of 1929. The three-part report of the Financial Crisis Inquiry Commission, the group Congress tasked to explain what happened, was, in my view, "a confusing and contradictory mess, part rehash, part mishmash, as impenetrable as the collateralized debt obligations at the core of the crisis." See Frank Partnoy, "Washington's Financial Disaster," *New York Times*, January 29, 2011. And although there already have been nearly two dozen books published about the crisis, one meta-review concludes, "No single narrative emerges from this broad and often contradictory collection of interpretations, but the sheer variety of conclusions is informative, and underscores the desperate need for the economics profession to establish a single set of facts from which more accurate inferences and narratives can be constructed." Andrew W. Lo, "Reading About the Financial Crisis: A 21-Book Review," *Journal of Economic Literature* working paper, January 9, 2012.

18. Some critics of government action might support inertia. For example, financial expert James Grant has noted that the one thing the federal government was unwilling to do in responding to the recent financial crisis was wait: "For the sake of recovery, there is seemingly just one action the US government refuses to contemplate. What it wants no part of is inaction." Grant favorably cites the "constructive inaction" of history, including the "forgotten policies, or rather non-policies, that allowed the deflationary depression of 1920–21 to run its course." Jim Grant, "Just Do Nothing," *Grant's Interest Rate Observer* 29(18, September 23, 2011): 2.

19. See James Gleick, *Faster: The Acceleration of Just About Everything* (Pantheon, 1999), p. 114.

20. Thomas C. Schelling, foreword to Roberta Wohlstetter, *Pearl Harbor: Warning and Decision* (Stanford University Press, 1962), p. vii.

21. See Donald Rumsfeld, "Known and Unknown: Author's Note," The Rumsfeld Papers, December 2010, http://www.rumsfeld.com/about/page/authors-note. The other books referenced are Frank H. Knight, *Risk, Uncertainty, and Profit* (Houghton Mifflin, 1921); Taleb, *The Black Swan*; Carl von Clausewitz, *On War* (1832); Perrow, *Normal Accidents*, and Plato, *The Apology of Socrates* (for a translation, by Benjamin Jowett, see http://classics.mit.edu/Plato/apology.html).

INDEX

Index

Index

Index

Index

Index

Index

Index

Index

Index

Index

Index